The Body Tourist

A Memoir

Dana Lise Shavin

LITTLE FEATHER BOOKS, INC.
NEW YORK

LITTLE FEATHER BOOKS, INC.

Library of Congress Cataloging-in-Publication data on file.
ISBN 978-0-9913329-4-6

Cover Design by Kat St. Vincent Studios

The LFB logo is a trademark of Little Feather Books, Inc.

The book *Atlanta: A Celebration* (Capricorn Corporation, 1978) mentioned in this publication was written by the author's father, Norman Shavin.

The epigram that appears at the beginning of this book is from *Comics: Anatomy of a Mass Medium* (Little, Brown and Company, 1972) by Reinhold Reitberger and Wolfgang Fuchs.

Excerpts of this book have been used in live presentations by the author and have been published in literary journals. "The Death of Charles Black" received Honorable Mention in Glimmer Train's 2012 Family Matters contest. "Tell Me About Yourself" appeared in Lime Hawk Literary Arts Collective's journal and anthology (Fall 2014). Portions of *The Body Tourist* were used in Dana Lise Shavin's presentation "Anorexia's Noble Heart: Illness as Illness and Cure" as part of the University of Tennessee at Chattanooga's 2012 Women's Speakers Series.

Author's Note

All identifying information has been altered to protect the privacy of those who did not ask to be written about in this memoir. With regard to my family, I'm fairly certain our stories about how things were will differ widely. In the words of Fernando Pessoa, "I will necessarily say what it seems to me, given that I'm me."

— Dana Lise Shavin

Dedication

To my husband, Daryl Thetford, first, foremost, and forever.

And to my mother, for her grit and humor and tenacious hold
on the best of what we've always had together.

To Mara —
For the journey — and
your beautiful magnetic
river.

The Body Tourist

Each super-hero chooses in the beginning of his career a disguise and a battle name... He dons a mask and in doing so reaches back to the age-old custom of exorcising demons and evil spirits by frightening them with a terrifying disguise.

— Reinhold Reitberger and Wolfgang Fuchs
Comics: Anatomy of a Mass Medium

Atlanta, Georgia

1971

I AM TEN YEARS OLD. I get off the school bus at the top of my driveway. My mother is running toward me, flailing her arms and yelling for me not to panic. A police car is parked in the turn-around. When she gets to me she grabs me by the arm and pulls me toward the house. I am overweight and struggling to run up the steep driveway hugging my books to my chest.

"We've been robbed," my mother says. "They took everything!"

"They took *everything*?" I am breathless. "My *horses*?" I break away from my mother's grasp and burst in the front door. Two police officers are standing in the entry hall, radios crackling. My father, who would only come home from work if something were really wrong, is leaning against a wall, talking to an officer who is taking notes. He looks up when I run in.

"Did they take my *horses*?" I shout, and then I stop. The kitchen table and chairs are gone. Sunlight floods the empty room. In the attached den, the sofa, rocker, recliner, TV and coffee table are all gone. I spin around. In the living room, the piano, gold velvet straight-back chairs, and mother-of-pearl inlaid table with tiny carved chairs are gone.

"Most likely they were watching your house," one of the officers says to my father. "Probably knew your routine."

Just past my father, the hall closet stands open. My mother's powder blue Hoover is gone. Down the hall, in my older sister's room, her belongings are untouched. My brother's room is untouched as well, and in my room, sixty-five molded plastic horses acting out almost every conceivable horse impulse stand where I left them that morning. But just a few steps from my door, my parents' bedroom is empty. Clothes lay in heaps where they were dumped from the tall dresser before it was carried away. Everywhere furniture has been, the carpet is a darker brown, unfaded by the sun. Rows of deep lines cut into the nap. I imagine our furniture tilted and dragged away on two legs, like people seized from behind and pulled on their heels into the shadows.

Chapter 1

Superhero

THERE IS A GREEN RECLINER at the center of my memory. It sits in my living room, facing the cornfields behind my apartment. When I think of it I can almost feel the hot summer breeze filtering in through the open sliding glass doors. I can hear my downstairs neighbor dragging a chair out onto her porch, ice cubes clinking in her glass as she settles in for an evening on the telephone. I can smell the tang of the South Georgia clay, offering up her iron-oxide guts to the plow, and I can see myself: legs curled under me, my cigarettes, ashtray and Diet Coke all lined up on the wide, flat arm of the chair. This is my command center when I am twenty-one. This is where I eat (when I eat), where I drink, watch television, talk on the telephone, write letters, cry, read---everything except have sex, though I might have done that in the chair too, had the opportunity presented itself.

I saw the green recliner for the last time in 1984. I was moving from the tiny, South Georgia town of Tifton to start graduate school in Clinical Psychology two hundred miles away in Augusta. While I could have strapped the green recliner to the top of my Honda and taken it with me, it seemed that its rightful place was, and would always be, in that apartment, facing the cornfields. Just the empty room and that chair. Exactly as it had been for a year.

* * *

A hundred miles north of the Florida border lies Tifton, Georgia, nine square miles of flat farmland whose claim to fame in 1983 is that it is home to the world's second largest Magnolia tree. That no one I ask seems to know or care where the largest one is surprises me, but then the town is little more than a mecca of churches and dollar stores anchored by an undereducated agricultural community, the majority of whose members live below the poverty line and power a climate of religious fundamentalism. There is one movie theater, one tiny shopping mall, one rock music radio station, and—this is where I come in—one halfway house for recovering drug and alcohol addicts. It is here, in a town rich with folly and illness, that my superhero dreams spring to life.

I discover Bridgeway House at the end of my senior year in college, through a government matchmaking agency for job seekers and employers. By the time I join the State Merit System register, I have attended three separate colleges, one of them twice, spent half of my junior year on a hospital psychiatric floor relearning how to eat, and been fired from two of the only three jobs I ever had. But because the Merit System has no way of knowing about the lost time or the lost jobs, or the fact that I am five-feet, nine-inches tall and weigh only ninety-five pounds, I get several invitations to interview, one of which is from Bridgeway House in Tifton, Georgia, two hundred miles—a solar system, to me—away from my parents' home in Atlanta.

"Hurray!" my sister crows, "You're free!"

But I am not free. Although I have had three years of psychotherapy and am no longer losing weight, remnants of my anorexia live like rats in the dark corners of my mind. There are periods of despondency laced with paranoia, when I lock myself in my bedroom for hours or entire weekends, too prickly to even pick up the phone. There is the fact that I refuse to weigh in the triple digits, somehow believing that the invisible line between ninety-nine and one hundred pounds is all that stands between me and my complete disintegration. Above all (or maybe underneath all), there is a fundamental lack of understanding about how to take care of myself, which includes not just eating enough and weighing enough, but also managing everything from my medication (a cocktail of antidepressants, anti-anticonvulsants, megavitamins, and birth control pills) to the oil level in my car (it will bravely make one hundred thirty thousand miles without a single oil change and die on an exit ramp). And then there are the simple things that I also cannot grasp, such as the importance of outfitting myself in well-fitting clothes instead of child-sized sweaters that a client will suggest make me appear to be flaunting my thinness, or the necessity of every now and then allowing myself to relax, to (as my brother says, with exasperation), "have a little fun."

"What *do* you do for fun?" a therapist once asked me.

Long, expensive minutes ticked away while I thought. "Fun," I repeated, drumming my fingers on the side of my chair. "Well, I enjoy women's magazines," I said at last, not sure if this technically counted as fun or whether it more aptly fit into an "educational" category. But then I was compelled to qualify my answer anyway, by admitting that the magazine models inevitably led me to further disparage the way I look, which was decidedly not fun.

* * *

Although my own precarious state of recovery is unclear to me, what is abundantly clear is that, while I want the counseling job at Bridgeway, my true calling is actually much loftier than counseling. Because I have narrowly escaped being one of the one-in-five women who succumbs to (i.e., dies from) anorexia nervosa in the US, and because people have always brought me their problems ("I've never told this to *anybody*" and, "You are *such* a good listener," are phrases I heard over and over again from friends and acquaintances), I believe I have a calling. Not a penchant for, not a proclivity toward, but a spiritual injunction that doesn't care about any plans I might have already been making to the contrary (to be an English teacher, for example). In keeping with this calling, I often see myself (with the razor-sharp lucidity common to addicts) as a kind of Sherpa, leading a flock of followers up the treacherous mountain of self-awareness, or as the guru at the summit dispensing lifesaving messages of healing. Needless to say, I never see myself as the girl in the brown-paneled office filling out paperwork in triplicate for the State.

Whichever superhero form I will ultimately take, Sherpa or guru, that I have this higher calling is clear. Never mind the black moods, the inability to weigh more than an eight-year-old, or the fact that I don't have a clue how to take care of my own health or happiness—these inconsequentials, these failings and flailings I sweep under the cape of denial. I have survived, and this, to my mind, is a stellar credential. It doesn't occur to me that I am little more than wounded rescuer, that there are chapters in textbooks dedicated to just this specific brand of grandiosity. Saving the day isn't my choice but my duty. After all, it is written in the annals of superheroes everywhere that saving is the price we pay for having survived.

* * *

Of course, the irony of interviewing for a job at a drug and alcohol halfway house when I am so newly out of the woods myself is not lost on me. But just as there's a moment of darkness in every addict's life, when it first occurs to her that a drug will change her for the better (heroin for some, starvation for me), there is a counter-moment when it occurs to her that it might not. Here I recall the voice of my therapist in the hospital, working to get me to see the fallacy of my "thin equals happy" theory. I was eighty-two pounds.

"If being thin holds the keys to your fountain of self-worth, why didn't you stop when you got there? Twenty or thirty pounds ago?"

"Because I couldn't see it," I said.

"You couldn't see it," he said, "because you'd have had to admit your whole premise was faulty. If self-worth is inversely proportional to size, then you should be practically knighting yourself. But here you are, struggling with the same issues of self-worth at eighty-two pounds that you had at a hundred and thirty pounds. Funny how the thing you thought would cure you just keeps making you sicker."

* * *

"I know too much to go back there," is my standard line now when people suggest (and they do) that I'm not yet out of the woods. And it's true—I do know too much to go back. What I don't know yet is how to go forward, and I don't know that I don't know that. Occasionally I get glimpses of my ongoing conflict—*there I am squeezing the guts from cherry tomatoes into the trash,* a holdover from the days when I ate only things that could be divided or mashed, or *there I am weighing myself for the twentieth time in one day.* But these behavioral remnants, these odd posturings around food and size are just moldering pastimes, I tell myself, vestiges of a self in search of some sustenance I still can't reliably name from some source I still can't reliably identify. Safe to say I do not see them as the undertow they are.

And so it is here, amid the lush soil of denial and self-aggrandizement, that the invitation to interview for the counselor position at Bridgeway House in Tifton, Georgia, arrives in my parents' mailbox. Although I have never been to Tifton and know nothing about the job other than that it's full-time and that it pays ten thousand dollars a year, the invitation kicks off a chain of preposterous fantasizing: I will move to Tifton and buy a house with several acres for horses and a fenced yard for my beloved dog, Keithan. On weekdays, I will spend my time curing people of their addictions, in part by lending the compassionate ear for which I am famous, and in part by sharing the Sherpa/guru wisdom of my own struggle with anorexia. On the weekends, I will date a variety of handsome, Jewish men, and rather quickly I will find myself at the center of a social circle made up of attractive, single professionals, in whose company I will frequent noisy dance clubs, enjoy dinners out, and celebrate the major holidays. Over time, I will build a family of choice from a carefully culled roster of friends and beaus, and in doing so, lay my reclusive, melancholic, weight-obsessed, mother-dominated past to rest. At which I time I will be truly free.

What I do not fantasize is that I will rent an apartment in Tifton that doesn't allow dogs because I will be hypnotized by the ocean of cornfields visible from the living room. I don't fantasize that I'll have no idea how to help (much less cure) people, or that I will discover, thanks to my clients, layers upon layers of my own illness still stubbornly intact. I don't fantasize that my only outings will be the visits I make to a coworker's trailer park where she lives in a double-wide trailer with a dog chained to the sofa and a husband I never see, or that one of my two dates all year will be with a chubby evangelical youth minister who will set his face on fire in my living room drinking flaming alcohol. I don't fantasize that there resides in Tifton in 1983 exactly one Jewish family, and that they do not have sons. And I most certainly don't fantasize that I will fall in love with a married, cocaine-addicted client, and that this will bring me face-to-face with the truth of my own grandiosity. Lastly, I do not fantasize that in the year-long unfolding of everything I never would have imagined, I will discover the most important lesson of all: that the superhero and the saved are one and the same.

Chapter 2

Tell Me About Yourself

M Y MOTHER IS DRIVING ME to the interview. The part of me that is on top of things knows that this is a bad idea, and that I must hide her existence from my prospective boss. But her presence is not, in my twenty-one-year-old mind, the main obstacle to getting this job, any more than is my alarmingly low weight or the fact that I bring no counseling experience to the counseling position for which I am interviewing. No, the major threat to my plan, as I see it, is my outfit. I am wearing a sheer, sleeveless, white blouse with enormous ruffles at each shoulder and a third ruffle that frames my face like an E-collar for dogs. With this blouse I have paired a blue-and-white skirt with matching cascading ruffles that—wait for it—*dust the floor*. It is the fashion equivalent of a prom dress. The absurdity of the outfit hits me two hours into the four-hour trip.

"I look ridiculous!" I gasp, as if I have only just now caught sight of myself. "I look like Scarlett O'Hara!"

My mother glances over from driver's seat.

"Don't be silly," she says. "It's a very cute outfit." This is part of her job, to act as a foil to my emotions. Also to make sure I eat lunch on the way and to keep me from falling asleep and crashing the car.

Dressed in tight black jeans, a white silk blouse, and smart, low heels, my mother looks more professional than I do, a fact I hurriedly push away from myself. She is fifty-three when this scene unfolds, and glamorous, with short, shiny black hair, expertly lined and shadowed eyes, and a beauty mark she draws in every morning just above her angular jaw line. She loves clothes, shops often, and dresses in visually and texturally unrelated separates, a fashionable collage of funk and high style. But my mother has a fatal flaw, an Achilles heel, which creates a vortex of worry and grief in her otherwise stylish life: she is petite. And because as a young child she was also briefly plump, she has never allowed herself to eat as she wants to. Her adult life has been a never-ending maze of diets, exercise, and, if our frequent conversations about delicious foods we would never eat is any indication, unrelieved hunger. As a child, at lunches with her at my favorite sandwich shop at Lenox Square Mall in Atlanta, I watched her discard the cap of bread on her sandwich.

"A half-sandwich is the hallmark of a whole woman," she would say. Ten years later I would be fired from my job as a pizza waitress because I was alarmingly thin and growing thinner but never ate lunch.

"I'm going to call your momma and tell her you don't eat," said my boss, to which I replied, "My mother doesn't eat either."

My mother's supposed weight problem (which in actuality was a height problem) is why everything in our refrigerator was a low-calorie version of itself: Weight Watcher's butter, low-cal salad dressing, diet soda, "diet-sliced" bread, sugar-free jelly, skim milk, and tiny saccharine pellets for coffee and tea. In my lifetime, I have never seen my mother eat a whole sandwich, drink a simple glass of juice, indulge in an ice cream cone, a sliver of cake, or even a little tub of flavored yogurt. At the most, if my father or brother ordered dessert out, she would dip her pinkie fingernail (I don't exaggerate here) into a cloud of icing and suck out the contents, groaning orgasmically.

"I'm so *f-a-a-a-t*," she would moan, leaning into me, tenting her brow and whispering the ugly word that would become the key to the private room we shared. In the kitchen drawer underneath the stove, my mother and I kept a little pink and white calorie guide, our bible. Sometimes we looked up a specific food ("Is fat fattening?" I once asked my mother, about the thin whitish veins snaking through my steak, and we pulled out the book to see), but other times we simply flipped through, looking for the biggest portion sizes for the fewest calories (lettuce weighed in nicely, with iceberg beating out darker, more robust spinach) and vice versa: those foods that could kill your diet in just a few bites (we would never eat pâté, mayonnaise, or cheesecake). To further arm herself in the war on fat, she race-walked our three-mile road every day, regardless of the temperature, illness, or her schedule. Even in stormy weather, she could be seen powering down our street in her raincoat and sneakers, my father trailing her in the car, windshield wipers throwing off water in wide arcs, ready to fling open the doors in case lightning made her think twice. It never did.

* * *

I look over at my mother in the driver's seat. She smiles a wide, silly smile meant to ease my nerves. Whether she wants me to get this job isn't really clear. She's tired of dealing with my eating disorder, that much I know. She wants me to get better, to get on with my life. But I also know she's lonely, and that she isn't excited about being left alone with my father. It is something I could worry more about if I let myself.

A sign announces we are sixteen miles from Savannah. I look at my watch. My interview is in thirty minutes.

"How close is Tifton to Savannah?"

"You're the one navigating," my mother says.

I open the map to the page I have folded down earmarked and see that I have failed to guide us around the spur that funnels traffic due east toward the coast. We should be headed due south. We are at least an hour off course. A sudden surge of perspiration jets out onto the ruffles encircling my underarms.

"Mom, we're going the wrong way!" I yell.

"What?" She begins to pump the brakes, as if she is going to turn around in the middle of the interstate. The speedometer needle, which has been hovering at fifty the whole way, takes an excruciating dive into the low forties.

"We weren't supposed to get off I-75!"

"Well why didn't you tell me?" She aims the car toward an exit ramp. "We'll have to find a pay phone and you can call the center and explain what happened."

"How can I explain what happened?" I yell again. "It's a straight line from Atlanta to Tifton! If I say I got lost they'll think I'm an imbecile and they won't hire me, and if I tell them it was your fault they'll know my mother is driving me to the interview!" I'm shaking so much my ruffles are vibrating.

There is silence in the car as my mother considers what I should do.

"Just say *we*," she says at last.

"What?"

"Just say, '*We* took a wrong turn, *I* will be there at two o'clock.' Period."

I jam my folded arms across my chest and wait for my mother to pull up to the pay phone at the Gulf station. It's a perfect solution, which only further annoys me. I get out of the car and am careful to slam the door as hard as I can. Then I poke my head through the open window.

"I *hate* this outfit!" I say. "I'm never wearing it again."

* * *

In a nutshell, this was anorexia's opening salvo: one day when I was eighteen years old and a sophomore at Bard College in Upstate New York, I was sitting in my boyfriend's car in front of Stereo World eating an apple. As I ate I felt for the pudge beneath my shirt: ten unwanted pounds that I had tried unsuccessfully to lose for three years, and that I had blamed for everything that was wrong with my life, including why I never won a ribbon at a horseshow, my mediocre grades, my "unpopularity" at school—in short, the wallpaper of gloom that was the backdrop to everything I did and everywhere I went. As I ate and pinched my pudge and wondered whether the apple could hold me through dinner, I was visited by an extraordinary understanding that I would later liken to a bird falling out of the sky. It was this: that *I had the power to fix myself.* Like Dorothy and her Oz-bound traveling mates, the key had always been with me, its existence hidden in the place where all important knowledge is kept from the self: in plain view. Weight loss was the stuff of the magazines I read, the goal of my aerobics classes, the substance of my self-help books, and of almost all of my conversations with my mother. I had always believed that losing weight would be the answer to all my problems. I had always known that the means to it was an uncomplicated mathematical formula that even I, a terrible math student, understood: calories burned over calories ingested equaled pounds lost. But in this extraordinary moment I saw, in a way I had never seen before, that losing weight— *that fixing my life*—was within my grasp. I simply had to lose *enough.* By the time my boyfriend walked out of Stereo World my epiphany was fifteen minutes old and I was anorexic.

* * *

I rummage in my mother's pocketbook for a stick of gum and unwrap one for us to share. She takes her half gratefully and folds it into her mouth. It has been an hour since we stopped at Wendy's for lunch, and although we won't admit it, we are both hungry again. I had a baked potato, dry, with chives. My mother (unable to resist blurting *don't you at least want a little butter on it?*) ordered a side salad and black coffee.

"What kind of dressing?" asked the girl, to which my mother said she wanted a cruet of vinegar.

"A what?" said the girl.

"A cruet of vinegar."

"A what?" she said again, with the exact same intonation, at which time my mother looked at me, a tiny light of rage coming on in her eyes. I leaned over the counter and asked whether they had any vinegar (they did not). Disgusted by all of it—my butterless potato, the girl, the unavailability of anything other than full-fat salad dressings—my mother turned away from the counter with her tiny plastic plate of lettuce and, under her breath, but not so low the girl couldn't hear, muttered, "Idiot."

"Mom, shhh!" I looked back at the girl. She was fingering the tiny gold cross around her neck and watching us tack away, my tiny mother with her protruding collarbones erupting from the neck of her crisply ironed Ralph Lauren blouse and her six pale lettuce leaves, and me, nearly six feet tall in my long skirt and platform sandals weighing barely a hundred pounds, a lone dry potato on my tray accompanied by a drink cup bigger around than my own face.

I knew what she was thinking: we looked like the starving people in the tabloids with the annoyingly trite caption "Dying To Be Thin." I knew because when you have an eating disorder, everyone tells you exactly what they are thinking in an effort to force some sort of reality on you, and it turns out that everyone thinks exactly the same things: *You must not be able to* see *yourself. You can't think you look* good. *You're going to* die *if you keep this up.* These thoughts they share because they think they are original, and that if you just heard the truth about how you look, it would make a difference.

Twice my mother asked how my potato was, and twice she suggested it wasn't too late to get some butter. She cut up her lettuce leaves into twelve bite-sized pieces, ate them, drank her coffee, and reapplied her lipstick. When she was through with everything, she looked up just as I was chewing a rubbery part of the potato skin. I could see her mouth moving, working it right along with mine. I asked if she was still hungry and she said no, she was stuffed, but if I wanted a Frosty, I could have one.

"Do you want one?" she asked. As if a Frosty were a real option.

"No," I said.

"Why not?" She licked the corner of her mouth where I had a little piece of potato caught on mine.

Rage and frustration welled up around the hunks of potato listing in my belly. Every so often, my mother felt it necessary to suggest I do something so extraordinary that it didn't even merit answering. Always they were things she herself would not or could not do. It might be something seemingly simple, like eating butter on a potato or ordering a Frosty, but other times it was something complex and far-fetched, like calling the head of the State Merit System and explaining that the jobs they offered did not pay well and suggesting they pay more. And if I said that was ridiculous, that I was in no position to challenge the State Merit System, she'd say, "Of course you are," as if, just like that, I really was. At times, the absurdity of it made me want to scream, because her suppositions were at once so naïve and so confident. Later I would understand that they came from a lifetime of raising children rather than working a professional job. But before I understood that, I sometimes worried she could be right, that maybe people who were ordinary (like me) but didn't see the world as withholding and unforgiving (as I did) were the very ones who became catalysts for change.

"A Frosty wouldn't hurt you," my mother said at last. "It might even help you."

* * *

Interestingly, I never mentioned my mother's food and exercise habits to my counselors when I was hospitalized. Looking back now, this surprises me, but I recall at the time it seeming too facile and too ordinary to make note of, as if these cravings, these denials, these grim hours of fanatical calorie-counting and calorie-burning were the foundation, not of obsession or illness, but of ordinary womanhood. And therein lay part of the problem: restriction and denial, as my mother and I saw it, were *worth* the trouble and discomfort for the reward of rendering our bodies disproportionately thin. And the myriad ways the game of extreme weight management announced itself, which included not just diet and exercise but chilling tenets such as *empty is full, hunger is good, eating is dangerous,* and *food is the enemy,* had something of the flavor of anorexia in it from the beginning. Food terror—and it was safe to say my mother and I both had it—was a labyrinth, a web of anxieties spun by one generation that caught the next. My own mother's mother policed her size, denying herself and her chubby daughter sweets, dangling the promise of happiness through self-control. A generation later, my mother would spin the twisted web forward into my life. Of course, by the time I was caught up in it, it felt not like a web, but normal.

* * *

In the car, I push my half of the gum into my mouth and chew, the giddy, peppery bite of cinnamon floating up around my face and masking the dark rouge of hunger raking at my belly. TIFTON, 40 MILES says a little green highway sign. I roll down my window a few inches, creating a vacuum that sucks in the warmth and dampness and earthy smell of soil, and inhale deeply.

"Roll that up," my mother says. "You're letting the cool air out."

* * *

Within a year of anorexia's opening salvo, I had lost not ten but fifty pounds. My thighs were black from the spontaneous bursting of blood vessels (the result of not enough protective fat encasing them) and my long, ropy hair was falling out in chunks. It was in the midst of this high-speed, yet (I somehow believed) clandestine descent into the landscape of wasting away that I was summoned to the Bard College administrative office at the start of my junior year for what I thought was the presentation of my Dean's List certificate from the previous semester. It was a cold day in Upstate New York and I was dressed in odd, capricious layers of clothing (two skirts, one atop the other, and two sweaters, plus striped tights and furry boots) meant both to keep me warm and also conform to the level of funkiness expected at Bard. In truth, the outfit, which hung on my gaunt frame, made me look rag-dollish at best, homeless at worst, as if, lacking a suitcase or grocery cart, I was forced to wear everything I owned at once.

Despite the layers, the hard wooden chair in which I awaited the dean's arrival sent piercing pain through the skin on my butt bones. I was restless, hungry, thinking of the quarter of a stale bagel waiting for me back at my room in my sock drawer. When at last the dean appeared, accompanied—troublingly—by the campus psychologist with whom I'd been sharing my weight struggles, I was numb with cold and discomfort. The dean and psychologist sat down across from me. The dean spoke in a monotone as the campus psychologist tented her eyebrows and grimaced, the effect a kind of emotional ventriloquism. Later I would recall words like "medical danger" and "student in your condition," but at the time, all I heard was that I was being expelled and that my mother would arrive in the morning to get me, and all I saw was that this was very painful for the psychologist.

I was incredulous. By the following night I would be back to lying on the shag carpet in the bedroom next to my father's home office doing leg lifts and sit-ups until I lost count. Back to long, unmattering days and nights unbroken by sleep. Back to the unspeakable boredom of wasting away. It was all too unreal.

"I'm going *home?*" I said, incredulous, to which the campus psychologist finally composed herself and her eyebrows and said, "To a hospital."

My mother did arrive on campus the next day. In a last desperate attempt to prove I was fine and that she could leave without taking me with her, I bought a bag of sunflower seeds and ate four of them in front of her. We boarded a plane at six that evening. My brother and sister were home when I got there, which was nice but also alarming because they rarely came to the house anymore to spend the night. The next morning, my sister made hot chocolate and asked if I wanted some, and then erupted into laughter. I was admitted to the hospital at eight a.m. Four months later, owing to a carefully scripted routine of cottage cheese, corn bread caps, and Raisin Bran, I was released at ninety-five pounds. The addictive cycle, I told friends and family, had been broken. Except that addictive cycles, as a rule, have a purpose, and while I had done the initial work of recovery, true healing, the kind that involves not just eating enough to survive, but also the ability to tolerate the complexities of soul and spirit (i.e., real-live living in the real-live world) was still years off.

* * *

My mother and I pull into the parking lot of Bridgeway an hour and fifteen minutes late. In addition to getting on the wrong highway, we drove around town for twenty minutes looking for the halfway house, only to discover that "house" was a misnomer. Bridgeway is actually a wide, three-story red brick building sandwiched between a library and a church in the middle of downtown Tifton. The only features that suggest something other than "State office building" are a basketball hoop in the parking lot and a narrow concrete front porch with two rocking chairs. I have instructed my mother to drive away as soon as I get out of the car so no one will see her; I am mortified now, to see two people rocking and watching us pull in. I jump out of the car before she comes to a full stop.

"Go!" I say, slamming the door and waving impatiently at some unknown destination up the street. Then I turn, gather the train of my skirt, and run up the steps like a bride.

"Well, well, well," says one of the men on the porch.

"Uh-huh," says the other.

Just as I am about to reach for the handle, the door swings open. Standing in the threshold is a tall, trim, black man dressed in blue jeans, a red shirt with loopy white stitching, smiling a broad, lopsided smile.

"Young lady," he says.

"I'm here for an interview?" I push my long hair out of my face. "I'm a little late," I say breathlessly.

"You're here's all that matters." He introduces himself as Rodney Jenkins, director of Bridgeway. He shakes my hand. Waves me in with a flourish. And then his eyes take a worried tour of my body.

* * *

Here's the real truth: a year-and-a-half after leaving the hospital, my recovery is far from complete. If I have any doubt, I need only walk down the street—or into an interview—and register the way anxious gazes travel the vertical axis of my body. *Oh, come on, people*, I want to say. *I'm not that thin.*

"Yes, you are," said my mother.

"Yes, you are," said two employers, who fired me for it.

"Yes, you are," said my friends, my siblings, my ex-boyfriend, who just a few pounds earlier had taken close-up photographs of the outline of my spinal cord, visible through the skin on my back.

"Do you see it *now?*" he said, thrusting the pictures at me the way one might shove a mischievous dog's nose into the piddle in the floor.

And so I have learned to keep my protestations to myself, the way schizophrenics learn not to stop hearing voices but to refrain from answering out loud. I vow that regardless of how not-thin I feel, I will not argue with others' views of me as skeletal. I agree to agree. While this will not make me any heavier, it will make me look less crazy.

* * *

Rodney Jenkins leads the way into the main office. It is a large, open room with six smaller offices off it. Mismatched chairs—some aluminum, some wooden, two on casters—are lined up against the brown paneled walls, forming a wide circle. The floor is a dirty, mint-green linoleum that looks unswept. The smell of weak coffee and Clorox mingle in the chilled air. The whole place feels like the waiting room you are confined to while expensive repairs are made to your car.

Mr. Jenkins motions me to a chair beside the only desk in the big room. "Sit," he says.

I sit down and hand him my resume, which suggests, by omission, that I attended not three colleges but only the one that conferred my degree, and which lovingly details a six-month internship at the State hospital but says nothing about my collection of lost jobs. As Mr. Jenkins looks over what I have typed, the hard, cold, aluminum chair presses uncomfortably against my butt bones and an unpleasant memory of the dean's office pops into my head. A chill touches off in my spine and goose bumps erupt up and down my arms like a time-lapse film of moss growing on a damp log.

Mr. Jenkins returns my brief resume to its folder and lays it on the desk. He nods at my arms. "You cold?"

"No, I'm fine." I clamp my teeth together so they won't chatter.

"Well then, young lady," he says. "Tell me about yourself."

I sit quietly in my chair. The intensity with which I want this job at Bridgeway is in exact inverse proportion to my preparedness for it. I know that. My actual counseling experience—*as* one, that is, not across from one—is practically nil. Suddenly, everything I thought I had going for me on the way here—my survival credential, my renowned listening abilities—seems both too large and too small to mention. Without those, all I have is my bachelor's degree, one six-month internship that I wasn't fired from, and an eagerness I am trying not to let spill over into desperation.

"Well, I'm from Atlanta," I begin. "I graduated from Oglethorpe University in May. In my senior year, I did an internship at the State hospital on the alcohol and drug unit. It was great experience. I sat in on rounds and assisted with treatment planning and counseling sessions." ("Assisted" is pushing the envelope. What I did was watch, and, in truth, what I watched more often than not was a handsome young counselor named Stuart.)

What I do not say: At the State hospital, chronic substance abusers checked in and out like traveling salesmen, most in search not of help but of food and a place to sleep ("three hots and a cot," spat the nurse almost every time she admitted a new patient). My job was mostly to shadow the counselors, and glean what I could from the questions they asked. *How does your drinking interfere with your life? Who has been impacted? What's been the cost? How will you do things differently?* Hard questions whose answers, I knew from personal experience, demanded time and space to flower, rather than the days or hours allotted.

What else I don't say: Prior to securing the internship at the State hospital, I took a volunteer position on a private eating disorders unit, a tightly run program that boasted holistic, individually tailored treatment plans for the eating disordered daughters of families with money. It did not occur to me to dress carefully so as to camouflage my emaciated frame; in my mind, release from the hospital was proof that I was as good as cured. After a morning touring the warm, sunny, residential unit, appreciating the blue-and -peach color scheme and hefty, overstuffed sofas perfect for passing long, hungry, weepy afternoons, the director invited me to lunch. A part of me suspected this was a test: *Would I eat? Could I eat?* And yet it did not register that, by her very need to test me, she was already having doubts about me. Technically, I could eat. But not without engaging in a few of my more tenacious food compulsions: the mashing of my food with a fork and eating off the back of it, only eating things I could divide, like the whites of eggs and the crusts of breads, eating while tapping my foot. And so I explained—in a casual voice that I somehow believed conveyed matter-of-factness rather than lingering food terror—that I would leave for lunch and report back for work at one p.m. The director nodded.

"All right, then," she said.

Twenty minutes later, I was standing in my mother's kitchen meticulously hollowing out half of a bagel in preparation for a thin smear of low-calorie Weight Watcher's butter when the director called.

"I don't think you're quite far enough along in your recovery to be a good role model for our patients," she said.

* * *

"Enjoy your internship?" Mr. Jenkins asks.

The question jolts me back into the moment. "Oh! Yes," I say.

Mr. Jenkins waits. I grope for something to add. "I learned a lot about addiction. And relapse. And I got to see how an inpatient unit operates." I don't tell him about all the counseling conversations not had, all the ins and outs of dealing with addicts not learned. I certainly don't mention Stuart, though it would thrill me, even now, to utter his name out loud.

"Tell me about relapse." Mr. Jenkins's eyes are fixed on my face, where the sharp angles of my cheeks have been chiseled by three years of six-hundred-calorie-a-day dieting. My heart, the one organ I cannot will into submission, does a little triple axel.

"People—addicts—relapse because they lose touch with how they feel and what they need. They get overwhelmed and stop working their program. When they stop working their program, they're more vulnerable, which makes it easy to start using again." I stop talking but my heart is spinning like a noisy fan in my chest.

Mr. Jenkins looks down at his hands. "Spoken from experience?"

A ripple of pain shoots from the pointy ends of my butt bones all the way up to my neck. My arms are ice cold and rubbery.

Mr. Jenkins flicks a piece of lint from his blue jeans. The clock on the wall, a gift from Camel cigarettes, ticks with obscene patience. Outside, a gassy truck lumbers up Worship Avenue. I wrestle with how much to reveal and what constitutes lying. Mr. Jenkins looks up at me carefully. "Are you speaking from experience?"

"I-myself-have-never-had-an-alcohol-or-drug-related-problem," I say. A wall of formality and absolutes, practiced and false-sounding. "I'm extremely responsible," I add, as if to say, *and anyway, addictions are simply a function of dependability.*

There is a long pause. I wonder whether Mr. Jenkins is waiting for me to say something else, something reassuring about myself, or brilliant, or personal. I think about what he is seeing, that I am twenty-five pounds underweight ("Thirty," says my sister; "Forty," says my mother), and about how it takes something outside of me—a job interview, for example—to break the opaque ice of body blindness and reveal the truth of me to me. Because suddenly I can't *not* see that my collarbones protrude from the neck of my ruffled shirt like etched mountain peaks, or that my shoulders, narrow and birdlike, are more befitting an eight-year-old child, or that the faintly visible, knotty rungs of my spine are screaming in protest because they are protected from a hard metal chair by only a thin sheath of skin. It is a maddening game the anorexic consciousness plays with itself, a kind of *Now I See Me, Now I Don't,* which is further complicated by the fact that the longer one goes without being able to see oneself clearly, the harder it becomes to know, in any given moment, what clear really is. It is like living in two worlds whose intersection is brief and small and always a surprise.

"Fair enough," Mr. Jenkins says at last.

Bridgeway House has a problem. Hundreds of clients pass through the program in any given year, and the State would like to increase this number. But for six long months they have been in need of a third counselor, the required number just to keep their doors open. The pay is low, admits Mr. Jenkins, but the experience invaluable. Did I have any questions?

My extremities are so numb that I can no longer feel them. I wag my foot in little half-circles to keep my blood flowing. What I have heard is that Bridgeway needs me. That I am going to save Bridgeway.

"No questions," I say.

"How do you feel about relocating?"

"To Tifton?"

"That's where we are."

I practically jump out of my chair. "I'd love to relocate!"

Mr. Jenkins smiles. "Then go tell your momma you got the job."

Chapter 3

A Map of Destruction

I AM A CHILD OF THE NORTHWEST Atlanta suburbs. I grew up in a ranch house surrounded by woods that bordered other ranch houses with landscaped lawns and backyard swimming pools and neatly fenced tennis courts that never seemed to have anyone on them. Our house was modest, with barely more room than we needed for a family of five, but it was, owing to my mother's artistic sensibilities, a blend of farmhouse antiques, original art, and contemporary furniture. Once, in my mid-twenties, I brought a new boyfriend home to meet my parents. We sat in the stylish warmth of the den, just the four of us, my father in his soft chair by the globe lamp, my mother perched on the edge of the sofa. Behind her on the wall, extending from the kitchen to the white brick fireplace, were a charcoal rendering of Moses, a black-and-white lithograph of Abraham Lincoln, an oil rendering, by my mother, of my father's flute, and another oil rendering, also by my mother, of John F. Kennedy. There was a framed photograph of my sister, nine years older than me, at the piano, and another photograph, taken by my brother, five years older than me, of a Jamaican child standing outside a shack. On the antique hutch, along with framed pictures of our family's first granddaughter, was a handcrafted silver menorah. Had I told my boyfriend nothing about my family, he could have known, from this room alone, my parents' religious and political leanings, their values, their passions, what they wanted. I myself had never seen my parents so clearly as I did that afternoon.

Like our neighbors, my family spent most of their time indoors, even in the comfortable seasons, with a few noteworthy exceptions. I loved horses, and took riding lessons from the time I was six. And twice a summer, my father, in khakis and dress shoes, hauled out our temperamental push mower and, sweating and cursing, his face growing redder each time the machine sputtered and quit, mowed an area the size of a parked car. For a few inspired summers, we rented a houseboat for a week on Lake Lanier a few hours east of Atlanta— trying times for a family illiterate in sunshine and deep water. True to our nature, we kids spent much of our time below deck where it was cool, playing cards and eating peanut butter sandwiches in our bathing suits while, elsewhere on the boat, my father slept and my mother searched endlessly for a can opener. These trips to the lake invariably ended badly. Once we docked on a small island, and my brother, fifteen, ran away for the afternoon. Once we thought our dog had fallen overboard. Once we ran out of gas in the middle of the lake and had to be towed back to port. And once my sister threw the anchor overboard, not realizing it wasn't tied to the boat.

* * *

We were terrible at play because we didn't know how. We were a family that placed a premium on seriousness: on education, on liberalism, on language, and on good deed. We were conservative Jews but not religious, observant but, as my friend Sara would later put it, without the comfort one expects from affiliation. Both of my grandmothers were deceased, and both of my grandfathers remarried women uninterested in—and in the case of my maternal grandfather, downright hostile to—children. There was an uncle and an aunt on my father's side, but we almost never saw them or our six cousins. Friends were discouraged; for companionship, we kept a steady stream of Welsh corgis and tropical fish.

And just as we were terrible at play, we were terrible at love, because we didn't know how to do that, either. Granted, as a family, our crimes were small crimes. We didn't talk about what bothered us. We honed a sense of humor that was sharp and cutting, and we took great pleasure in forcing others to laugh at their own expense. We were poor listeners. We were insulting and sarcastic, withholding and unsympathetic. Our jokes welled up from a fountain of subconscious anger, and our laughter ricocheted around the dinner table in wicked epithets. We were untrusting and judgmental, as bitter to one another as we were to outsiders, as condescending as we were openly critical. And strangely, we believed deeply in the myth of our family closeness, mistaking insularity for intimacy and feelings of superiority for pride. There were no bruises, no harrowing tales of abandonment, no drunken pillages or public shamings. But ours was a family that ate at itself like a cancer.

I can hear my brother, five years older, already disagreeing.

"Mom and Dad weren't perfect, but they were respectable people with good intentions and they loved us."

Which is true.

Here's what else is true: My mother did not like being a mother. She was prone to sudden rages whose triggers shape-shifted: one day it might be shoes out of place or an unexpected guest, another day it might be dishes in the sink or a phone ringing at dinnertime. Her rage neatly followed the narrative of her unhappiness with my father, the gist of which was that he saddled her with children, quashed her creative energies, and turned all his attention to work. He had everything—independence, celebrity (he was the author of several books and a newspaper columnist), a social life, and stimulation, while my mother had children and a housekeeper and a suburban enclave, all of which added up to a domesticity she didn't know she despised until she got it. Rage in all its forms—impotent, seething, weepy, diabolical—was her only recourse. Once, on a family trip to Gatlinburg, my father tried to get off a shopping mall escalator that hadn't quite crested and tripped over the little step that remained, falling forward onto his hands and knees. I had never seen my father fall down before; it had never even occurred to me that he *could* fall down. My brother, sister, and I stood with our hands over our mouths, holding our breath, waiting for him to get back up, while behind us, I could hear my mother laughing.

This glee, this schadenfreude, I saw again and again until my father's death, anytime he stubbed a toe, dropped a fork, tripped over a word. These tiny misfortunes were the little cracks in my father's so-called perfect life through which my mother's rage clawed its way in. This was his punishment, his comeuppance, for disallowing her potential while going on to have himself a life.

My mother's anger was so predictable that, by the time I was ten, I could gauge her moods by the way she moved from stove to refrigerator, how much milk she put in her coffee, the way she lit a cigarette. These barely perceptible actions were like forecasts to me, unspoken promises of what lay ahead. Her intensity segued neatly with that of my brother, who was smart and popular but angry for reasons I could not know then. Like a magnet, my mother's anger drew him out of his room, and soon he and I would be fighting.

"He hit me!" I seemed to always be saying, to the bored audience of my parents.

My father let himself out through the back door of sleep. He napped after work and through weekend afternoons. At dinner, he stared drowsily past me, leaving quickly to return to his bed. Later, from the hallway, I would hear above his snoring the tinny laugh track from *All in the Family*. It was an eerie juxtaposition, like a silly song with a tortured beat.

It was in this way that my father left our lives. He never walked out, and my parents never divorced. Instead he made his graceful, gradual exit by backing out of the picture day-by-day. When my mother could no longer stand the isolation, she raged louder, and my father, surprised every time, would wake briefly to her dissatisfaction. A short period of reconciliation would ensue, during which time they might go to therapy, but this always drew to a predictable close when one parent or the other proclaimed the therapist intellectually inferior. When the crisis had passed, my mother retreated and my father went back to sleep. It was a scenario that played out every several months, like hapless drunks who drink and fall down, then drink and fall down, then drink and fall down.

"Why don't you divorce?" I asked my mother when I was fourteen. Hadn't my father disappointed her in a hundred small ways, his dress uninspired, his hygiene questionable, his attentiveness to her needs unapparent? Hadn't he slept through most of our lives? Hadn't he allowed himself a covert addiction to Valium and painkillers, and didn't he deny this to us, his rummaging family, who found evidence in all the obvious places: pockets and dresser drawers, medicine chests and loose change bowls?

"He doesn't drink or run around," my mother said.

"Why don't you divorce?" I asked my father. Hadn't my mother expected too much, and hadn't my father given enough? Money and comfort, cars and classes, fine clothing and parties and overseas vacations, plus the perks that came with being the wife of a well-known author, all of which she accepted and thrived on, while pining for a life of her own?

"Marriage is a contract broken only by death," my father said.

Since talk of divorce invariably ended with the proclamation that my father was behaviorally appropriate and my mother was an obligation to be kept, we continued as we always had. My father slept and my mother raged. My brother and I enacted our own messy version of the drama between them, alternately fighting with and ignoring each other. I was, for years, closest to my sister, nine years older, a brilliant student, pianist, and later, poet, who sequestered herself in her room under a noisy hairdryer with her books and her lined notepaper and her diary and her quietly mushrooming depression.

By the time I was fifteen, a ghostlike thread was all that remained between my parents. They slept at far ends of a wide bed, clipping their words and referring to each other as Him and Her.

"Go tell Him it's time to eat," my mother would say to me.

"What's wrong with Her?" my father would ask me.

And so they stood on the chasm of disappointment, angry and lonely but neither at fault, and neither strong enough to lead the way back from the brink. My mother pulled me into the emptiness, and left my father hanging weightless, like a floating piñata in an empty back room. Occasionally, we might try to spear him for something we needed—money, his presence at a dinner—but mostly we let him float, silent, unnecessary, and pleased to be left alone. If we talked about where he had gone, our eyes went to the ceiling and we shrugged our shoulders. This is how, at fifteen, I married my mother, becoming for her what my father wasn't: someone to talk to, someone to eat with, and someone to race-walk with, and later, someone to diet with, someone to make fun of my father with, and finally, someone to loathe him with.

For years the progressive dissolution of my family worried me in ways I couldn't articulate. I was restless and unhappy at school, lonely and lost at home. I joined no clubs, attended no parties or proms, and avoided the telephone. On afternoons and weekends, I wandered the house, stopping at the dining room window to watch the trickle of cars on our street. Where were they going, I wondered? What did people do all day, and how did they convince themselves it mattered? I was sad for them, sad for their weary cars, sad for their pointless expeditions.

"Everything is sad to you," my brother said one day, which was the first time it occurred to me that everything wasn't sad to everyone.

This is how a family's unhappiness compresses you: by encircling you like air, obscuring you like fog, then drowning you like water. Anorexia would be just the first stop on the archipelago of my family's illnesses; down the chain, we would also drop anchor at heart disease, depression, panic attacks, chronic fatigue syndrome, and two kinds of cancer.

This is what I bring forward into my life. This is what I bring to Bridgeway House.

Chapter 4

A Cure for Death

A T BARD, THREE WEEKS AFTER I received my message of healing at Stereo World, I had lost five of the offending ten pounds. Within six weeks, I had lost the other five. To say that my success was intoxicating is to grossly understate the way I felt about it. My success was, for me, like winning an Oscar, or discovering a cure for polio, or cancer, or for that matter, death. To understand why it felt so big, you have to consider the story that came before, the one that had been building up around my weight since fifth grade and that finally exploded on the Bard College campus. You have to consider what those ten unwanted pounds (I can't even say "extra," because this supposes that I was overweight by any standard, which I was not) said to me about my womanhood, my sexual being, my human being. You have to consider the way that those ten pounds were imbued with a kind of magical power, which I believed was responsible for every less-than-satisfactory thing that had happened in my life up to that moment in my eighteenth year.

In searching for the source of my weight's magical powers, I come back time and again to two particular events. The first takes place at my fifth-grade school lunch table. Classmate Randy Russell, upon watching me gnaw a chicken drumstick, says, "What happened to you?

You were cute in second grade."

What had "happened" was that, for a few months before I would reach my full height of five feet, nine inches tall, the weight which would be distributed nicely on my new lanky frame pooled in a rounded belly, an extra chin, and jiggling thighs. In addition (though I add the following only to give a narrator's full account of things as they were and not to suggest that anything other than the weight mattered), I had recently gotten my long ropy hair cut into heavy bangs, transitioned into a pair of oversized, octagonal, wire-rimmed eyeglasses whose lenses were distorting and too thick for their frames, and been fitted for braces on my teeth.

I can't think about this interaction with Randy Russell without recalling the cold metal frame of the folding lunch table pushing into the tops of my thighs, and the acrid smell of yeast rolls comingling in the air with the sickly-sweet perfume of cornflake-marshmallow bars. Randy Russell's assessment of the ground lost between ages seven and ten is a psychic memento frozen in the fusty air of a schoolroom cafeteria. Along with the realization that I had been deemed "no longer cute" is the concomitant realization that an earlier assessment had taken place, that of "cute," but this kinder analysis doesn't matter. *Assessment* is the operative event here, and it wakes me to all kinds of realities about my life, the main one being that I have never and can never putter happily and invisibly around the playground of my own head immune to the appraisals of others. It is this sudden thrusting into the (as I see it) cruel light of outside opinion that means I will have to forevermore divide my attention between the blissfully private inner park of imagination and the problem of outer image. Later I will read that anorexia is the embodiment of the struggle between a desire for invisibility and a yearning for recognition, and will marvel at the irony of it: how vanishing makes others look harder at you. But until then, there is the problem of Randy Russell's commentary, the sudden jolt that is the beast of self-censure now waking in me, asking now and forever, *what happened?*

* * *

And the second event is this, also from my tenth year: I am in the upper parking lot of my synagogue. I've asked my mother for a dime for the Coke machine because I dropped the first one she gave me down the radiator in my Sunday School classroom. My mother doesn't believe me and thinks I am angling for a second Coke. There is a pause, a gathering rage. Then she throws the second dime at me.

"Here," she says. "You fat ugly pig."

The first time I talk about this in the hospital, I defend my mother.

"She thought I hadn't really lost the first dime," I explained. "She thought I'd already had one Coke, and that I was lying to get another one."

"That's not how you talk to a child," the counselors said. "How did it make you feel?"

"The ice was good," I joked, remembering the soft little ice cubes that fell into the cup ahead of the Coke and that crunched up cold and delicate as snow in my mouth.

The second time I talked about the episode, I expounded: "You don't understand. My mother's anger might have been misplaced, but that doesn't mean it wasn't justified. She was a slave to an institution that was failing her!" (This eloquent summation, of my mother's feelings about marriage and society and child rearing, would, I believed, win me insight points with the counselors. For wasn't this what the conversation was really about: my *mother's* feelings, not mine?)

"Okay, so she was a slave to her marriage," the counselors said. *"But how did her words make you feel?"*

The third time I talked about it—*my mother was unhappy, I was the last child at home, a burden*—the room was silent, the only noise the buzzing of the overhead lights. Ten faces—two counselors and eight patients—stared at their laps. No one said, *how did you feel about being called a fat ugly pig by your mother?* No one said anything.

"I felt," I said finally, but I didn't know how I felt.

"What did you *do?*" someone asked.

I thought back. I caught the dime against my chest. I walked back across the parking lot and into the synagogue, through the dark sanctuary and out the other side to the Coke machine. I dropped the dime in the slot and punched the button and waited for the little red cup to fill. I drank the entire thing and chewed up all the little ice cubes. I walked back across the parking lot to my mother's car.

"I can see it like it was yesterday," I said.

What do you notice?

Nothing. I'm staring at the ground. No wait—I'm staring at my *thighs*—they're slapping together.

What else?

My belly—a round mound beneath my stretchy shirt.

What do you feel?

Fat.

Fat is not a feeling. Happy, sad, angry, lonely, tired are feelings. Which of those emotions *do you feel?*

Fat.

* * *

Of course I didn't know at the time of the Coke incident that the real source of my mother's anger was lying at home in front of the television set eating a lunch of hard salami and Saltine crackers. What I couldn't fathom as a ten-year-old was what I knew all too well as a fifteen-year-old: that my mother was unhappily married and the discontented mother of three. That she was in a world of grief that had nothing to do with me or my need for a second dime. But in the way that unrelated consequence can seem to answer earlier inquiry, what arrived at the doorstep of my consciousness that day in the upper parking lot of my synagogue was my answer to Randy Russell's lunchroom question: *What happened was that I became a fat ugly pig.*

* * *

On my first day of work at Bridgeway, I wake at seven a.m. I have to be at work by eight, but as I stand in front of my closet looking for what I will wear, every pair of pants bleats out a story of discomfort and displeasure. It is a curious irony, like that of the vanishing, spot-lit anorexic, that all of my clothes are somehow both too tight and too loose, their tale the tale of living at both ends of every spectrum at once—in this case, somehow both too large and too small, physically of course, but psychically as well. At last, I settle on a pair of gray jeans, a gigantic faded pink T-shirt belted at my waist, and flat-soled, black Chinese slippers. Whether I think this outfit is professional is lost on me now, though I suspect I bypassed the "professional" question by telling myself it was "creative." However, since my awareness of how I look to the outside world flits in and out like a nervous bird (which is how the interview prom dress happened) what will happen today is that I will get to work and the bird of awareness will flit in and I will see the gray jean/pink T-shirt ensemble for what it is: weekend wear at best, and even then, ill-fitting. Imagine (if you can) a mirror over which a curtain falls every few seconds while you are fixing your hair or getting dressed. Now imagine the mirror is a rippling lake. This is body image distortion, and while the fat/thin juxtaposition is what the anorexic is most famous for (seeing her skeletal body as waddling and gelatinous), her ideas about how to present herself—what to wear when and how her clothes should fit, for example—are also shifting and unstable. Certainly starvation wreaks havoc on acuity, but poor self-regard plays a part here as well, given that body image distortion often lives on once nutritional stability is restored. Here I think of a hydroponic plant, growing in the absence of soil. Certainly something is feeding the roots—in my case, a rich mix of rigidity, self-contempt, and anxiety.

* * *

It seems to me a glitch in city planning that Bridgeway sits in the middle of downtown Tifton. Before my interview, I romanticized the idea of halfway houses, envisioning them in remote, idyllic locations removed from the pressures of city life and the glare of the public spotlight. This I now recognize as my younger self's own escapist fantasy. I recall that, in response to a therapist's question, I once asserted that desert-island living was the place for me, as it would remove me from public scrutiny, thereby allowing me to eat whenever and whatever I pleased (suggesting that I believed my problems with eating came from the simple condition of existing side-by-side with other humans). The therapist wasted no time debunking my preposterous proposal, by suggesting that the glare in which I found myself so uncomfortably caught was none but my own.

"I think you already live on a desert island," he said. "You need *more* of the real world, not less."

He was right of course. Over a span of twenty years, I'd virtually never listened to a news story all the way through. I'd never given thought to my religious upbringing (except to quit Sunday School out of a boredom I couldn't even disguise as moral disagreement because it didn't occur to me to morally disagree with conservative Judaism). When called upon to give my views on the "Israel/Palestinian problem," I recused myself by calling the topic "too heated" (though I didn't know why it was heated; I'd only surmised it from the fact that people felt compelled to ask me, a Jew, about it). Certainly I had never voted, and though I could name who was on the ticket, I could not discuss what was at stake, nor did I care. No, over the span of my twenty years, I had done little besides chronicle, in a succession of carefully chosen lined and unlined blank books, the mostly miniscule moments of my existence. Bad tennis days were dissected, but there is no mention of the Manson family murders. Trips to the Chattahoochee River on horseback were recounted, but nothing about the young black boys (thirteen of them by the time Wayne Williams was convicted) who were being abducted and murdered, including one or more whose bodies were dumped in—yes—the Chattahoochee River. At college in 1979, I meticulously made note of my ever-changing moods, even describing how seeing the chalk phrase "Free the Hostages" on the sidewalk fueled my sadness about a world whose machinations terrified me, but my compassion did not extend to the actual men and women being held hostage in Iran. Mine was an insular world where everything that happened boomeranged back to me for the sole purpose of inflaming or frightening me.

There is a joke about a man who hears that the hostess of a party he was supposed to attend has died tragically, which forces him to cancel his plans. Bemoans the man, "Why does everything have to happen to me?"

This was me.

* * *

And so my first lesson this first day at Bridgeway is a basic one. Isolation-as-cure, while dreamy, is dangerous, and flies directly in the face of the actual mission of halfway houses, Bridgeway notwithstanding. Their purpose is to stop the addict's flight from society (through alcohol, drugs, and geography), and to serve as a stepping stone (a bridge, if you will) between the world of addiction and the world of everything else. Bridgeway clients, having already been through a requisite detox and 21-day treatment program, are in the slippery emotional terrain between "addicted" and "recovering," whereby they haven't yet learned the coping skills that will protect their sobriety. Therein lies our job: to give clients something to hold onto as they make their way back into society without alcohol or drugs or fantasies of disappearing. Individual and group therapy, Alcoholics and Narcotics Anonymous meetings, and education groups are all a part of the effort we mount to bolster the newly sober addict's ability to resist the pull of relapse. This is Bridgeway's sole raison d'être. This is why Mr. Jenkins's interview question—*what did I know about relapse and was that knowledge spoken from experience*—hung uncomfortably in the air until I answered satisfactorily, because I looked, for all intents and purposes, like the greedy arms of addiction were still wrapped around my bony shoulders, like it was only a matter of time before I would again be yanked (or go willingly) into that inglorious pit of self-destruction, which would be (as the director of the Eating Disorders unit knew) very bad role modeling, indeed.

* * *

"Good morning young lady," Mr. Jenkins says when I walk in. He scans my outfit and I see his mouth working over words that he doesn't say. He is seated at the desk where I had my interview just two weeks ago, with a large mug of coffee and the newspaper. He points to my interview chair. "Take a load off."

Although he has his own office, Mr. Jenkins will spend most of his time at this desk because it is a hub of activity and he likes being in the center of things. Staff offices—including mine—are off this main room. The front door of the house is visible from it, and clients must pass by it on their way to the group room, the dining room, and the upstairs sleeping quarters. Behind us, in the irregular collection of chairs that encircle the room, sit Henriette, the staff RN, and Margery, the staff secretary. Henriette has been at Bridgeway for fifteen years, and if the grim, hard face and slightly stooped, mannish body are any indication, it's been fifteen hard ones. She's fifty-two, I would learn later, but looks seventy. It's hard to recall whether I disliked her right off or whether it was gradual, an outgrowth of the contempt she seemed to have for me from the start. Margery is around Henriette's age, and has been at Bridgeway twenty years. She is soft-spoken and painfully prim with a blouse buttoned up to her chin, but when I go into the ladies restroom after her, I will be surprised to be enveloped in a cloud of cigarette smoke, and I will somehow understand that it is unmentionable.

I sit down in the chair facing the center of the room and Margery and Henriette. Margery is telling Henriette about taking her grandchildren to Disney World in July and how excited everybody is, including her. Even in animation, Margery is rigid, her smile masklike and brittle.

"Yeah, I did that once." Henriette shakes her head fiercely. This, I will come to understand, is her trademark expression, and it will punctuate every emotion from amusement to disgust.

Margery's mouth pulls into a line and she stuffs down the rest of her cheerful vacation logistics.

"Let's get you hired." Mr. Jenkins pushes the mountain of papers at me that will make me an official employee of Bridgeway House. As I go through them, only scanning and not really reading (working hours, health insurance coverage, workers' compensation, salary, client confidentiality, house rules, grounds for client expulsion, discrimination disclosure, floor plan of the house, fire escape routes, emergency numbers, grounds for employee dismissal . . .) he explains my duties. I will carry a caseload of eight to ten clients, each of whom I will see individually for counseling at least once a week. Along with the other two counselors—Linda, who hasn't shown up yet, and Henriette—I will lead something called Big Group, which is exactly what it sounds like: a group with all twenty or so residents in attendance. Twice a week, I will lead, by myself, something called "Split Group," which will be made up of five or six clients who are not on my caseload. The purpose of this smaller group is to deal with emotional issues that arise in response to Big Group, or to a client's individual therapy session.

"Uh-huh. Okay. Uh-huh. Yes." I am nodding my head gently (to the observer I look like any new employee taking in the information about her duties) but behind the scenes, my heart is acting out a tragic drama in articulate palpitations. *I've never done individual therapy before,* it's screaming. *I've never run a group! I don't know the first question to ask, or the second, or the third. Look at my collarbones* (taps out my heart)*! Look at my oversized pink T-shirt, at the terror in my eyes, and tell me how you think I'm prepared to do any of this?* And then the nervous bird of awareness flits out and I find a perfectly coherent question waiting in the part of my brain that feels reasonably, supremely even, prepared for the job.

"How do you know when a client is making progress?" I ask.

Mr. Jenkins laughs. "It's an art."

* * *

In 1983, the year I found myself at Bridgeway, America's obsession with anorexia nervosa was in full swing. The women's magazines were playing both sides of the industry: models were getting thinner, daughters were starving trying to emulate them, and the magazines responded with not fewer but more skeletal models, alongside alarming (yet somehow titillating) articles and statistics about anorexia. The movie *The Best Little Girl in the World*, about a young woman secretly struggling with anorexia, had been released two years earlier, but it was the death of thirty-two-year-old singer, Karen Carpenter, on February 4, 1983, to cardiac arrest brought on by anorexia, that catapulted awareness of the illness into the mainstream. By the time I arrived at Bridgeway, I had had two close friends who were anorexic. One would never recover. In light of what I knew about addiction—and this included, in my mind, starvation, as the forces that drove not-eating were interchangeable with the forces that drove alcohol and drug abuse—the "art" approach to treatment seemed to me a flaccid arsenal against so steely an opponent. To say I did not understand the spirit of what Mr. Jenkins was saying—that therapy is bigger than techniques and progress notes, and that people are not predictable or all the same—is an understatement. That there was not some acid test or thermometer to determine psychological health and wellness, that recovery was more than anything an agreement between two parties— the addict and the addict's non-addicted side—should not have surprised me. I was living testimony to the wide gap between what appears to be true and what is actually true.

* * *

The front door bursts open. A tall, busty woman of about thirty, with a dragon tattoo on her neck and black hair cropped so tight it looks like it hurts, barrels in. With enormous blue eyes and heavy mascara, she is beautiful in a larger-than-life, dramatic way that terrifies me. I pray that she is not one of my clients. Mr. Jenkins doesn't look up.

"Glad you could join us today," he says.

"Go to hell, Rodney," says the woman, who shoots into one of the offices, throws her purse into a drawer, and slams it. I hear the flick of a cigarette lighter followed by the crackling sound of tobacco igniting. Soon there is the welcome smell of new cigarette smoke.

"Your counterpart," Mr. Jenkins says to me. "Linda, come meet Slim. She's about to make your life easier."

The rustling in Linda's office stops abruptly. She walks out and stands in front of me, hands on her wide hips, tattoo writhing at her neck. Behind her, Margery is grinning and Henriette is scowling.

"Your name is *Slim*?"

"Actually no," I say, blinking up at her, but I don't tell her what my name really is because I'm certain she won't like that either. Her eyes journey up and down the limited expanse of me, taking in the pink T-shirt, the skimpy Chinese slippers, and what isn't there, the other ten to forty pounds I can't allow. She opens her sensual mouth to say something but Mr. Jenkins, thankfully, waves her away.

After signing papers, Mr. Jenkins points to what will be my office, in the corner off the main room. I walk in and lay my purse down on the desk. Mary Tyler Moore's triumphant hat-throw to her own independence on the streets of Minneapolis springs to mind as I turn around and around in the space, taking in the paneled walls, gray metal desk, black plastic trash can, rolling chair, and three large windows with colorless metal school-room blinds. There is one troubling detail: a door that opens onto Linda's office, which, because she is on the telephone, she slams.

My head hurts. For breakfast, I had half an English muffin with a teaspoon of sugar-free strawberry jam, and now, although it is only nine-thirty, there is an ancient, gnawing hunger in my stomach. I know better than to let this happen. I know better than to eat sixty or seventy-five calories and call it a meal, but without my mother standing over me in my kitchen, there is what feels, to my unrecovered self, like a well of freedom into whose dark maw I will be content to tumble for many more months. It is a part of the anorexic playbook: the joy of realizing that no one (and by no one I mean my mother, eyeing me over her own dry half-bagel) is dictating my food choices, leaving me free to make what I know to be terrible ones, followed by pounding hunger headaches and the embarrassing roar of my own caved-in stomach, all reassurances that I have won—i.e., that for one more day, I have not displaced an ounce more space in the universe than I did the day before. I close the door to the main room, sit down, and lay my head on my desk. Slowly, stealthily, my hands find their way into my shirt, and I feel for the pudge underneath.

Chapter 5

The Four Questions

HERE IS A KNOCK AT MY DOOR. My head snaps up. I've been an official Bridgeway employee for ten minutes, during which time I've done nothing but sit with my forehead touching my desk. Without waiting for me to answer, Linda pushes the door between our offices open. She leans a hip against the doorframe.

"Hi," she says.

"Hi."

"You smoke?"

I nod. There is a pause and then she points a finger at her throat. "Do you *aack?*"

My heart makes a little exclamation point. Only shrinks have ever asked me openly if I vomit.

"What? *No!*" I say, making a face to convey how truly unacceptable the idea is to me. It's a point of pride among women who control their weight through starvation that they do not binge or purge. The very idea that someone might think they ever lose control and stuff monumental amounts of food down their throat or that their weight loss is somehow "unearned" by cheating (i.e., throwing up) is unbearable. In part, not binging/purging is about not wanting to seem out of control. But it's also about the audiovisuals. Vomiting is a deeply private act and profoundly disturbing to witness. As an anorexic, I am already ashamed of my desire for food, so the last thing I want is for anyone to think I give it more than a cursory thought. Gorging on bread and chips and ice cream and who-knows-what else and then bringing it all back up before the calories have time to assimilate? That's a lot of thought.

"Okay," Linda says. She glances over her shoulder to the main office, then looks back at me. She lowers her voice. "You should come to supper at my house. I'll tell you everything you need to know about this place."

"Thanks," I say, managing a smile though the invitation annoys me. Because of course I can't "come to supper," for reasons just explained (I can't be seen desiring food), but also because my suppers, like my breakfasts, are carefully meted out resources that must be consumed in a specific place. At night it's either air-popped popcorn sprinkled with water to hold the salt on or a hollowed-out bagel with a paper-thin spread of diet margarine, eaten in the green recliner I bought at the Salvation Army store the day after I moved to Tifton. The food and the recliner are inextricably linked. While I can sit in the recliner without eating, I cannot eat the food anywhere but in the recliner, a combination of ritual, familiarity, and comfort, all of which I believe I have consciously created for myself but which in fact has bloomed out of random chance, fear, and the obsessive need to control my environment and my consumption. A web of contingencies I could no sooner recall building than I could have torn down for a single night's supper out. The same way it would come to irritate me when people wished me a Merry Christmas, never considering the possibility of my Jewishness, Linda's invitation to supper—having established that I do not "aack" but without consideration for the world of possibilities beyond "aack," irritates me. And so, although I have no plans for my evening except to go to my apartment and wait for the next day, I decline.

"Thanks, but I can't," I say.

"Ooh, you found you a *man* already?" Her syrupy Southern accent coupled with her carnival-style make-up and neck tattoo makes the suggestion sound lewd. Linda's bifurcated world of puking and fucking is already beginning to wear on me, and I've known her for less than an hour.

I can hear Mr. Jenkins' deep laugh in the main room. "Linda!" he says. "Be nice. She's new!"

"She can take it," Linda says watching me.

"Show her around," Mr. Jenkins says. "Show her the upstairs, take her to the kitchen."

"You show her around," Linda yells back.

Mr. Jenkins pokes his head in the door. "You skatin' on thin ice," he says. "Show Slim the ropes."

And so with a jaded and practiced boredom, Linda leads the way out of the main office and begins our tour of the house. She waves her hand absently toward the end of the hallway.

"Down there's the group room," she says. "Next to that's the poop room." She laughs at her own rhyme. She points to a plain wooden door just outside the main office that has a hole in it the size of a fist. "Up there's where they sleep and shower. Most of them are at work right now. We have a contract with a factory in town."

"Can we go up?"

Linda stifles an eye-roll and pulls open the door. A curtain of hot air falls over us. We clomp up a long, narrow flight of steps at the top of which we emerge into an open area with ten or twelve cots. Heavily scratched and grafittied communal dressers and thin, stand-alone closets line the perimeter. A few yellowed posters with slogans like *One Day at a Time* and *Hang in There* cling to the wall. Several box fans work to keep the air circulating; still, it's humid and smells like mildew. It is nothing like the private, sunny bedrooms in the remote, idyllic house I'd imagined.

"This is the women's side," Linda says. "The men's looks the same, only there are more beds and it smells worse." Without waiting for me to say anything, she turns around and clomps back down the steps. We emerge from the fist-punched door, make a U-turn, and start down a second flight of steps, this one wider, leading to the kitchen and dining area. The lurid, tropical smell of bananas envelopes us. My stomach churns hungrily. I pray that Linda can't hear it.

"Banana puddin'," Linda says, looking back at me. "You'll love

Miss Hattie's banana puddin'. We'll get some after dinner."

"I hate bananas," I lie.

Linda rolls her eyes again. I hold my breath, waiting for the confrontation about food, eating, about my weight—Linda could take aim at any one of these and hit her mark. Remarkably, she doesn't. Instead she says simply, "She makes a mean cherry pie, too," and follows it with the thing that is like a bomb: "Oh, and staff and residents eat together. It's just a perk; it's free."

* * *

The supposedly wonderful news of Bridgeway's free and social lunch agenda hits me like a punch in the stomach. Because it isn't just that I couldn't eat at the eating disorders unit where I wanted the volunteer job; it's that I can't eat in public *at all*. But while I can construct a lie like "I hate bananas," to excuse me from one specific pudding, I can think of nothing that will excuse me, for the duration of my employment at Bridgeway House, from the communal noonday meal.

"Oh, that's nice," I say. I glance at the menu board. Today's generous offering is macaroni and cheese, corn bread, fried okra, salad with ranch dressing, banana pudding, and sweet tea. The tickertape of numbers flashing in my brain estimates that dinner, were I to eat a serving of everything, would set me back by about eight hundred calories, a number so far above what I currently eat in an entire day (sometimes two) that even now I can recall the horror I felt standing in that kitchen surrounded by those smells and the expectation that, as a fully recovered, non-relapsing superhero to the addicted, I had no recourse but to scarf down whatever amount of whatever food was ladled onto my plate—at a strange table far from my green recliner no less—and pretend that there would be no fallout: that I would not go home and do four solid hours of aerobic exercise followed by a week of fasting.

I scour the dining area for somewhere I can (pretend to) eat out of the public eye. But the room is agonizingly, fluorescently bright with ten square metal tables, all in plain sight of one another and the kitchen. There will be nowhere to take my full milk-fat mac-and-cheese and salad greens with their blanket of dressing and push them around on my plate until it looks as if part has been carelessly eaten, part carelessly left.

A gray-faced resident, who I remember seeing the morning of my interview, is at the large metal sink, washing a deep pot. She turns off the water and plucks her cigarette out of her mouth.

"How's your momma?" she calls out, but I ignore her.

"There's no privacy here," I whisper to Linda. "Everything's so open."

"Yep," she says. She starts us down the hall to the social room. "Keeps 'em honest."

Don't I know this? Don't I know from my Psychology classes, from my internship, from my own treatment, from life itself, that visibility is the best deterrent to crime, including crimes against the self, including relapse? I am beginning to see it clearly now: like the house set (inexplicably, I thought at first) amid the watchful eye of the town, the residents live amid the watchful eye of the house. Here I think back to the hospital, to the forced trips to the cafeteria where I was allowed my choice of food but not where to eat it, exposing everything I ate (and didn't eat) to public scrutiny, every dinnertime having at its core a kind of Passover-inspired litany of Four Questions: *Why on this night do you only eat the whites of your eggs? Why on this night do you mash your food with your fork? Why on this night do you cut off the crusts off your bread and then throw the* bread *away? Why on this night do you not eat at all?* An excruciating running commentary that prevented me from doing what I had been doing for nearly two years, which was to tuck awareness of my own strangeness away where I would not have to explain it or confront it.

This is how we know ourselves, through the eyes of those around us. Here I think about a Fig Newton episode from the hospital, whereby I was working to separate the sugary fig middle from the less caloric and therefore "legal" dry crust. In a defining scene, I am sitting high on my bed, working a little plastic knife between the crusty skin and the subcutaneous fig, a surgical intervention of grave importance that day. At the same moment that the wide door of my room pushes open and my counselor Elaine (of wire-rimmed-glasses-and great-swimming-goldfish-eyes fame) steps in, my hand *slips* and my trusty knife plunges deep into figgy territory. I freeze, but I do not look up. Elaine, undeterred by the fact that I do not acknowledge her presence, sits down next to me on my bed. It sags significantly under her weight (she is not fat but neither is she thin and I register both of these things while still pretending not to know she is there) and her eyes (I can feel them, even now, thirty years later) light first on the eviscerated cookie in my hand and then come to rest on the side of my face. At the bottom of my trash can, which she (mercifully) cannot see from where she sits, are the lifeless bodies of three other Fig Newtons, their sticky middles glued so firmly there that it will require a small amount of force for the cleaning woman to pry them loose (a task that will engender disgust although about what exactly she won't be certain).

What matters here is not Elaine's reaction (I have no recollection of what she said or if she in fact said anything) but what her arrival did to me, which was to awaken a shame so intense over the fact that I had been caught *caring about* food, in this case a snack cookie, that I redoubled my efforts to lose weight after that, which accounted for my additional five-pound weight loss early in my hospitalization. To explain how multilayered and profound is the shame I felt, you have to think in terms of the politician who gets caught with his hands in the coffer, or worse, up the dress of a mistress. Anorexia is in fact a kind of mistress, a beloved other that you hide from the public eye in the belief that the world can't understand your kind of love and will therefore mock it, try to show you how it isn't really real. And so in the interest of protecting what you know to be true, which is that your beloved is the thing that will ultimately save you, you engage secretly in your relationship—in the beginning, to throw family and friends off your trail as you winnow your daily calorie count down to next to nothing, and later as well, as you maximize the amount of time you spend jogging or leg-lifting or sit-upping off the calories you still allow yourself. What starts as a plan to protect that which gives your life meaning and that which you adore morphs into a kind of terror and embarrassment about your own passion, and about the possibility of having it taken away.

We leave the cafeteria and walk down another short hall.

"And this is the social room," says Linda. Another wide open space without partition or privacy. There is the rank smell of old cloth sofas and platter-sized ashtrays overflowing with cigarette butts. Magazines pressed into service as coasters lie rippled and coffee-stained across two long tables. Linda introduces me to the residents waiting for morning AA, pointing at each person as she says their name. *Aline, Larry, Johnny, Mike, Katy, Eli, Sid.* No one gets up or smiles. Their eyes travel my torso, taking in the big pink T-shirt, the little slippers. They are dressed better than me: the men in fitted blue jeans and button down shirts, the women in a long flowing hippie skirts. Linda points at me. "New counselor. She'll kick your ass." And with that she whirls around and starts back up the stairs, leaving me speechless in the smirking, headlamp gaze of seven scary addicts.

"Nice to meet you," I say, then turn and run up the steps two at a time. A smattering of laughter follows me up.

* * *

At eleven-thirty, Linda pokes her head into my office. "Dinner is served."

I look up from the chart I've been flipping through robotically for the last hour, while fretting about lunch and hatching a plan.

"I'm heading out to the Humane Society," I say. "I'm getting a cat."

"Really? Right now?"

"I wanted to bring my dog, but my apartment complex doesn't allow them." By the time I say this well-rehearsed line out loud, I have already envisioned every Bridgeway lunch hour for the foreseeable future: *Wish I could stay for lunch but I have to go home and feed my cat.* I don't know that cats can go for days without human contact, that a few dry nuggets in a bowl and some water is all that's needed to keep them happy.

But I don't go to the Humane Society. Instead, I drive the two miles home, sprint up the steps to my apartment, slam the door behind me, and compose a resignation letter.

* * *

There's a story in my family that goes like this: When my mother took my sister to the University of North Carolina at the beginning of her freshman year, her roommates had already moved into their dorm room. My mother carried my sister's belongings from the car as my sister lay on her bed, and, as her new roommates looked on, instructed my mother where to put things. I shook my head when my mother told this story. It reeked of entitlement, I thought, a complex and arrogant exhaustion.

Now I see it differently. I think about when my parents dropped me off at Bard College in Upstate New York, nine hundred miles from home. It was February, three months after my seventeenth birthday, halfway through what should have been my senior year in high school. I'd applied for early admission and was ecstatic to be accepted, but staring out my dorm window as a heavy snow fell and the reality of being on my own set in, I was suddenly terrified. In an effort to calm myself, I set to work arranging my room and putting away my clothes. I made hospital corners on my sheets, and tucked my ivory down comforter around them. I lined up my shoes and new furry boots in the closet, set my hot-pot on my desk next to my typewriter, and opened a ream of paper. As I worked, my fear lessened, and in time, I was no longer thinking about my parents speeding south down Highway-9G toward Atlanta without me.

An hour later, I was pulled from my reverie by the sound of a lone car making its way down the icy campus road. I went to my window. There, unbelievably, were my parents, just then leaving. Unbeknownst to me, they had gone to meet the dean and look around the college.

The car moved at an achingly slow speed, my father at the wheel, unaccustomed to icy roads. I could see my parents both facing rigidly forward, as if to look elsewhere would pull the car astray. As the noise of the tires faded and the swirling snow swallowed up the car's red taillights, my terror returned: I was far from home and completely alone, with no friends, no family, and no real idea of how to take care of myself.

I stood at the window for a very long time, fantasizing about them coming back. Maybe I'd left something in the car, and they would have to bring it to me. I would run down the dorm steps to greet them, slipping and sliding through the snow to their car.

"You forgot this," my mother would say, extending a sweater out the window, and I would grab it and her arm and beg my parents to take me back home. They would agree (how could they not? They had to know I was too young, too immature to be on my own) and I would curl up in the back seat under the ivory comforter that moments earlier had hugged my dormitory bed, and be restored by the murmur of my parents' voices over the rush of the highway beneath us.

But my parents didn't return. The sun set and the icy road glistened, then turned a bluish white. Clots of students emerged from my building and from other dorms, wrapped in coats and scarves and their own fuzzy boots, and made their way, laughing, toward the dining hall. My stomach rumbled, but I didn't move. An hour later, the same students made their way back, still laughing. The campus grew quiet again, and my fear crystallized into sorrow. I stood motionless at my window, unable to take my eyes off the place in the road where I'd last seen the red glow from my parents' taillights. *Immobilization.* This was our signature, my sister's and mine, our individual response to terror: she on the bed, an oblivious dictator; me at a window, alarmed and weepy.

Four years later, everything expected of me—from dressing professionally to eating publicly to interacting appropriately and fearlessly—exists on a plane of wellness and capability that I am so far below I can't even make out the underside. But there is a filmy awareness, even as I compose my resignation letter, that, if I give up now, I will fall back down the rabbit hole of my illness.

And there is memory of just such a retreat not far off in my past. It is this: after my hospitalization—after I'd returned to Bard and then transferred to Oglethorpe University in Atlanta to finish my senior year, and just as I was beginning to make real strides toward recovery and independence, I had a grand mal seizure. I would have been driving if not for the fact that my car had mysteriously refused to start that morning. The seizure—a full tonic-clonic, consciousness-erasing behemoth—left no clues to its origin on the EEG, and so I was simply handed a prescription for Dilantin and instructed not to drive for six months.

Herein lay my dilemma, and my rabbit hole: I could either continue to live on campus, where I didn't need a car, or I could move home with my parents and be taken back and forth to school. If I continued to live on campus, I would be forced to go to the dining hall instead of driving to the convenience store down the street for my meals. I would have to go to the student center to watch television, would have to make friends if I didn't want to spend my evenings and weekends alone—no more driving the few miles to Lenox Mall every time I got bored. If, on the other hand, I moved home, I could resume a salad-only regimen. I could watch TV in my parents' den in my sweats while my hair air-dried at night. True, the climate at their house was stormy and they existed on separate planes and my mother's ire hung in the air anytime she was forced to interact with my father. True, moving home would set me back in my recovery, were my mother and I to resume our old patterns. In fact, moving home was so clearly the wrong choice that I didn't discuss it with my therapist until after I'd done it.

For the next six months, my mother drove me back and forth to school like a kindergartner. At first, she did her walking while I was at class. Then occasionally she would wait for me. Soon enough, she was waiting for me all the time. Once we were again walking together, it was only a matter of time before we were also grocery shopping, cooking, and sitting at the dinner table together long after dinner, reading the paper and eating air-popped popcorn. It was a carbon copy of the relationship we'd formed in the storm of anorexia, except with a twist. One condition of my recovery was that my mother and I stay away from discussing inflammatory topics, which included dieting, her weight, my weight, and her unhappiness with my father. And so, with most of what we knew to talk about off limits, we were like dogs in a delicate stand-off. Together we traversed the exoskeleton of our lives, careful to stay clear of the meat.

But if there was danger in talking, there was an unutterable loneliness in not talking. We were like lovers gazing longingly at one another from across a wide plain. Unsurprisingly, a few weeks into the arrangement, no longer able to resist temptation, we ran at each other, helpless in our desire, desperate for the taste of each other's obsessions in our mouths. In letters to friends I complained of the seizure-imposed return home (leaving out that it was my choice), but in the quiet cave of my therapist's office, I came clean. I explained how being back home relieved the pressures I'd felt at school to eat and behave and act as an adult. I told him that, while I understood that what I was doing looked to the outside world like a bad idea, I was exultant. I compared the coming home to the gentle tug of an undertow. The irresistible pull. The warm suck of water.

"That sounds like drowning," he said, but I said no, it was nice, more like a yielding. Later of course, I would know that it was drowning.

* * *

I jerk out of my reverie as if from a deep sleep. I have twenty minutes to eat lunch and get back to Bridgeway. I splash my face and boil a small package of frozen string beans with an onion bouillon cube, drain the water, and sprinkle a pinch of shredded mozzarella cheese on top. Four saltine crackers and two large sugary pieces of bubble gum round out my meal. *Two hundred calories,* announces the ticker tape in my head. In the hazy distance, a tractor putters down one of the red dirt paths that crisscrosses the cornfields.

Chapter 6

Be Not Aware

I SURVIVE MY FIRST TWO WEEKS at Bridgeway House. I do so by clinging to a routine driven equally by everything I must accomplish in my workday, and everything I feel I must control. Breakfast is always half an English muffin with a translucent layer of mozzarella cheese, and coffee with skim milk. While my English muffin is toasting I feed Erica, the skinny gray cat I got from the Humane Society my second day at Bridgeway, and then put on the outfit I've decided on the night before. I eat and get to work by eight, co-lead Big Group (*co-lead* is a bit of a misnomer—what I actually do is comment occasionally on what Linda and Henriette say), meet with one or two of my clients for individual therapy (another misnomer— they sit across from me in my office and I ask softball questions like *how are you feeling* and *are you working your program)*, then drive home "for Erica" and eat my string bean bullion at eleven-thirty. From twelve-thirty until it's time to go home, I might have Split Group (do I need to say this is just more softball questions?), more individual sessions, staff meetings, or some combination of all three. From five to six p.m., I take a fast walk, regardless of how tired I am, how hungry, or the weather. Famished (string beans are not exactly a powerhouse of energy), I charge through my dinner of air-popped popcorn and then try on everything in my closet before settling on an outfit for the next day.

* * *

It is Monday morning and Linda and I are in my office sharing a cigarette before Big Group. This is our ritual. She tells me about her evening—what she made her husband, DeWayne, for dinner, or who stopped over for a drink from the doublewide trailer across the way. I never have anything to recount—I don't cook and no one ever stops over—but I like these mornings. There's an intimacy that I haven't shared with another woman in a long time. I know Linda likes them too; she started the ritual, after all, by coming into my office each morning uninvited and plopping down in the chair beside my desk. Still, there's a guardedness I can never quite broach and can't read. It is embodied in the way she exhales smoke straight up into the air, in how her eyes forever move around the room, in her crossed leg that is never still.

"Good grief," Mr. Jenkins says, poking his head in. "It smells like a train station in here." He extends a chart to me. "She's nineteen. Valium. She a pistol."

I take the chart and look at the name Margery has typed and affixed neatly on the tab: *Estovar, Lila Marie.* Inside are progress notes from her 21-day treatment program in Florida. Words like *uncooperative, defensive,* and *prone to explosion* jump out at me, along with *immature, weepy, anxious,* and *sociopath.* This is the summation of Lila Marie Estovar's character, salient descriptors collected and assigned by a counselor in a treatment center trained to see the worst. I'm reminded of finding a folder in the day room of the hospital with notes from the morning's support group. It was left there by a careless or distracted counselor, and I'd have returned it had I not peeked inside to see what it was first. There, in neat cursive handwriting, were progress notes on each of us: how we appeared in group, whether we participated, recommended courses of action. I squirreled the folder back to my room where I devoured every progress note on every one of my fellow patients, my heart pounding in anticipation of the moment I would come to my own name. I read hungrily, taking in words in huge chunks like a bulimic consuming a pie. Finally I came to my name. *Weight 82#. Depressed, defensive, rigid. Not making progress. Psychiatric consult requested. Antidepressants indicated.*

Did I know these things about myself? Of course I knew my weight. And I knew I was depressed. But defensive? Rigid? Not making progress? These were harsh words to take in, and there was something haunting about them. As they were not meant for my eyes, they were somehow realer than real, and they came to me almost as a plea. *Look at yourself* . That something was really wrong with me must be true, because it said so in absence of me.

Either that, or the counselor who wrote the note got me dead wrong.

"Have fun curing her," Mr. Jenkins says of Lila, then throws back his head and laughs.

"You're a shit, Rodney," says Linda. She smiles at me, her dreamy blue eyes glittering, her right foot tapping out its steady tale of restless apprehension.

* * *

"Your shirt is too small."

I have just returned from lunch. At home, I changed from the button-down denim blouse I was wearing into a lightweight tan sweater because while the air outside the halfway house is a stifling ninety-four degrees, the air inside is a frosty seventy-two.

Standing in my office doorway making the pronouncement is a young, slender female with long, streaky, blonde hair, dark eyes, and a face that has not lost its baby fat. She's wearing an old-fashioned green-and-white striped dress that is belted at the waist and comes to the top of her knees. Except for the hair, she looks like a 1950s housewife. I look down at my torso.

"It's like you're needing to show how thin you are."

My stomach begins to roil with string beans and Tab and not enough starch to soak it all up.

"I can even hear your stomach growling."

"It isn't growling, it's digesting," I say. "I just ate."

"What did you have?"

I sit back in my chair, pen poised over a chart. I wrestle with what is happening here—a surprise confrontation around a meal from a client—and I search for the words to describe my green bean concoction.

"Soup," I say finally. "And who are you?"

The girl walks in and sits down in the chair by my desk.

"I'm Lila," she says. The name curls off her tongue and Lila smiles demurely after it. Then she frowns. "I'm bored. Can I have a session now?"

I glance at my watch. "This afternoon," I say. "Come back at four."

"FO-ur?" she whines, then loses interest in her own frustration. She breaks into a mischievous smile, climbs onto her knees in the chair like a child, and shakes the hair out of her eyes. She leans over my desk toward me. "You're not much older than me," she whispers confidently. "And you're one of those people that throws up when they eat!" With that she leaps from the chair and bounds through the outer office, then out the door to the porch. Even though she doesn't know the truth—I don't eat and throw up—she knows the scaffolding of the truth. An old familiar terror begins to wind through my belly.

What I didn't know before about working with addicts, I am learning: theirs is a culture of confrontation, of accusation, of confession. If the client didn't do anything, he probably thought of doing it, and if he thought of doing it, then he's probably not working his program. It is perhaps only natural that these unending allegations of wagon-falling and program-failing make their way out of the group room and therapy sessions and into the general milieu of the house. Mr. Jenkins, who is about to get married, is peppered with questions about fidelity and parenthood. Linda with her dragon tattoo endures questions about her wild past. Henriette gets "Henry." And I get called a puker. The only person spared interrogation or mockery is Margery.

At four, Lila comes and stands at my open door. Her hands are interlaced in front of her and she is smiling cautiously.

"It's four," she says softly.

I wave her in. She sits down and eyes the open chart on my desk. "Is that mine?"

I nod.

"They didn't like me there," Lila says.

"It doesn't mention not liking you," I say. "It does talk about some negative behavior. Want to tell me about that?"

Lila smiles cherubically. "*Moi?*" she says, splaying her hands over her chest. "Why, I think you have the wrong girl!" She is smiling larger now. "But enough about me, let's talk about you. Are you married?"

Just a few words out of her mouth and I can tell Lila is smart and funny and spunky, and I'm tempted to believe that the counselors in the 21-day program just didn't know how to engage with her intellect. They probably lumped her in with the other addicts, immune to her glow, her youthful promise. Since I don't know yet that in the operating manual for sociopaths, charming other people is the first order of business, I do not tread with anything remotely resembling caution. Very quickly, I adore sweet, innocent, smart, spunky Lila. I don't know what Mr. Jenkins meant by calling her a pistol, but then I didn't know what the hospital folder I found meant by calling me defensive. People, even counselors, make mistakes of judgment, I decide.

"No," I say, "I'm not married. Are you?"

Lila shakes her head distastefully. Her hair zooms cutely around her face with the effort. "I'm too young to be married," she says. "I have things to do. I want to go to college. I want to be a lawyer."

I could ask her, at this point, how drugs figure into her plan. I could ask her what she's doing in a treatment center at nineteen instead of at college. I could ask her what her next step is, what kind of family support she has, what kind of financial support she has. I could ask her any number of things that might open and move the therapeutic conversation forward, but the fact is *I don't believe her diagnosis.* Looking at Lila, supposedly Valium addicted, drama-loving, and immature, sitting across from me in her knee-length dress, with her girlish smile, her blemish-free complexion, and hands folded into her lap, I'm pretty sure somebody got it wrong. So I don't address the drugs.

"So tell me what you like to do," I say, and the "counseling" conversation progresses, or I should say, devolves into banality.

There are, of course, reasons why I got tripped up, could not possibly see Lila for what she was. At the time, Valium use was so widespread (and, the message went, so innocuous) it was the butt of many jokes. In a scene in the 1979 movie *Starting Over,* Burt Reynolds is having a panic attack in a furniture store. "Does anyone have a Valium?" his brother calls out, prompting every woman in hearing distance to reach into her purse.

And there is this: from the time I am twelve and until his death, I will have listened to my father complain of chronic headaches and backaches, heart palpitations and anxiety, and a myriad of mystery pain, the source of which will never be found but for which he will be supplied with Valium. This he will keep in the right pocket of his pants. The rattle of his pills was not unlike the jingle of a dog's collar; even now, when I think of my father, the thought is accompanied by that signature sound, as if announcing its own arrival.

Neither of these two stories—not the panicked shopper ministered to by a legion of blissed-out housewives, nor the mysteriously and chronically pained life of my father—can possibly have anything in common with the coy young woman in my counseling chair, and so I simply decide that she is, if not fine, also not the girl suggested by a list of unsavory descriptors pinned on her by some under-trained former counselor itching for an addict to call her own.

Chapter 7

Pukerhood

R ATHER QUICKLY, I DEVELOP a preference for the smaller "split" group over Big Group because I run it by myself with only a few clients. Three weeks in, I am feeling brave enough to try out some exercises I learned in the hospital. One of them is called "Write Your Obit." Its purpose is to get people in touch with what they hope to accomplish before they die. This goes over well for recovering alcohol and drug clients, because death—tempting it, barely escaping it, musing about it—is a kind of high. Clients Eli and Ben, restless coke addicts with multiple ear piercings, inflate themselves posthumously (they die a rock star and an astronaut, respectively). Darla writes that she sobered up at forty-three (her current age) and got her college degree, married a well-established businessman, and traveled the world. Sid and Michelle decline to read theirs aloud, a guardedness it would behoove me to emulate. Instead, I let go of everything I know about boundaries, about keeping my private life separate from my work life, and most importantly, about keeping crazy thoughts to myself so as not to appear crazy, and proceed to read my future obituary aloud.

"Dana overcame a lifelong weight problem, became a well-known psychotherapist, and ran a sanctuary for homeless animals." I smile and look up to astonished silence. Five mouths are hanging open. One is covered with a hand. Darla is the first to speak.

"A *weight* problem," she says. "*What?*"

All mouths close and looks of amusement begin to flicker from person to person like a spreading fire. Eli leans forward and smoothes his mustache with two fingers. "You a puker?"

At this late moment, I realize my mistake. My disclosure is inappropriate, recklessly offered and ill thought-out, meaning I have only a vague idea why I am disclosing in the first place.

"What?! No!" My ears flame and my heart kicks into a gallop.

"She's a puker," Eli says, sitting back again in his chair.

"No I'm not," I say. "I have a—*condition*—that makes it hard for me to gain weight." My body shakes as I offer up this deeply abridged explanation of myself that is the technical truth but not the emotional truth (and I love this word abridged, suggesting as it does a river of calamity flowing beneath my sterilized version of things). I follow this with an arrogant, condescending admonishment: "And besides, counselors' lives aren't important to the business of healing." As if it were the residents' fault we were now talking about me.

Blind to what I'd hoped would happen (some version of *Look how far you've come! Please oh please help us do the same!*), blind to the fact that in the scope of things, I actually have not come that far, I don't know how my plan—to disclose just enough to win me points and make me look wise—goes so horribly wrong, and I don't know because, in the absence of terror (i.e., because I'm more comfortable in my Split Group now), I'm no longer in my own crosshairs.

"That's why she don't eat with us. She has to go puke it up real fast." Eli explains to the group, meeting each person's eyes in turn as if he were a doctor conducting rounds.

He turns to me. "My sister was like that. She looked just like you." He leans in again, his face so close to mine I can smell a dirty braid of cigarette smoke, played-out spearmint gum, and coffee. "It's okay," he whispers, "we all got something." Then he winks. And it is this wink— or more specifically, the *complicity* implied in the wink—that wakes me up, that lets me know that if I do not offer up my narrow body for sacrifice (and sacrifice is exactly how I see it) to macaroni-and-cheese, fried okra, dressed salad, sweet tea, and banana pudding, then my identity as a practicing puke-artist will become a terrible secret— possibly even a point of blackmail—between the residents and me. But only until it goes public, at which time news of my pukerhood will come to Mr. Jenkins' attention, and I will be forced to disprove it by happily and without outward terror eating a massively fattening lunch at Bridgeway.

I feel, at this moment, like throwing up. I dismiss group early and race home.

* * *

My apartment complex sits at the end of a dead-end road on the outskirts of town, two miles south of Bridgeway house. To the east is Route 130, a long, rural road that winds through the countryside, incomprehensibly unpopulated by gas stations or shopping centers of any kind. To the west is the ramp to I-75. In between the two, and directly behind my complex, is a cornfield that is like an ocean: green and vast and undulating.

Mr. Jenkins lives with his fiancée in the building perpendicular to mine, and for my mother, who was with me when I looked at the apartment, this "someone familiar close by" was its most important (if not only) selling point. Certainly it wasn't the useless rural road leading to nowhere-land, and certainly it wasn't the cheaply constructed, one-bedroom apartment itself, nor was it the magnificent cornfields with the red dirt tractor paths that disappeared deep into their unknowable depths. If anything, these were marks against it, in particular the cornfields. I can still remember my mother chatting with the apartment manager in the kitchen as I stood at the open sliding glass doors in the empty living room. On the other side was a deck just big enough for two chairs. In my memory, this deck extended out over the cornfields like the prow of a ship, and had the movie *Titanic* already been made in 1983, I'd have leaned out from the railing with my arms extended behind me, Kate Winslet-style, pretending to feel ocean spray on my face.

"What do you think?" my mother called out.

"I love it," I called back, without removing my gaze from the leafy green ocean. "I just *love* it."

I did not love the apartment. I had not, in fact, even walked through it. Once inside, I caught sight of the cornfields through the sliding glass doors, and that was where I stood the whole time my mother was in the kitchen with the apartment manager, learning things about the apartment I should have been learning, like that dogs were not allowed. The endless cornfields, with their undulating leaves and their whispered promises of limitlessness and possibility, distracted me. It was their fault my mother signed the lease that would bind me to an apartment I had yet to even see. When she was finished signing, she came and stood beside me.

"My God," she said, a note of disgust in her voice as she straightened her collar and looked out over the sea of corn. She pushed me out of the way and sent the glass door careening down its narrow track till it clicked shut. Then she slid the latch into place and yanked the cord that sent the vertical blinds scurrying across the view, plunging the living room into dim, cool shade.

"Keep these doors locked at all times," she said. "You don't know who could be out there."

But I don't keep them locked. Most days, I don't even keep them closed. Heat and dampness filter in, at times stifling, but after spending all day in the dry, chilled air of Bridgeway, it feels good, like a hot bath.

And there is, in fact, someone out there. Me. Every night after work, as the sun begins its slow descent, I change into shorts, grab my Walkman and earphones, and run down the apartment steps and out to the dirt road that borders the complex. After ten minutes on this hot, sun-baked road, I step into the lush, green world of the cornfield. Some evenings I walk around in there for an hour or more. It's my most comforting time of the day, when I feel far away from Bridgeway, and anxious thoughts about my next meal, and the difficult conversations I am having with my parents who want to know about the wonderful time I am having with all my new friends (my life as a recluse having been, in their minds, magically transformed into one of celebrity and social pandemonium). For all of this, I love the cornfields more and more each day. For how they swallow me up in their belly, hiding me from the world. For how the corn is planted on a giant grid, every stalk equidistant from every other stalk, a marriage of order and destiny. For the warm, pure smell of earth they exude and for and way the growing leaves chatter in the breeze, like they are talking to me, like they are saying *everything will be okay*.

* * *

And so it is into the cornfields I head the evening after my obituary/ weight disclosure at Bridgeway. It has not rained in two weeks and the road to the cornfields is dusty and dry. Deep ruts with high edges, carved by tractors in the wet spring months, are baked solid. A red dust cloud envelops my white sneakers as I walk, as fast as I can go, toward the embrace of the fields. Once in, I start to cry.

I cry so hard I can barely keep up my pace, wiping my tears and my nose with my T-shirt sleeve as I go, powering my way deeper and deeper into the belly of the cornfields, trying to lose the moment of Eli's knowing indictment and the vision of five mouths gaping open. I think of my mother, powering her way up and down our street all those years, in sickness and inclement weather. Runners, both of us, chased by our own private demons. I know that I have no recourse but to eat, and eat heartily, of things I would otherwise never go near, beneath the blinding fluorescent lights of Bridgeway's downstairs cafeteria, and overseen by twenty-five gawking residents eager to witness just such a spectacle.

The fact is, I have never eaten normally. I have never had an easy, unthinking relationship with food. There has always been dieting, or thinking about dieting, or wishing I didn't have to diet. That there were people in the world who ate without guilt, without thought, without recrimination, fascinated me, and at eighteen, newly anorexic and working at the pizza restaurant from which I would ultimately be fired, I decided to find out how they did it.

I watched the faces of my customers as they ate. I searched in their eyes for what gave them permission to devour things I could only fantasize about. When I was younger, I would stare intently at a movie screen to see if I could catch an actor off guard, catch him *not* acting— believing that if I watched closely enough, I would discover in his eyes some moment of self-awareness, an admission even, of pretense. I believed I could learn something fundamentally important in that nanosecond between an actor's acting and his self-conscious *awareness* of himself as acting, and this was my goal again as I stole glances into the faces of the men and women who ate their pizza robustly, as if their lives, their sanity, their core connectedness, didn't depend upon them *not* eating, as did mine.

But if the key to our differences was in their eyes, I couldn't find it. I cleared away pans and plates and re-filled empty glasses of Coke, I listened for clues in their conversation, their laughter. I watched the way they walked away, still laughing, without concern for what roiled about in their stomachs. At ninety pounds, I was fired.

* * *

My tears dry quickly in the heat. My face is a frightening map of red rivulets that I will have to scrub off when I get home. I take a right at the end of the cornrow and then another right, following the grid in reverse to go back home.

Later, in my bed, a thought about the mathematics of healing that seems to have been sparked by the cornrows themselves: that mental health is a moveable plot point, as on a grid, fluid and flexible and infinitely more complex than any colorless description of character or grim-sounding diagnosis. Likewise, recovery is squishy, imperfect, jagged around the edges, *an art*, Mr. Jenkins called it, meaning there is no finish line, no test to determine whether the point of completion has been reached, the thing (recovery) done correctly and finitely. There is only variable growth and variable setback, intersecting always, and the most we can say about our position, at any given time, is *this is where I am now.*

Chapter 8

The Case for Intercourse

ROSE, THE CHURCH VOLUNTEER who comes to Bridgeway once a week to talk to the clients about their spiritual life, knows someone who knows someone nice. Would I go out with him?

"I have a date," I tell my mother over the phone.

"Dana!" she says, happily.

Emboldened by the impending date, though I don't know why, I tell Linda I will come for dinner.

"Well blow me down," Linda says.

"But I don't eat pork. Or meat and dairy mixed together. It's a Jewish thing."

Mr. Jenkins, who always seems to be listening from the main office, laughs. "She don't eat pork," he says, though there is no one else in the room.

A week later, Rudy Milsaps, whose heart, according to Rose, makes up for what he lacks in looks, knocks on my apartment door. I open it, expecting the worst. But he isn't the worst. His hair, while too short, is clean and a nice chestnutty color. He is about three inches shorter than I am and has a flat, chubby face and close-set eyes, but they are kind and hazel and they seem to gleam from behind his gold-rimmed glasses. He isn't my ideal man—or even my type—by any stretch. That man will drop into my life three years from now. His face will be strong and stony and his eyes blue and his sense of style disastrous, but he will also be a half-foot taller than me and doting and brilliant. But until Fisher makes an appearance in my life, Rudy will have to do. He gives a hearty little wave from the threshold of my door followed by a nervous, snorty laugh. Then he hands me a bottle of vodka.

I open the door wider and wave him in. Rudy's eyes travel my body, but I don't care what he's thinking. I've had a rum and Tab already, to take the edge off my anxiety about the date, so I'm feeling confident, even a little sexy in my tight black jeans and short black sweater and long silver earrings. I feel like flirting and don't care that nervous, slightly rotund Rudy turns me off. In fact, I'm glad. I have nothing to lose.

"I thought we'd have drink here first," Rudy says. He looks anxiously around the apartment. "Do you have any shot glasses?"

I go to the kitchen and fish out a University of Georgia shot glass with a picture of a bulldog on it that I found in the cabinet the day I moved in. Rudy takes it from me.

"Oh, are you a fan?" he asks.

"Of what?"

He holds up the shot glass.

"Oh, definitely," I say. "I love dogs."

"No..." he says, pointing to the glass.

"Oh! Of vodka?"

"Never mind." Rudy sits down in the green recliner and opens the bottle and pours the shot glass full of hundred-proof vodka. His hands are shaking slightly.

"Do you want some Tab to mix it with?"

"No," he says. "Do you have a match? I'll show you a trick."

I hand Rudy a lighter. He holds the tiny flame to the rim of the shot glass until the vodka wears a sudden crown of fire.

"Watch this," he says.

He opens his mouth wide and throws the flaming alcohol down the back of his throat. Only he miscalculates and, within a split second, his whole face is engulfed in blue flames and he is screaming and slapping at it. It takes a second for me to realize this is not part of the show, and I run to the kitchen for a dishtowel. He grabs it and smothers the fire out quickly but I can hear him whimpering from behind the towel.

"Oh, God! I'm sorry! Do you need some ice?" I stare at his towel-covered face, hands over my own face in mirrored horror. I don't know whether to touch his arm or try to comfort him in some way. Rudy shakes his head. His shoulders hunch in and out. I pick up his glasses from the floor.

When at last Rudy lowers the dishtowel, I see that his eyebrows and lashes are gone and his chubby cheeks are an angry, bright pink. The gleam is gone from his eyes. He exchanges the dishtowel, which is still warm, for his glasses, and puts them on gingerly.

"I'm just going to go," he says, "I'm sorry," and he walks quickly to the door without meeting my eyes. I can hear his feet take the stairs down several at a time.

For a minute I just stand in the middle of the room. I can hear a car start in the parking lot and roar away, and then the faint sounds of a laugh track on my neighbor's TV downstairs. I go to the kitchen and put the bottle of vodka in the cabinet next to my rum and a six-pack of Tab. Then I open the sliding glass doors and drag the recliner up to the threshold. Erica pops up onto the arm of the chair and lies down in the V of my lap. The cornfields are still in the early evening air.

And that's it. I'm alone in my apartment again, just Erica and me and the cornfields. And I'm happy. I don't have a second thought about Rudy's burned face. I don't wonder what he will tell Rose or how the information will make its way around Bridgeway. The whole Rudy event—he isn't even Rudy anymore, but a happening, an incident—is already losing ground with me, already surpassed in importance by the slant of light on the cornfields.

"How was your date?" my mother wants to know. She calls at ten o'clock when she feels fairly certain Rudy will have left. I am still sitting in the green recliner, smoking.

"It ended quickly," I say. "He left at about seven."

"Seven! Why?"

"It wasn't a good match," I say.

"Dana, you're always so quick to judge."

"It was mutual," I say.

"How do you know?" my mother asks, and I can hear the worry rise in her voice, like Rudy Milsaps was the last possible suitor on earth, and now I've ruled him out for some minor infraction like too much eyebrow or a dim sense of humor.

"He set his face on fire and had to go home," I tell her. She might as well know it wasn't my fault. I tell her about the alcohol trick and how he miscalculated the plot points of his own mouth.

"*What?*" she says, we both start to giggle.

* * *

A few weeks later Rose tries again. There is someone else who is more promising, she says. A nice looking young man, she assured me (and he was) who didn't have to drink to bolster his ego (what I told Rose about Rudy but not about myself) and who was "having trouble meeting eligible women." Of "eligible" I take note. It seems to suggest a kind of fitness for duty, in this case the duty of being a wife.

I say to Rose, "Is he looking to get married?"

Rose, who at forty-two seems a world-and-a-half older than me, smiles sweetly.

"Aren't you?" she says.

I'm twenty-two. My best friend from high school will have gotten married the year before, but I still won't be able to believe it. She was always the independent one. She married the second man she slept with.

"I'd been married two years and had a nine-month-old by the time I was your age," says Rose. "If you aren't thinking about a husband, you should be."

Thirty years later I can almost feel my face fall into the shape it must've arranged itself in at that moment, a kind of horrified grimace. Rose's comment reminds me of my high school friend, Louann, who used marvel aloud at the perpetually astounding (to her) thought that her husband-to-be existed somewhere in the world. She would try to imagine what he might be doing at the moment she was conjuring him. At a football game, like us? Having dinner at The Magic Pan at the mall near his house, like us?

"Don't you wonder what your husband-to-be is doing right now?" Louann would ask me, and my expression would collapse into the horrified grimace that would become my trademark "marriage face."

"Not at all," I'd say.

I told myself it wasn't that I didn't want to or could never imagine a future with someone, but that I wasn't ready to tether my thoughts to another person, especially a person I'd yet to even meet. Of course, there was more to it than that, otherwise my "marriage face" might have been curiosity or amusement or one of a hundred other expressions, instead of horror.

The fact was, by the time Louann was dreaming cheerful dreams about her unknown future husband, my parents had been stonewalled in marriage for years. At fourteen, I was tired of hearing about my mother's feelings of imprisonment, her overlooked creative side, and her unsatisfying sex life. I knew all about the day-to-day grievances, the small but specific hurts: how she felt ignored by my father at parties, felt she lived in the shadow of his writing career, how she tired of tending to his myriad physical ailments. When they went to therapy, I knew about that as well, and that the outcome resulted, for a short time, in a surge in sexual activity, but that it quickly retreated to the impasse from which it had temporarily emerged.

I recall, at fifteen, how the titillating details about my parents' marriage filled my mind and senses with wonder, how privileged I felt to be ushered into their private world. I felt lucky to be getting firsthand "facts" about marriage, facts that would come in handy later, when I navigated through my own relationships. But the news was all negative, it turned out, and so I flip-flopped between my desire to know the ugly "truth" about marriage and coveting Louann's unfailing matrimonial optimism, the charming way she pined for her anonymous man, already loving him as she tried to tune into his frequency without even knowing his name. Had I given any thought to marriage? Yes. Did I wonder what my future husband was doing? No. I was pretty sure that whatever it was, it would, in time, come to drive me mad.

"Marriage has never really been high on my list of things to do," I tell Rose.

"Well maybe Scott will change your mind," she says, patting my arm.

And although I have absolutely no curiosity about a somewhere/sometime husband, and no childbearing urge propelling me toward an "eligible" male, I am moved to accept the date. Because now, thanks to Rose, I'm beginning to wonder if there might be some as-yet undiagnosed problem—a poverty of heart and mind, sibling to the bodily poverty I have lived in for so long—that explains why I do not, at twenty-two, inhabit a loving relationship.

* * *

Let me just shorthand it by saying that Scott was not my sometime/somewhere husband-to-be. He was handsome—dark-haired, with a well-manicured beard, crisply dressed in jeans and a button down shirt—and I was attracted to him. Bolstered—again—by rum and Tab, I dressed myself in my snug-fitting black sweater and a pair of new, size-3 black jeans that were, I was delighted to find when I put them on, slightly loose (depending on which way I leaned the scale said a hundred and one or ninety-nine, so I leaned toward ninety-nine). I felt sexy and alive, and happy to be out on a date with such a good-looking man.

We chatted easily on our way to the movie. Anytime Scott said something remotely witty, I lightly smacked his leg with the back of my hand and laughed. After several of these smack-and-laughs, he shifted his leg away, so from then on I smacked his arm. But our relationship didn't stand a chance. I suspect Scott knew this from the moment he saw me and tried to hide his alarm behind a cough, or if not then, then by the time the movie was over and he sat quietly watching me pick croutons out of my tiny Red Lobster house salad. By then the rum had worn off and I was anxious—anxious about eating, about eating in front of Scott, about eating too much. I tried to cover my anxiety by talking about the movie we'd seen, *Flashdance.*

"I thought Jennifer Grey did a great job," I said. "I'm jealous of her. I always wanted to be a dancer."

"Is that why you're so thin?" Scott asked.

I smiled at what I thought was a compliment, and put my hand to my chest demurely. "Oh, I don't think I'm that thin," I said.

We rode back to my apartment in silence. Scott pulled into the parking lot, politely thanked me for the date, and, without making eye contact, waited for me to get out of the car. He was gone before I even got to the top of my stairs. Embarrassed, ashamed, I pretended to blame Rose's abysmal matchmaking acumen.

"These guys just aren't my type," I tell her when she stops by Bridgeway on Monday. "Don't set me up with anyone else."

"You're too picky," says Linda, exhaling a thin line of smoke. "This is Tifton, not New York."

* * *

Of course the problem does not lie with Rudy or Scott or the town I live in, not completely anyway. It's true Rudy isn't my type, and Scott was scared off by my weight and what he perceived it said about my mental health. But the bigger problem here lies in the fact that I have not dated or had sex in three years, and beneath that is an even bigger problem, which is the full story of my sexual life, which, because it is short, I can tell in its entirety. It's a coming-of-age story of immense complication and grief, and it begins (as I suspect all coming-of-age stories of immense complication and grief do) with my parents.

A week before my sister left for college, our father sat her down and issued a warning: "Your mother and I were both virgins when we graduated from college and we expect the same of you."

But this was 1970, not 1950. The sexual revolution was in full swing. Birth control pills made sex without fear of pregnancy possible. Not surprisingly, by the time my sister came home between semesters of her freshman year, she was full of chatter about a number of boys she liked, and by the end of her sophomore year, one of them would accompany her home to Atlanta. His name was Dick.

"As in big one," my sister whispered.

If my father suspected she had ignored his caveat—a no-brainer given the sexual electricity that surrounded the new couple that even I, a twelve-year-old, felt (there I am flirting with Dick in our driveway, there I am, hugging Dick's legs)—he didn't say anything. Eight years later, when I left for college, he issued no warning against sex. It's possible that my interest in boys up to that point was so lackluster (I'd gone on just two dates in my entire five years of high school), that my father felt there was nothing to worry about. Or perhaps (though this seems least probable and I only mention it to give him the benefit of the doubt) he *wanted* me to have sex, fearing I might otherwise seal my fate as a loveless spinster. Whatever his reasoning, even if he had sat me down and said, "Don't have sex in college," I'd have likely looked at him with disbelief and asked, "Why would I do a thing like that?"

Six months into my freshman year, I knew why. It wasn't for love. It wasn't even for sex. My case for intercourse came down to the simple fact that I was, at seventeen, one of the youngest freshmen on campus, and by all indications, the only virgin. In addition to already being sexually active, many of my peers had spent time in Europe, while my entire travel history spanned a few family trips to Gatlinburg, Tennessee, and one high school band trip to Mexico City. Overseas travel lent my peers an air of worldliness, which they embellished with flouncy Parisian dresses and tales of foreign lovers. Sex, as it is abundantly clear to every young woman who aches to trade her virginity for the ineffable glow of womanhood, would imbue me with the sophistication I lacked, confer on me a worldliness independent of a passport. Sex would grow me up, sculpt my curves, flatten my belly, sharpen my intellect. It would lend fluidity to my gait, glitter to my eyes, and mystery to my personality. Not least of all, it would put an end to the homesickness I still felt, since you can't pine for your old room while passionately copulating to the slurry beat of "Sittin' on the Dock of the Bay."

And then one day as I was lumbering across campus in my Burlington Coat Factory waffle-down parka and my pointlessly intact hymen, I met Neil. Neil, also a freshman, whose offer to sleep with me would seemingly solve all my problems.

The night of my intended deflowering, Neil stayed in my dorm room. There were a few tense giggles and some tentative kisses. Neil lifted my T-shirt. Out in the hallway I could hear my neighbor come in and slam her door, rattling every other door on the floor. Books landed on her desk with a muffled thud. Neil cupped a breast in one hand, and laid his mouth over mine. Down the hall, from its little closet, the payphone let out a tinny jingle. I wondered if it was my parents calling. Neil put his mouth on my nipple and his hand fumbled in my underwear. Another door slammed. Laughter erupted from the phone closet. A searing pain ripped through my vagina. Neil rolled over.

"Is that it?" I asked.

"It'll get better," Neil said.

If there was an absence of passion going into my first sexual experience, a tepid prologue, this passed, and soon it seemed all Neil had to do was look at me, and like flame to gas, without foreplay and sometimes without even undressing, we would be lying where we had been standing, bucking and fucking. My peers' outward accoutrements of sophistication paled in the face of my American boy and our king-sized box of condoms. Just as I'd believed it would, sex lifted me out of the sleepy valley of self-doubt, and set me down in a vivid, fertile land. Heady pheromones emanated from me like sweet fumes from a chocolate-chip cookie factory, bringing men of all ages to my doorstep. The charms of interested suitors blotted out the tender memory of fifty-odd model horses still prancing and grazing on my desk at home, the wrap-around picture windows that framed the moon illuminating the horses' backs on clear nights. No longer would I race home between semesters to sleep alone in the twin bed of my girlhood. Orgasm and the hierarchy of excitement leading up to it paved over the sad artifacts of my youth. Sex was magic. Did it matter that my father, when he found out, called me promiscuous, and alleged, in a family meeting I was not privileged to attend, that I was stuffing my veins full of heroin and my belly full of alcohol? Did it matter that my mother was furious?

A year into our relationship, Neil and I sailed out to the horizon of my sexual ocean and found, to our great surprise, not more ocean, but the edge of our world. Off the side our little boat tumbled, taking with it all the components of my newfound, finely-tuned sexual self: the near-constant physical longing I had for Neil and the easy way I slid into bed regardless of time or competing plans, the power I felt in being admired, the pleasure-giving at which I'd become adept. There we stood, suddenly celibate, gazing into an abyss, my sexual charms visible but irretrievable, like a handful of half-dollars shimmering at the bottom of a clear, deep pond. While I at first believed the timeline of my desire had simply expired—didn't people get tired of other people all the time, move on, find others?—the fact was that I wasn't tired of Neil at all. If anything, I was more in love with him than when sex, and our relationship, were new. The depth of my emotional engagement with Neil was more profoundly satisfying than I ever would have imagined that first day he approached me on campus, swinging a tennis racket and blathering on about how pretty I was.

But something larger and more important than sex had exploded in my mind, something complicated and terrifically, maddeningly vague. Within a few months of meeting Neil, I had turned serious about a weight loss mission. The goal was twofold: I wanted to be prettier, sexier, for Neil. And I wanted to be happy. Not simply the kind of happy that having a boyfriend and no longer being a virgin made me, but the kind of happy that the attainment of some heretofore unknown pinnacle of joy, a joy that originated in and also celebrated my core, would bring me. It was a nonspecific, highly rarefied, and deeply entrancing state of bliss that I suspected was only available to those willing to sacrifice much for it, and although I may not have known it then, had I been willing or able, to throw open the doorway to this spellbinding bliss, I'd have seen, spotlit, a certain fifth-grade lunchroom table at which sat a young girl, wrestling with the question of what took her down.

The mission was to lose weight until all was exultant and spectacular in my life, and it played out in the dining commons and on the bathroom scale and in the mirror every morning, afternoon, and night, and as it required my utmost concentration, I had no energy left over for looking into my sudden sexual troubles with Neil. While I suppose I knew it took a certain number of calories for the human body to walk, talk, sleep and breathe, and more to support the completely elective function of intercourse, I dismissed my sexuality with something like corporate bravado: when resources start to dwindle, it's last-hired, first-fired. Sex, in other words, got the ax.

Of course there was more—there is always more—to why I no longer wanted to have sex. The clues were everywhere; many of them the same clues that would later help me unravel the strands of my anorexia. Yes, my father's accusations mattered. And yes, it especially mattered that my mother was furious. Our relationship had been built on a foundation of information-sharing, and yet I hadn't told her about Neil. There are many possible reasons why she felt angry, but ultimately, because I never asked her, I don't know what they are. I know that she felt I was too young for sex, I suppose she may have felt deceived by my not telling her about it, and I believe she was envious of my flourishing sex life.

Add to my mother's disapproval the fact that, several months into the heady and delicious world of sexual delight, during which time Neil and I were as likely to be careful about birth control as not, I missed my period. It returned, but then I missed it again. Each time the terror was like a mini volcanic eruption in my mind. For three or four days I would monitor my toilet paper for the scantest sign of blood, praying feverishly, thinking of nothing but the devastating avalanche a baby would be in my life. I would have to either get an abortion, after which I, like many women (according to *Cosmopolitan* magazine, my bible at the time) would live a life of regret and guilt, or I would have to drop out of college and raise it. With each scare, Neil, in characteristic adolescent fashion, went about his life unconcerned with the drama surrounding my womb, the potential for a real, live baby entering his unready life the furthest thing from his mind, even though we were doing all the right things to make it happen.

Each of these elements, I suppose, could have accounted for my loss of interest in sex. The pain of my mother's anger, the sense that she did not support my becoming what I should have been becoming (a sexually functioning woman) was a part of it. The surprising, unkind and untrue accusations, issued by my father, that my sexual self was whorish and drug-fueled, was a part of it. The specter of unwanted life emerging, unbidden and unwanted, from that place that had just begun bringing me such pleasure, was a part of it. But it is only now, in looking back, that I see another possible explanation for my loss of sexuality, this one more sinister. This one involves a quest for independence, for maturation, for, in the terminology of my later graduate texts, *individuation.* Sex, as I began to see it, was the embodiment of my march away from my girlhood and, therefore, my mother, a "punishment" she did not deserve. After all, hadn't we been so close? Hadn't we dieted together, exercised together, maligned my father and suffered his absences together? That I owed her something valuable was clear suddenly. And there was nothing more valuable I had to give than myself.

And thus began my sorrowful retreat from autonomy. The tamping down, the repacking of my sexual self—not inside the body of my fully functioning womanhood, for that would never have held—but inside a prison of bone—was how I could do it. So it was that I got out of bed and stopped eating. In every anorexic body there is an apology, and this, the sacrifice of my sexual self, was mine to my mother. Such was the body over which, a year into our relationship, Neil and I found ourselves, confused, grief-stricken, and mourning the ghost of my sexual audacity.

Chapter 9

Handbook for Sociopaths

E LI IS GONE. He left Sunday morning after a fight with another young resident named Billy. Mr. Bob, the weekend house manager, says he doesn't know what they were fighting about, that the shouting was over with by the time he got downstairs. All of the residents were either out on the porch or still asleep, except Darla, who was in the kitchen with Miss Hattie.

My heart leaps when I hear the news. But my relief is cut short by Mr. Jenkins.

"That ain't good," he says. "He yours?"

"He's Linda's," I say. Linda isn't in yet and I wonder what he will have her do. Go look for him? Drag him back? I'm glad Eli isn't mine because I don't want to go prowling around where ex-Bridgeway clients go to make up for time lost using, which is Hogg's Bar on the south end of town near the Salvation Army. Mr. Jenkins hands me his chart.

"Call his PO," he says. "Tell him Eli done flown the coop."

I take the chart. "Do I tell him why?"

Mr. Jenkins wrinkles his forehead comically. "Do you know why?"

This is such a simple question it floors me. "Oh," I say. "No."

"Then no," says Mr. Jenkins.

I go into my office and call Eli's probation officer.

"Eli left last night," I say. The PO says nothing beyond, "Okay," and hangs up. When I come out of my office, Lila is waiting for me in the main room.

"I missed you over the weekend!" she says. "It was so boring around here. I kept telling Mr. Bob he should call you and tell you to come down here and bring us some books or games or something but he said we couldn't bother you. I told him you'd like it that we miss you when you're not here!" Lila is talking fast and playing with a strand of her hair like a little girl when Henriette steps out of her office.

"Lila, get downstairs," she says. "You've got no business up here."

"She's my counselor," says Lila, grabbing for my arm. "I have business with her."

I am a microsecond away from uttering, "Yeah, she has business with me," when Henriette's eyes flare and she approaches Lila, enunciating slowly.

"Did you not hear me, young lady?"

My own heart pounds as I wait to see what Lila will do. If there is something professional, something counselor-like that I should say or do, I don't have a clue what it is. Since I have pardoned Lila of pathology, I am confused as to what Henriette's beef with her is. Lila, with an expression more of amusement than fear, looks from Henriette to me and back to Henriette before making a show of letting go of my arm. I don't dare move. Just before she skitters out of the main office, Lila looks back at me and smiles beatifically. "I wanna sit with you at lunch," she says.

Henriette shakes her head. "That girl is nothing but trouble."

* * *

Here is everything I know about therapy when I am twenty-one: a good therapist never charges in with answers. A good therapist is like a loyal dog, following wherever the client leads, waiting while she journeys ahead, overjoyed when she comes back with something of value. Or nipping at the client's heels, herding her, in closer and closer approximations, toward insight. A good therapist never drags a person kicking and screaming toward a cure.

Here is everything I know about how to run Big Group: nothing.

And yet, today, I am to find out what happened over the weekend. What were Billy and Eli fighting about? Why did Eli leave?

"And I ain't talking," Mr. Jenkins says. "I'm just there to watch the fun."

"You always say that," Linda says. "Then nobody can get a word in edgewise." Henriette (uncharacteristically) laughs.

I sense Mr. Jenkins knows more about what happened than he's letting on. "How do I get them to tell?" I ask.

"Pick around it," he says. "Let the pressure build. Make 'em think you already know, but get them to spill the beans."

Like the dining room, the group room is fluorescently lit, with nail holes in the walls that have left yawning vertical gashes in the sheetrock. It is several degrees cooler than upstairs, and a chill encases me like a cold suit of armor. I can feel the residents' eyes on me. As usual, my heart is throwing itself against my chest, and the roar of blood through my ears is deafening. My fear is a symphony that keeps me looking around the room for signs the noise is leaking out. This is how I go into every Big Group, carrying with me a terror that this will be the group that turns the tables of confrontation on me, that points to my concave stomach and my birdlike shoulders and demands to know what they say about recovery.

For ten minutes, there is excruciating silence as I pretend to be collecting my thoughts. Lila looks around expectantly, like a happy, energetic puppy. Darla sits quietly with her eyes closed. Mike, Carlos, and Billy—twenty-something pill users—and new residents, Mary, Annabelle, Sylvie, and Robert, all between thirty and forty, alcoholics who will relapse and be kicked out before their time is up at Bridgeway House—stare intently at the floor. Maria and Tom (cocaine, alcohol, respectively) steal furtive glances at one another, and the three oldest residents, Leonard, Frank G., and Frank C., all in their fifties, repeat alcoholics with jail time under their belts, sit with their arms folded across their chests, watching Mr. Jenkins. There is a cigarette pack on almost every lap, a Styrofoam coffee cup in every hand.

"How come no one's talking?" Lila asks at last, breaking the silence. "It's like a morgue in here!"

"Why don't you start?" I say. My heart leaps at the sound of my own voice.

Lila looks around nervously. "Why me?"

Mr. Jenkins laughs. He is slumped down in the padded desk chair he keeps in the group room for himself. His head is resting on the back of it, his face pointed straight up and eyes closed. The residents look at him, then back at me.

"Tell us about the weekend," I say.

"Oh, it was lovely!" Lila smiles sweetly.

"I bet it was," barks Henriette.

And then, as he does every morning, Mr. Jenkins loses patience. "How was it, Lila?"

Lila looks at him with wide, startled eyes. "How was what?"

But Mr. Jenkins doesn't move. He is still slumped with his head back and eyes closed. I glance over at Linda, who smiles knowingly.

"Was it worth it, Lila?" says Linda.

"Was what worth what?" There is alarm in Lila's voice.

"Aw, come on," Mr. Jenkins says. "Was what you *got* worth what you *gave*? Was it worth being kicked out of Bridgeway?"

Lila's face goes white. My heart, unbelievably, picks up speed. When I was twelve, I wrote a short story about a horse race in which I said that the leading horse lunged forward. "Can something already going that fast go faster?" my brother asked gently, helpfully.

"Oh, yes," I said, though I knew he was right and I was wrong. knowing I was wrong and that I was just trying to defend my story. Now I know I was right after all.

Lila looks to me for help but I can't help her. I don't know why she is being kicked out of Bridgeway. I feel like I have come in on the tail end of a movie that I do not understand and yet will be forced to explain later.

"Why isn't Billy in trouble? He's the one who gave me the pills!" Lila says, eyes still wide.

What? *Pills?* What? I'm like an unsuspecting mother discovering a dead body under her teenaged daughter's bed. I feel sick.

"Ah," says Mr. Jenkins, not looking at Billy. " 'Cause Billy's a pothead and don't know any better. Do you, Billy."

Billy stares at the floor. "Yes, sir," he says. "I mean no, sir." He plays with an imaginary bit of dust on the floor with the toe of his shoe. He looks twelve instead of twenty.

Mr. Jenkins laughs. "See Lila? Billy's too dumb to know the rules. He don't even know he in treatment. But you do, don't you?"

A flash of anger goes across Billy's face. Without looking at anyone, he bolts from his chair and out of the group room. We listen to him charge up the steps and out the front door, letting it slam behind him, not even bothering to collect his things before he's gone for good. Everyone looks at Mr. Jenkins. Several tense seconds pass. Then Mr. Jenkins throws his head back and laughs. "Have a good life, Billy!"

I feel like something huge has just happened, a wreck or a robbery. I am breathlessly both afraid and relieved. In the hospital, where I was only thin and the other patients were only sad or had imaginary back pain, these kinds of scenes did not happen.

The residents look furtively at one another and at each of us. Henriette is frowning and scratching notes into a chart with a noisy pen. Linda is sitting with one leg folded under her, her outstretched foot vibrating as usual. No one goes after Billy. Tears are streaming down Lila's face. No one speaks to her. I envision standing in the hallway with her after group, murmuring some words of solace only she and I can hear, the other residents giving us a wide berth, knowing I am doing the business of healing. Thankfully, I will be spared from enacting this absurd, self-aggrandizing scenario by Lila herself.

"Why do we have rules?" Mr. Jenkins says finally, his voice bored sounding and patronizing.

"They're guidelines to live by," says Darla.

"They're for our safety and stability," says Henriette without looking up from her chart. Without thinking, I cut my eyes over to Linda and we share a private eye roll. Even I know not to answer questions meant for the residents.

Mr. Jenkins nods. "It's very simple, people. If you can't follow them here, you can't follow them out there."

No one says anything. Suddenly, Carlos blurts out, "Lee-la, sex should be 'be-yoo-tiful! You should not use as bargaining cheep!"

Sex? Bargaining? It takes me several seconds to piece together that Billy got pills on the street and traded them to Lila for sex. Had I not read and then discarded every single thing the treatment center in Florida said about Lila, this would not have come as a surprise at all.

Mr. Jenkins looks at Carlos. "She's an addict, Carlos! Don't you know? She's got no choice! It's a proven fact that everything that happens to an addict is someone else's fault. Am I right?" He looks from resident to resident. "Am I right, Mike?"

Mike looks down at his shoes.

"Am I right, Franks?"

The Franks nod.

"Am I right, Lila?"

Lila is crying softly, wiping her face with her sleeves. She doesn't look at him.

"Am I?" he asks again, more forcefully this time.

Lila stops wiping the flood of tears. "You're *baiting* us!" she screams. "You're just trying to see who's gonna crack!"

Mr. Jenkins, undaunted, smiles a big crazy smile and nods his head ridiculously. "You're right!" he says. "Cause the world ain't gonna tiptoe around you! The rest of you don't learn to deal with it in here, you'll never make it out there."

Lila stands up. "You all think you're so fucking smart," she says, and before Mr. Jenkins can laugh and nod his head, she jumps up from her chair and storms out. Her wooden Dr. Scholl's make thunderous *thwhack thwhack thwhacks* on the steps as she runs up them, then makes a U-turn and runs up the second flight to the sleeping quarters. An hour later, a car will pull up out front, Lila will get in, and I will lose my first client.

With Lila gone, the room is plunged into quiet, the only noise the whamming of my heart and the clamor of blood still rocketing around in my ears, a sound like a thousand soldiers marching down a gravel path. This is Big Group: scary, out of control, emotional. It is everything I am afraid of: confrontation, rage, impulsivity, accusation, all things I have attempted to drag and push and exercise and not-eat out of my life. I pray for it to end.

"Is that all we have for today?" Mr. Jenkins asks.

"Believe so, sir," says Henriette, frowning.

Mr. Jenkins stands up. "Good," he says walking out the door, patting his stomach. "Miss Hattie's got banana puddin'."

In the main office, I wait for Mr. Jenkins to return from the kitchen with a dinner plate piled high with dessert. His eyes light up when he sees me.

"You want some puddin'?" he asks, sitting down at the desk and shoving the plate toward me.

"She hates bananas," Linda says from her office.

"Hates bananas!" Mr. Jenkins says.

"Honey, I think you just hate to eat!" Henriette says from the coffee maker. She's looking at me over the tops of her reading glasses. "You best get over it, too. Folks here won't let you get by with that nonsense for long." She sniffs loudly, shakes her head, and disappears into her office.

"She's right," Mr. Jenkins says, not unkindly. He takes a giant bite of pudding and smacks his lips. The smell of bananas and sugar and vanilla wafers rides the current of his breath into my nose. "Miss Hattie, you have out*did* yourself!" he yells into the air.

And there I am. Caught in a lineup of cars, each with its own set of failed brakes, a pile-up happening so fast not only can I not stop it, I can't even swerve. Because I completely dismissed Lila's previous counselor's findings, I missed that she was still using, which has now gotten her thrown out of Bridgeway. Second to that car is the one wrecking right here and now, the one Henriette has just driven into me and that I fear will skid all the way into Big Group. And the third car in the pile-up *is* Mr. Jenkins, and the possibility that what he chose to overlook in my interview is now disconcertingly clear.

But there is more here. There is something of the dismissal of boundaries in Henriette's sudden "outing" of me. That I fear she might take me to task in Big Group is absurd from my vantage point thirty years later, of course, but it is testimony to my middle-placed-ness at the time, evidence of how I did not quite understand the line that divided me from the clients. And so I fretted about her plan to expose me, and in my head, I mounted the argument I would never have with her: the one about how counselors require anonymity where clients are concerned, and how it is this that creates therapeutic distance and builds a façade of capability, like a wall that clients can't see over. Behind that wall (I would explain to Henriette), all hell could be breaking loose in a counselor's life, but theoretically, it wouldn't matter. Counseling is an art (I would continue eloquently) but it is also an artifice. When my mother discovered that our family therapist was divorced, she went into a quiet rage, showing up for sessions at the hospital but refusing to participate, tearing tiny pieces of paper into smaller and smaller squares, before finally confronting him: "How can you help us if you can't help yourself?" Her cry was angry but also plaintive; as far as she was concerned, she was fighting for the life of our family.

"Because the health of your family doesn't depend on the health of mine," our therapist said simply, truthfully.

But my mother never recovered from the information. Of course there is no way to know what the outcome of our family therapy would have been had the therapist not been forthcoming with this bit of personal disclosure. But for my mother, in search of artifice, it was all she needed to close the gap, and to embody his failed relationship. And so, in the auditorium of my own head, I implore Henriette not to expose me for the addict she knows me to be. For my protection, of course, but also for the clients'.

Mr. Jenkins extends his last bite of banana pudding out to me. "Mmm?" he says.

I shake my head. "I didn't know you were going to kick Lila out."

"The rules is the rules. Sex and drugs in the house equals bye-bye." Mr. Jenkins waves a silly little five-finger wave as he says it. "They know that." He licks his plate.

"I know but she's so young," I say.

Mr. Jenkins laughs loudly, delightedly. "You gonna have to toughen up, Slim!"

As if in response, the front door swings open, and Eli, trailed by his PO, steps inside.

Chapter 10

Joe Blow

I GAUGE LIFE THESE DAYS—the residents', my own, and the cornfields'—by growth or lack thereof. Darla is gone, and according to her outpatient counselor, doing well. Eli stayed after his PO found him (amazingly, still straight) at the Salvation Army and brought him back to Bridgeway, but something had gone out of him, a spark. Later he would confess that he was in love with Lila, and that her sex-for-drugs exchange with Billy was why he left. The Franks both found jobs in town, but came back to Bridgeway smelling of alcohol and were kicked out. And my new client, Judy, a straight-laced alcoholic housewife, spends a good part of each of our sessions asking me about my personal life, which I find irritating, until Linda's client, Maria, tells me Judy has a crush on me, which, upon hearing this, sends Mr. Jenkins into paroxysms of laughter and provokes a round of teasing by him and Linda and Henriette and even Margery, centered on the prospect of telling my parents I am a lesbian. This is 1983, when such things were somehow scandalous and hilarious.

But the big news is that I at last eat lunch at Bridgeway.

Here is how it happens: I designate a Friday as "eat lunch at Bridgeway" day. (This gives me Saturday and Sunday to spend all hours exercising, should I find that I need to.) I follow Linda and

Henriette and Mr. Jenkins downstairs to the kitchen ("*What did we do to deserve this honor,*" they crow). The residents, already in line for food, turn one by one to look at me as I come in. I smile—as if I am calm— as if eating a monstrously fattening Southern meal at midday is exactly what I want to be doing—but in fact my heart is pushing blood through my ears like a snowplow and my vision is slightly compromised. Because I have never been downstairs at lunchtime, I don't know what to expect: whether the staff sits together, or whether, as the counselors did in the hospital, we are supposed to disperse and eat among the residents as if we are all just equal, hungry individuals. I don't know whether we serve ourselves, buffet style, or if Miss Hattie or one of the residents doles out the food, leaving no control over portion sizes. I don't know whether I can have preferences (pretending to hate bananas, for example) or dietary restrictions (I keep kosher) without people thinking I'm "sick," though I do know that the quieter I can be about both preferences and restrictions, even ancient, legitimate ones, the better off I'll be.

Linda hands me a plate. I see with some relief that lunch is spaghetti with tomato sauce (tomato sauce is relatively innocuous, calorie-wise, if it is meat-free, which this is), not macaroni and cheese (dense, heavy fat calories), and that both Linda and Henriette, who are ahead of me, take only a modest amount, about two-hundred calories worth, and don't take any garlic bread at all. They spoon out a tiny amount of salad, an amount that would be easy enough to spread around on a plate and make it look partially eaten, and so I do, too, and when we get to the end of the line I am elated to discover that water—delightfully, mercifully, calorie-free water—is the alternative beverage to sweet tea. Not only that, but Linda asserts that we don't need to eat the cherry pie right now, we can come back later in the afternoon. *Later,* I think, as in *never.*

"We're sitting against the wall," she says, motioning with her head, and I see that there are five chairs, one for each of the staff and none for any residents. Heart still pounding, but with a confidence that comes from feeling somehow vindicated by my plateful of unmashed and unsqueezed or divided, or completely avoided (or to be puked up later) food, I stride past the two tables where my Split Group clients are sitting together. In a move that surprises even me, I *dip* my plate ever so slightly as I go by so they can see it. Maddeningly, Eli winks, just as he did in Split Group the day he called me a puker. At the staff table, I look around at the other plates of food, and, excepting Mr. Jenkins's, which is piled high, if you didn't know whose was whose, you'd never have known which was mine.

"I'm glad to see you eating," says Henriette, frowning.

"A few more meals like this and Rodney ain't gonna be able to call you Slim no more," says Linda, the words oozing out of her mouth like a long ribbon of taffy, but I squash down the apprehension this arouses in me. It all goes on the grid, I remind myself, a little point gently nudged toward "better."

A surprising thing happens after lunch. As I am sitting in my office flipping through charts, my stomach wrapping itself lovingly around something other than green beans and onion bouillon, I feel wonderfully *unhungry*, maybe for the first time in three years. This unhungry feeling, new and thrilling, requires a metaphor all its own. It is like ice skating, I decide; or more accurately, it is like that moment on the ice when you finally let go of the railing for a few seconds and coast, suddenly aware of the strength of your ankles, or the cold air stinging your eyes, or the smile on your best friend's face. Aware of that space between grasping and grasping.

* * *

And then, one Saturday morning, a week after my Bridgeway lunch, I am sitting at the desk in the main office working a crossword puzzle when the front door swings open and a hot July wind pushes through. I put down my pen. A pair of scuffed, blonde suitcases maneuver their way in the door, followed by a tall, dark-haired man in his mid-thirties in white painter's pants and a light blue denim shirt.

"I'm Joe," says the man. "From Panthersville."

I extend my hand. My fingertips are ink-dirty. "Welcome to Bridgeway," I say.

Joe starts to cry.

* * *

When I was eleven, I saw a story in *Life* magazine about a sixteen-year-old boy named Richie Diener who was shot and killed by his father. I read the story from beginning to end, then read it twice more. I scrutinized the accompanying photographs, looking for clues to the family's future horror in the face of ten-year-old, freckle-faced Richie. In one picture, there was a butterfly on Richie's nose and his eyes were crossed, looking at it.

Richie was a normal kid from a loving, two-parent family. As many childhoods do, his slid into a difficult adolescence, marked by a drug problem that began with marijuana and escalated to pills. By the time Richie was sixteen, he had become violent. On the fateful evening on which Richie's story turned, he appeared at the top of the basement stairs, obviously stoned, with a butcher knife in hand. He announced to his father, who was in the basement with a gun, that he was going to kill him. He started down the steps.

The impact of the bullet stopped him. Richie sat down hard, a look of bewilderment on his face, though I am not sure whether it was the author of the story, or eleven-year-old me, who put it there. Seconds passed; Richie slumped forward and died.

I tore out the article and hid it in my closet where it lingered for years like a secret, dangerous companion. I was in love—not with freckled, butterfly-loving, ten-year-old Richie, but with the troubled boy-man with the mysterious, brooding core, the Richie undone by his own father, the bewildered, betrayed Richie who, in the moment before he died, might have looked up from the hole in his chest with a mix of apology and incomprehension. It was this Richie, *Richie at the moment of impact*, who I thought about and pined for, for years after reading the story. Eventually, I would stop thinking about him, but the foundation of attraction had been laid.

It's the oldest story in the book of love, the one about the damsel who is pursued by two suitors, one an upstanding man of the community who (frankly) bores her, and the other, a swashbuckling ne'er-do-well whose irresistible charms are his looks and (I imagine) his limitless reserves of testosterone. True, in my case, there was no other suitor. Rudy Milsaps would never call me again and neither would Scott. And now that I'd seen Joe, I wouldn't answer the phone if they did.

Joe takes a deep breath, wipes his face with his open palms and walks around the desk. He sits down heavily in the aluminum chair and slides his body forward until his head rests on the back of it. His auburn hair, cut in a messy shag, falls loosely into his eyes. I want to lean over and brush it out of them. I want to lay my cool hand against his wet cheek. Joe's long, outstretched legs are like a fence, corralling me between them and the wall. The residents are either at work or watching television downstairs. Joe could kill me—or kiss me—and no one would hear.

"Cocaine," Joe says, by way of explanation, still wiping the tears from his face with the heels of his palms. I slide the admission forms across the desk. Our eyes meet over the pen holder. In the well of his throat I can see his pulse racing. My own pulse wakes as if from a long sleep and builds, like a mounting crescendo, to a dead run.

* * *

A year from now, a graduate school professor will plant himself at a small podium in front of a chalkboard on which will be written, in all caps, ETHICS FOR PSYCHOLOGISTS.

"Ethics is the most important class you will take in your graduate career," he will say, and he will seem to be looking specifically at me. "Do you know why?"

Of course I know why. It's because the therapeutic relationship demands an unequal balance of power between therapist and client, because this is how transference (whether or not you buy into psychoanalytic theory doesn't seem to matter) is born. Without transference (the theory goes) you are just side-by-side equals talking about a problem, but with transference, you (the therapist) wear the mask of someone significant to your client, allowing him to come face-to-face with old rivals and allies and doppelgangers, to confront *mise–en–scène* that which (or whom) perhaps no longer exists in reality.

Ethics demands that you not screw up this important opportunity by, for example, letting loose with a noisy hello and a crazy wave from halfway across the Piggly Wiggly. Or discussing your client's no-good, sleeping-around wife and underachieving children with someone who calls claiming to be his mother. Or going to the movies with your clients, or, by God, *making out* with a client who had been gone from your halfway house for two weeks (therefore, in your mind, making him technically no longer a client). The problems that can result from ignoring these basic ethical conventions are manifold, and include (but aren't limited to) muddying of the therapeutic waters, destruction of therapeutic distance, and the general impaling of trust that is the cornerstone of therapy itself.

But Joe's arrival is like the sudden hit of a numbing drug. I am vaguely aware of opening some bottom drawer of my brain and stuffing what I know about ethics out of sight. That pesky bit of interference gone, I am free to focus on the way my nerve endings reverberate with obscene pleasure at the simple sight of his baby-fine hair, to enjoy the luscious way his brooding eyes take in my figure (no pitying or anxious looks, only appreciation!) my smile, my hair.

Thoughts of Joe dominate my waking life. I daydream about him on my walks through the cornfields. I imagine dates where he is witty and I smack him on the thigh and he *doesn't pull away*. I journal about him alone in my apartment, and fantasize about him at night before I go to sleep. I speak to him anytime I see him on the porch.

"How's your program going, Joe?" I ask, folding myself concernedly into a rocking chair on the porch beside his. On the surface authentic, counselor-to-client kindness.

"I'm doing great," he might say, or "I'm really struggling," but whichever it is, I always nod and invite him to say more, hardly able to hear him over the din of my imprisoned sexuality clamoring hotly for its release. Other days I volunteer to ride the afternoon bus to the industrial parts factory where many of the clients, including Joe, get part-time work. I sit on the edge of the bus seat as the clients file past, hot and dirty and tired from welding, stripping wire, and unloading trucks, but when Joe gets on I slide over discreetly so he can sit with me, the filthy smell of burned synthetics and sweat emanating from his skin and filtering into my nose like an aphrodisiac.

I mention my attraction to Joe to my old therapist in a letter. He writes back, a short note but to the point: *Important that you not pursue a relationship with Joe until he is no longer a client or you are no longer his counselor.* And so I play dangerous games with the language: at what point can I consider Joe a *non*-client (as soon as he seems to be feeling better? the second he's discharged?) or me not his counselor (after hours? on the weekends?) so that I can do what I want to do: brush his hair away from his eyes, wrap my long legs around his, embrace the alluring wounds of his past. These questions I ponder, secretively, deliciously, as I go about my day-to-day business at Bridgeway, business which has, thanks to Joe's presence, taken on a fuzzy yellow glow.

* * *

One morning for Split Group, I bring in an exercise that I learned in the hospital: draw yourself as an animal, then talk about what your animal says about you. It's crowded in my office. All five of my clients are new, except for Kathleen and Eli. We squeeze into a small circle, our toes almost touching. I open the window a crack to let the cigarette smoke out, and the sound of a soft rain filters in. Because it is my habit to notice those rare instances when I am not anxious, I smile to myself. I congratulate myself on how far I've come since I got to Bridgeway. No more heart-pounding anxiety, at least not in my Split Group. No more stupid and inappropriate revelations to my clients. Then, as if the universe must prove me wrong about this last, I begin to sketch right along with them.

Five minutes in, there's a knock on my office door. Mr. Jenkins pushes it open. Behind him, and towering over him by six inches, stands Joe. My heart rockets into my throat.

"You got a new group member," Mr. Jenkins says. Joe steps around him into the room. His hair is still damp from the shower and his eyes are black and shiny. He smells like baby shampoo.

"Hi, Joe." Kathleen and Eli scoot their chairs apart to make room for him. Mr. Jenkins leaves. I hand Joe a piece of paper and a pencil, both of which, I'm horrified to see, tremble noticeably in the air. Eli the winker sees this and winks.

"We're drawing ourselves as animals, Joe. Then we're going to talk about what our animal says about us." In Joe's presence the exercise sounds contrived and small.

"You're kidding, right?" Joe says. He gapes at me, ignoring the extended paper. I am wearing snug blue jeans, ankle boots and a short red sweater. This morning before I left the apartment I affixed a tiny, gold horse pin over my left breast. Joe's eyes consider the horse pin and then return to my face.

"She's not kidding," Kathleen says. Kathleen has appointed herself my co-leader, deferential to me but bossy to others. I should stop it but I don't because I find it empowering.

I hold up my paper. It too, shakes. "Like this, Joe." My picture features a sky and grass with a pushmi-pullyu sandwiched in between. The pushmi-pullyu is a favorite character of mine from *Doctor Doolittle*, a two-headed, four-legged beast like a horse whose claim to fame is that half of its body faces east and half faces west, and henceforth, it cannot move.

"My animal could suggest that I feel stuck," I say stupidly.

"Like there's something she wants to do but she can't because she's scared," Kathleen explains in an annoyingly patronizing voice.

Joe smiles. "Or some*one*." This dirty come-on travels my body like an electrical current. He says nothing more but tilts his head to one side like a dog listening to a familiar word. His shaggy hair falls softly across his forehead and brushes one shoulder. Our eyes lock. Suddenly I feel the heat of his kneecaps on mine and realize our knees are pressing into each other. Some slumbering network of nerves in my crotch lights up like a Christmas tree. I jerk my legs in and cross them under my chair.

"Oooh-*hoo!*" shrieks Eli, thrilled by this exchange. Like twelve-year-old me caught in the sexual energy field of my sister and her boyfriend, Eli is electrified, vibrating with excitement. And that's it, what little control I had over group, which was really just five residents too sleepy to protest my sketching games, is gone. Joe scribbles something on his paper, a grinning snake crawling into a hole, and the group cheers with delight. Even Kathleen laughs a loud, choppy, smoky laugh. I am mortified, furious. *We had a deal, you and me!* I want to scream. We had a deal to yearn for each other passionately but secretly, and most of all, *respectfully!* We had a deal to pretend that no one else could tune into our frequency, to pretend that the buzzy current that ran through us at every encounter was nonexistent, or if not that, then chaste, innocent. Decades later, the absurdity of this— the sweet juvenility, the complicity I invented out of thin air about a man whose addicted life was, I knew, defined by lies and overstatement and infidelity—will be obvious to me, but in the moment, I am speechless. We file out of my office fifteen minutes early, to Mr. Jenkins' raised eyebrows.

"Cure everyone already?" he asks, to which I will say nothing, thinking this is the end of it. And it would have been, had Mr. Jenkins been blind.

* * *

I'm on my way home that afternoon when Joe stops me on the porch.

"Can we talk?"

I look back into the main office. Mr. Jenkins is reading the paper. While I can't see her, I know Henriette is at her desk finishing up her chart notes, frowning, even alone. Margery is on the phone. I cross my arms and wait for whatever Joe has to say.

"Going home?" asks Melanie, rocking in a porch swing. She is a new client of Linda's, given the option of drug treatment at Bridgeway or jail for forging checks. She's tall and skinny and starts every sentence in group with "I don't know about y'all but." I don't like her.

"Yes," I say, without looking at her.

"Where do you live?"

It's an inappropriate question. "Not far," I say.

"Not far as in where?"

I turn and give her a hard stare. "As in not far away."

"Oh, I get it," she says. "You can't tell me because I'm a *client.*

Well, don't worry. I promise I won't come *visit* you." She looks at Joe. "Joe would visit you, though. Right, Joe?" She picks up a basketball and skips down the steps to the netless hoop in the parking lot.

Joe watches her go and then shakes his head. He turns back to me and offers me a cigarette. Hesitant, I take it. He produces a lighter and I lean in, cupping the cigarette against the breeze and looking up at him. His dark eyes reflect the tiny flame between us.

"Where *do* you live, anyway?" he asks. Then he laughs through his nose and waves the question away.

"Look, I'm sorry I embarrassed you in group," he says. "I don't know why I did that. You know how much I like you. It was..." he pauses to get the words right, looking down at his feet, then at my mouth, then back at my eyes. "It was *stinkin' thinkin.'* It was old behavior and I'm ashamed. Can you forgive me?"

Joe's eyes are soft, imploring. It's all there: the irresistible woundedness of a reckless youth, the incomprehensibility, the yearning, years too late, to stop the unfolding of luckless events that would spell his ruin. If this were a movie it would be that moment where the impassioned lovers-to-be can no longer hold back. Where they lunge clumsily and hungrily for one another and fall forward into each other's mouth in a ferocious gnashing of teeth, then collapse onto the bed or the floor or a table and fuck breathlessly.

"I'm leaving," Joe says.

A wave of shock rolls through me. It is equal parts joy (*no longer a client! Can have sex!*) and despair (*Bridgeway is nothing to me without Joe*). There is also a tiny part of me that fears for his sobriety, but that part is admittedly so far beneath the hots I have for him that it takes me some time to access it.

"You're leaving?" I say. "When? Are you—do you think you're ready?"

Joe laughs. "Oh, I'm ready," he says. "I'm goin' where there's snow."

My heart sinks. "What, up North somewhere?"

Joe cups my chin with his hand. Adrenaline floods my body. Out of the corner of my eye I see movement in the main office. Mr. Jenkins has shifted in his chair. Lowered his newspaper. I can't move away from Joe's cupped hand. The feeling is a tidal wave, an orgasm. "You are too sweet," he says.

I shake my head. "I don't get it."

He smiles. In his eyes there is an exhaustion and a longing that I recognize as battle weariness. He drops his hand away from me, sags against the open door.

"Snow," he says. "Blow. *Coke*, honey. I need some *coke*."

I grab his arm. "One more week," I say, more urgently than I mean to. "Just give it one more week. *Please*." Joe looks at my hand on his arm, then back at my face.

Of course, I have no idea what will change in a week. I have nothing up my sleeve, no healing magic, no plan, not even an inkling of what could possibly happen that would cause Joe to say later *good thing I stayed that extra week*. The truth is that I don't know how to do anything for my clients other than listen and lead them in ill thought-out sketching exercises. In fact, in my earliest visions of myself as a counselor, back in college, I was clearer about what I would be wearing (cable knit sweaters, Birkenstock shoes) than I was about what I would be saying, and three years later, not much has changed. Faced with the urgent business of helping Joe, I've got nothing but the fervent hope that something will come to me, and a head full of romance and horniness.

Joe squeezes my chin. "Where'd you say you lived?"

Chapter 11

Fucked

I T IS MY FIRST VISIT to a trailer park. Rusty charcoal grills, dirty childrens' toys, trash cans, and cars are scattered about; because one person's front yard is another person's back yard, it is unclear what belongs to whom. Linda's address is Row 16, Lot 10. Finding a house this way is like playing Battleship.

I knock and step up into Linda's trailer. I am afraid it will look on the inside the way things look on the outside. But I'm pleasantly surprised. The trailer is unexpectedly spacious and neat, and almost pretty. There are built-in cabinets and bookcases. The dining table and coffee tables are glass-topped and tinted dark gray. There is flowered wallpaper in blue, rose, and brown that picks up rosy tones in the carpet. White vertical blinds cover sliding glass doors, blocking out the heat of the South Georgia summer sun.

"Hey, I'm here!" I call out.

"Hey, Bitch!" Linda calls back affectionately, her deep drawl lengthening the word to sound like "bi-yatch." She emerges from the kitchen with a cigarette in her mouth and two drinks in her hands. Her eyes are already rimmed in red, though it's only seven-thirty on a Friday night. Somehow it seems wrong to get wasted while the sun is still high in the sky and the singsong voices of children can be heard outside. Linda hands me one of the drinks, a red, frothy mixture that smells of gin. Alcohol, like the sex of my past, like the starvation of my present, is magic. Its calories somehow don't count, and I'm always happy and relaxed while drinking, and feel thinner afterward.

"Thanks," I say, accepting the drink, still looking around. "Wow, it's like a real house in here."

Linda's eyes roll, as they almost always seem to do when I talk. "What'd you think it would look like?"

"I guess since they're long and narrow on the outside I thought everything would be lined up on the inside." I don't mention that I thought it would be filled with the detritus of other peoples' messy lives.

A large dog barks once from the living room. It sounds like, "Ha!"

Linda shakes her head, sputtering out smoke at the same time. Because she is thirty, married, tattooed, and rumored to have been married before, I feel impossibly naïve in her presence. And in spite of the trailer park address, the red-rimmed eyes, and the dog chained to the sofa, my perception, when I am twenty-one, is that Linda has it all together, that there's a lot she can teach me about Life.

Linda eyes me as I look around.

"DeWayne and I want to buy a little piece of land in Cordele and move the trailer up there," she says. "It's noisy here at night, with the air conditioners and people yelling and stuff." She smashes out her cigarette and twin highways of smoke erupt from her nostrils. "More?" she asks, holding up her own empty glass.

I hungrily suck down what is left of my red drink and follow her into the kitchen, where the smell of pizza is a heavenly, aromatic cloud. I watch while Linda refills my glass with one part sloe gin fizz mix and two parts gin. She lays a plate on top of the glass and gives it a quick shake to activate the fizz, then pops my old straw back in it and hands it to me.

"Drink up," she says. "Oh, and here." She hands me what is left of a joint in an ashtray on the counter.

I freeze. I haven't smoked pot since college, and it always made me jumpy and paranoid, although, back then, there wasn't much to lose. Now, I'm an alcohol and drug counselor, supposedly a role model.

Never mind the circus that is going on with my weight behind the scenes, the caloric computations and multiple, daily weigh-ins in the privacy of my bathroom, and the constant reconfiguring of whether half of an English muffin includes or does not include its bready middle. In my mind at this moment, the dancing and bargaining I do with myself around food is not equal to the bargaining and dancing Bridgeway clients do around drugs and alcohol. But this—this tiny joint butt now being proffered by Linda—is. Quickly, the second gin makes putty of my conscience, however, at which point, all that's left is the filmy fear of a misbehaving child: What if Mr. Jenkins finds out Linda and I are drinking and smoking dope? Will he take us to task in group (again, this somehow doesn't seem preposterous). Will he fire us?

"Should we be doing this?" I say at last.

"Aw, hell," Linda says, grabbing the half-joint and lighting it herself. She takes a long draw on it. "Do you really think A&D counselors don't drink or smoke, for God's sake? Or—*aack*," she says, making the gagging gesture she made the first day she met me. She exhales slowly. I stare at her until she's done.

"I told you I don't *aack*," I say, making the gagging gesture back at her.

"Whatever," Linda says. "Don't get your panties in a wad. I'm just saying we're not held to impossible standards."

She hands me the joint again. I take a timid toke as I consider the idea that refraining from drinking or smoking pot or puking when you are charged with helping other people do the same is an "impossible standard." It is, in fact, the reason I was fired from the volunteer position: it was obvious that I could not do the very thing I would be asking other people to do: eat.

So I do what I always do when I'm trying to justify: I play with the language. I decide that because I am not *addicted* to pot or alcohol, using them recreationally is perfectly acceptable and not hypocritical. I decide this in part because, on the heels of two strong drinks and no food since noon, the logic really does seem sound. But mainly I decide this because I need to talk to Linda about Joe, and I don't want to rock the boat. I sit down on the sofa next to where the dog is chained.

"That's Pete," Linda says. She unchains him and opens the sliding glass door. A blast of heat and blinding summer-evening sunlight blows through the living room. Linda shuts the door practically on Pete's tail and sits down across from me. "So, bitch," she drawls. "What's new since work this afternoon?"

At which time the words tumble out of my mouth. "WhatdoyouthinkofJoe?"

Although he's in my Split Group, Joe is Linda's client. Which means she has uninterrupted access to his thoughts and feelings for an hour every week, or every day, if he wants it. A privilege I would eat my teeth for. What I want to believe is that I am the reason Joe didn't leave Bridgeway last week when he threatened to. But it's possible he stayed because of something Linda said. Or because his coke deal fell through. Only Linda knows for sure why he stayed, and I will parse whatever she says in order to figure out exactly where I stand with him. Linda rolls a new joint, expertly working the paper around in her freshly licked fingers. My heart races, waiting for the information.

"Joe who?" she says. She hands me the slim package to light. I take it but do not light it. I wait for her to look up at me.

"*Joe!*" I say, as if repeating his name forcefully will identify him for her. Which it does.

"Oh. What do I think of him in what way?"

I light the joint, inhale, hold it, then exhale a narrow line of smoke. "*Any*way," I say. I lean forward until Linda looks up from the ashtray and our eyes meet. For a moment she says nothing. And then she sits back abruptly.

"Oh, my God," she says.

"What?"

"Oh, my God, no."

"What?!"

"Do *not* do it."

"What? Do what?"

"Do *not* fuck him. I mean it. Do NOT fuck him."

I fall back into the sofa and laugh. Inside my stomach, red sugary juice is throwing a dance party, and in my head, gin and marijuana are joining forces in a kind of thrumming salsa beat. My own laughter sounds far away and somehow not of me. I haven't had a girlfriend in a long time, and my next genuine, straight-shooting girlfriend is still eight months away, waiting for me in Ethics class. Her name is Moira, she's obese, and she will out me and my anorexia within a week of meeting me. But until then, I have Linda, whose blurting of the word "fuck" out loud makes me deliriously happy.

"Nobody's fucking!" I say, laughing. *"Yet!"* I laugh harder. My eyes are watering and I cover my mouth because I have the sense that my laughter is too large for the room.

But Linda isn't laughing. "Listen to me," she says. She leans forward, puts down her glass and points her cigarette at me. *"I am not kidding."*

I feel a slow draining of joy, and an unwelcome build-up of anxiety. Although I am no longer laughing, I hear the echo of my laughter still in the room. It sounds false, operatic, ridiculous.

"He was thinking about leaving the program, you know," I say, my voice suddenly tinny and elf-like. Then the urge to laugh again, disconnected from anything funny, wells up in me. I am too high.

"I know that. What, did you tell him if he stayed you'd *screw* him?"

"No! I didn't say that! We haven't even talked about sex!" This is technically true, although it is also true that we have been flirting, and by flirting I mean something that exceeds flirting and is, were I to be honest, more akin to verbal foreplay. Like Joe whispering *you're killing me* when I pass him in the hall and me mouthing back *me too.* Shame wells up in me like a geyser.

"Here's what I think of Joe," Linda says. "He's an addict. An *addict.* Do you have *any* idea what that really means?"

I am humiliated by Linda's scolding tone and broadsided by the sudden requirement that I be lucid and serious. Of course I know what being an addict means. It probably means being Linda, the person who can't see the irony of injudiciously engaging in behaviors that *make* addicts addicts. But she doesn't let me answer.

"It means you could be anyone in the world to Joe right now. You could be me. You could be Henriette, for God's sake, with her witchy face and her man's body, and it wouldn't make a bit of difference to him. If he thinks you'll do him, then he'll ride that horse as far as it will go, and *then* he'll leave, but with a hilarious story about a naïve little counselor who tried to screw him straight." Linda takes a long drag on her cigarette, exhales. She never takes her eyes off me. "How long do you think it will take for Mr. Jenkins to find out you messed around with a client? Or the entire A&D community for that matter?"

"We haven't done anything, Linda." I am fighting back tears now. "I just asked him not to leave. I thought maybe his urge to use would pass and he'd remember why he came to treatment in the first place. Maybe he'd recommit himself to the program."

Linda gets up to open the sliding glass door for Pete. The stabbing, bright sunlight pierces the room again. Pete shoots back inside like a cannonball and waits to be re-chained to the sofa.

"Re*commit* himself?" Linda squints at me from across the room. Her eyes are watery slits and she steadies herself on the handle of the door. "This isn't his fucking *wedding* anniversary, you know!"

"Well, he came to treatment of his own accord," I venture weakly. "I just thought maybe if he stayed, he'd turn a corner."

Linda shuts the door but doesn't move. "Let me tell you a little something about Joe," she says. "Joe's not in treatment because he's suddenly decided shooting coke under his nails is no fun and he'd rather be a scout leader. Joe's in treatment because, after decades of using, he lost his contractor business *and* his house, and now his wife is leaving him and taking their *kids*. He knows he's got to do something to make it look to a judge like he's at least fit for visitation. Joe's turned a million corners and never seen a straight road. And what you're thinking about is *fucking* him? *Really*?"

A wave of nausea moves across my chest at the mention of a wife and children. I pull myself up off the floor and lurch down the hall toward where I hope there is a bathroom. My heart is galloping, whamming against my chest like a fist.

"Hey!" Linda calls after me. I turn to see her staggering into the kitchen, one hand grasping the back of the sofa. She points her cigarette at me again. "Don't fuck with people whose stories are bigger than your own."

In the bathroom, I hold onto the counter to steady myself. My head is throbbing and my contact lenses are dry and scratchy. I splash my face and sit down hard on the toilet waiting for the nausea to pass, telling myself it isn't possible to throw up a lunch of only lettuce and shredded cheese eaten nine hours earlier, though for the first time in my life, I have a glimpse of true bulimia, which is the surface impulse to throw up food overlaying the deeper impulse to purge feelings. Right now, I desperately want to vomit what it is I have just swallowed: the realization that, far from being a healer to Joe, I have been a distraction, and because I myself am distracted by Joe, I have not been there for my other clients, either. I have been, in effect, cheating on my clients with a client.

When I'm able to stand again, I look hard into the medicine cabinet mirror. Gone is the youngest member of the psychological superheroes. Gone is the supposed fact of my own recovery leading the way for others. There, reflected along with a constellation of toothpaste spray, is the ordinary fact of my long, gaunt face. I lean forward and look into my bloodshot eyes and am surprised to see the same weariness I saw in Joe's, which is when I remember Mr. Jenkins confronting Lila and Billy several weeks earlier, explaining to Big Group that we invariably pair up with our emotional equals. From a lavender-colored bottle on Linda's basin, I squirt out a little dot of soap and scrub my forehead, my nose, my cheeks, everything that feels hot and greasy to the touch, then pat my face dry with a towel hanging over the shower. If it's true that we pair up with our emotional equals, then I have done nothing but fall in love with the face of my own illness.

* * *

Many years after I am gone from Bridgeway, when I am married, and a therapist, and fully recovered, Linda's comment will still be with me. If, as a result, I believed that my story of anorexia didn't deserve equal billing with stories of alcoholism and addiction, then it was because I trusted Linda implicitly, and I believed that, regardless of all outward signs (her own drug abuse, her many divorces, a scuffle with the law) she understood a thing or two about addiction and people, and the monumental toll that one took on the other.

But there would come a time in my life when I would revisit the conversation and understand that, in the theater of addictive illnesses, where alcoholism, drug addiction, and eating disorders took the stage, one was just as reckless, just as tragic, as another. But whatever Linda's point about who was whom and what was what in the arena of life mismanagement, the part of her message that would stay with me was this: don't pollute another person's struggles with your own. Especially when that person is drowning, and you're the one supposedly holding the life jacket.

Which is where the memory of the pushmi-pullyu, my visual metaphor for immobility, comes flooding back as well. While, at the time, I believed my conflict was whether or not to sleep with Joe, there was, in fact, another storyline entirely, having nothing to do with Joe. It harkened back, of course, to the story of my discarded sexual self, to how my wish for companionship, for sex, for a man, clashed with what I believed I owed my mother, which was to be without needs, devoid of appetite, utterly, injudiciously, celibate. In light of this belief, my solution was perfect, if unoriginal: crave a man who is off limits in a hundred different, dangerous ways, and when you cannot have him, chalk this up not to the fulfillment of your own sad story, but to environment, fate, other people. Later, outside the spotlight of attraction, I would realize that everything I thought and felt about Joe had nothing whatsoever to do with Joe, that he was less the desired object than the catalyst, the hand that flicked the switch, that ramped up the competition between wanting the things I'd forced myself not to want and finally admitting that I wanted them.

Linda bangs on the bathroom door. "You okay in there? You *aack*ing?"

I open the door. "I don't *aack*," I say. "And I'm leaving."

I pick my way through the quiet downtown Tifton streets, happy for the darkness and the solitude of the car. As I pass Bridgeway, I crane my neck to look up at the third floor sleeping quarters. It is ten p.m. and, per regulations, there are no lights on except in the main office where the night manager, Mr. Bob, sits drinking his coffee and reading the Bible. I imagine Joe stretched out on his bunk and breathing in the noxious air of sobriety, restless in the heat and dreaming of... what? It occurs to me then that I have no idea what Joe's dreams are about, because I know absolutely nothing about him. Until tonight, I'd never even considered there might be a wife, a family. All of my feelings for him, everything I thought I knew, grew out of the almost-fact of our touching knees, my chin in his hand, and how I was going to be the one to save him.

Chapter 12

The Topic of Cancer

MY PARENTS' HOUSE IS COLD. For a few minutes, I am happy for the air conditioning, since I have just driven the four hours from Tifton to Atlanta in my tiny Honda hatchback with nothing but a fan to blow warm, damp air at my body. October has bloomed hot and sultry in South Georgia this year, much like August and September.

Early this morning, I woke to the drone of a tractor making its way through the rows of tall, dark green corn, and I stood on my porch and watched it. I wished I could ride along, feel the hot sun on my back, let the lingering shame of the previous night at Linda's burn off of me the way school burns off of you at the beach in the summer.

"You're too thin," my mother says when I walk in the door. It has been four months since I've been home. I'm wearing blue jean shorts and an aqua-colored T-shirt, the fourth outfit I tried on this morning. I imagined Joe seeing me in it, nodding his approval. "What do you weigh?" my mother says.

I tug at my shirt. There's a dark line of sweat where the seatbelt pressed against my chest the whole way home. Keithan, who has just heard my voice, barrels down the long hallway to greet me, wagging her tail in exuberant wide circles like a flag. I squat down and open my arms, and she runs into them.

"How much do you weigh?" my mother asks again. According to the family therapist, whom we last saw two years earlier, she isn't supposed to ask my weight because it is invasive. *Whoever controls the weight controls the girl,* he said. But if I refuse to give her a number she will only think that I am losing again.

"One-oh-three," I say. A four-pound fudge upward.

She glances the length of my body. Her disgust is evident, though at the time I don't know if it's because she detects the lie, or if she's just tired of playing this same conversation out over and over. She turns back to the counter where she is cutting up carrots for the salad, *chunk, chunk, chunk,* a sound that is more like executing than dicing. I can smell the twin aromas of chicken broiling and potatoes baking in the microwave. A prickle of anxiety disguised as a chill creeps over me. It has been several months since I have eaten a meal with my parents, and my mother, like me, will be counting every calorie that goes into my mouth.

"Put your things away," she says with her back still toward me.

Keithan follows me down the hall to my brother's old room, which is the only room still a bedroom besides my parents'. I drop my overnight bag just inside the door, fish an oversized sweatshirt out of it, and pull it on over my head. Now that I'm cool again, it feels good to be covered up.

Next to my brother's bedroom is my old room, which is now my father's study. I can hear the steady clack-clack of his typewriter and the faint sounds of WSB Radio chatter. He doesn't come out to greet me, which doesn't surprise me. There were long stretches during my illness that I would lie on the bed and listen to the endless clatter of his typewriter, certain that if I or my mother disappeared, he wouldn't know it for months, so single-minded was his focus on work. Or that if he ever did happen to ask how I was doing, I could say anything from, "Fine," to, "I'm going to kill myself now," and his response would be the same: "Okay, Sweetie, have a good day."

I poke my head in his door.

"Hey," I say.

The clatter of typing stops. My father wheels around in his chair.

"You're home!" He looks genuinely glad to see me.

"Yep," I say.

"How is work?" he asks. "Do you like it, are you making friends? Are you learning a lot?" All questions he would know the answers to if we spoke on the phone, which we don't, or if my mother filled him in after we talked, which she doesn't.

"Yes," I say, "I like it. I'm friends with the other counselor," though, as I say this, a new bout of sadness and shame wells up in me. *And yes, I am learning a lot, for example, don't fuck a client. Don't even THINK about fucking a client. And, by God, if you do think about fucking a client,* don't *tell the most hypocritical person you know, because she's likely to tell you how wrong it is and how appalling you are while she herself is riding high atop her own client screaming woo-hoo! and waving a cowboy hat.*

My father is smiling at me, waiting for me to say something more than *Yes, I like it,* but I realize there is nothing more I want to tell him. And just like that, I am standing on a log of ambivalence, fighting feelings of anger that are so old I can't possibly unravel them to their start. This anger is about the fact that he doesn't leave his office or even his chair to greet me, even after not having seen me for four months. I'm vaguely aware of believing that if I just don't want the anger, it will go away. I am not, after all, the same sick girl arriving home from the hospital on a therapeutic leave (an amusing term because I always went home on leave and it was always precisely the opposite of therapeutic) to find that my father is too busy to come out of his office and say hello. (In his defense, he had likely seen me a few days before at the hospital, for family therapy or visitation; nevertheless I couldn't help but feel my visit home should have been worth a momentary pause in his day's work.) And so it is this age-old grudge I try mightily to push away, to tell myself is a casualty of my newfound maturity, a debt I owe to these last four months in Tifton. But I can't do it. I can't push away the memory of lying in my room, my thoughts an anxious whorl of despair and starvation punctuated by the persistent clack-clacking of typewriter keys, a feeling like drowning next to an ocean liner outfitted with all sorts of rescue gear.

"So how are you, what's going on?" I ask.

"Well," my father says, and here he inserts a shallow giggle, a laugh that isn't really a laugh but that is his classic stand-in when a real one is not available. "It seems I'm going to be making some changes in my life," he says. "The way I eat, for example—no more hard salami!" Another forced sounding laugh. "More exercise! I'm going to be getting lots more exercise. You're going to see a different me. I'm taking the bull by the horns."

I feel like there is a whole beginning conversation I've not been privy to.

"What? What's happening?"

"And your mother and I are going to get out more. I'm going to *romance* her! Oh, we're gonna have some fun!"

"What?" I say. "You're gonna romance Mom?"

"It's in the *cards*," he says. As if in some kind of eerie accord, the trees outside the giant windows I am certain my father never pauses to look through begin to rustle.

"What's in the cards? What *cards*?" My father's speech is cryptic and full of false enthusiasm. I know this talk. It's what ensues when my parents are having trouble, when my mother is threatening to leave and my father has been roused from his Rumplestiltskin sleep of work. "Don't you worry about a thing, Sweetie, I'll be fine."

I'll be fine is not a part of the language of divorce threats and romance re-upping, however. "What? Are you sick?"

"It's bladder cancer," he says. "But it's okay, we caught it early."

I stand at the door of his study, shivering in my sweatshirt, unable to make eye contact. I stare past his talking face to the now-still pines. I am vaguely aware of being angry now at my own anger, and doubly angry with my father for making me have to be mad at myself.

"How long have you known?"

"Oh, about two weeks," he says cheerfully.

"What are they doing?"

"The usual. Chemo right now, later maybe a little radiation. Really, I'm going to be fine. It's so early."

"They said that?"

"I'm saying that. I'm taking charge. I'm telling you, you're going to see a very different me." He's smiling still. He is smiling bigger than I have ever seen him smile.

It makes me want to scream.

* * *

When I was eighteen, I read a memoir called *Mars*. The author, Fritz Angst (under the pseudonym Fritz Zorn), asserted that it was his family's emotional repressiveness, their utter unavailability to him for anything approaching true human discourse, that caused his cancer. The book made sweeping claims about the psychic origins of physical illness, and as I neared the end of it, I understood Zorn to be speaking not only of cancer but of something larger and more sinister, a whole family systems-engendered forest of illnesses from which there could be no more logical source and little hope of recovery.

I think about the memoir from time to time when I am older, after my father is gone. Perhaps this was us. Perhaps my mother, angry and unforgiving, rejoicing in my father's mishaps, and planning, if only in outspoken fantasy, her escape to an apartment, a life of her own, laid down the first tiny cell outposts in his body. Maybe the burden of my illness, the cost of my hospitalization, the sorrow it caused him to watch his youngest daughter turn away from all that was positive and life-affirming (my horse, my womanhood, other people, him) and turn instead toward negativity and sorrow and despair furthered the progression of his own illness. Malignant, my mother and I were.

But when I look back on that day my father announced he had bladder cancer, I see something I couldn't have voiced at the time. A well of feelings, a prism of fear and sadness and dread and hopelessness and anger, all of it radiating out from the core of ambivalence I had always had about him. Because he had always complained—of headaches, anxiety, back pain, neck pain, fatigue, a life spent reeling in an endless stream of doctor visits, Valium, aspirin, back rubs, sleep, work—this ongoing anguish and the quest for its cure was the backdrop against which all other aspects of our relationship, including its demise, unfolded.

Perhaps predictably, this conversation in the doorway of his study is all I remember of that visit. Whether I ate dinner, whether my mother said anything, what we talked about the rest of the weekend, would now be nothing more than conjecture. What I am certain is true however, (because this was the truth of every visit, including those untainted by the specter of illness) is that the three of us felt, despite the company of one another, epically alone.

Chapter 13

Faking Well

B Y THE TIME I PULL INTO my apartment complex on Sunday evening, the runaway pounding in my chest feels normal, like my new resting heart rate. I have been with my parents for two full days, and because my mother was preoccupied with my father and therefore not watching me not-eat, I have also been hungry for two full days. My hand shakes as I try to put my house key in the lock, and I steady it with my other hand. Inside, I drop my pocketbook on the floor and go into the kitchen. I reach into the freezer, but as I consider having a snack of bread crust with a thin smear of Weight Watcher's butter, I decide I don't like the math. Crust plus butter equals about forty calories, whereas if I have bubble gum instead, at eight calories for a piece the size of my knuckle, I could apply the extra thirty-two calories to dinner. This is a kind of mental savings account whereby I "deposit" the calories I forgo at one meal or snack for theoretical consumption at a later time. The fact that I never cash in those calories doesn't matter. They accrue interest in the form of pounds not gained, pounds lost, or just a good feeling for not having eaten them.

Two years post-hospitalization and six months into superhero counselor-hood at Bridgeway, this is not how I am supposed to still be thinking. Instead of trying to construct a façade of capability that will trick my employer and my coworkers and my mother into believing I am a healthy, mentally stable young woman, I should be spending my time developing a pool of bona fide emotional integrity that I can draw upon to heal my life and help my clients. But this isn't happening because at the heart of my predicament is the relationship I have developed with my illness: the aforementioned love affair I have with feeling in exquisite control over my appetite, in focusing on food instead of real issues—my loneliness, for example, my many fears, and now my father's illness—and the resultant exacting form my body takes. It is this love affair that erases the boundaries between healthy, recovered eating and the kind of caloric juggling I still do: bread crust instead of bread slice, bubble gum instead of bread crust.

If that were it, of course, addicts would not be addicts, or at least not for long. Were there not some other, ultimate payoff for our time spent gathering up our substances or planning for their ingestion or expulsion or avoidance then we might not be caught in such a grip. But the fact is, addiction is a raft, a bobbing pontoon in a wide river that floats us dreamily away from the shores of our discontent. Bread crust over bread slice? Bubble gum over bread crust? How much more pleasant to wrangle with these choices than to wonder if my father is afraid, if my mother feels more trapped, if the cancer is terminal? And regardless of whether the answers are all yeses, there is still, will always be, this: *Calories burned over calories ingested equals weight lost;* my magical formula that isn't magic at all but that nevertheless transports me to a place far away.

* * *

I cram two pieces of gum in my mouth and, before the sugar can play out, put on my sneakers, grab my sunglasses and my Walkman, and head downstairs for my cornfield walk, which I am too hungry for but which I can't choose not to do because I promised myself the exercise.

Mr. Jenkins is pulling into the apartment complex with his fiancée, Barbara. He rolls down her window, leans over her to talk to me.

"Out for a walk?"

I nod. The gum in my mouth is too huge to say anything. He leans further over and takes a good look at me in my sunglasses, with my earphones in and my gob of gum. He smiles.

"You got all your senses plugged," he says. "You look like..." He pauses. "You look like the reincarnation of *Tommy!*" He throws his head back and laughs, then says it a second time, only louder. Barbara bursts out laughing. They are still laughing when they get out of the car and walk up the sidewalk to their apartment. A hard knot of shame forms in my belly.

I click on my radio and head down the badly rutted dirt road into the cornfields, kicking clods out of my way and jumping tractor tire ditches. The dirt is a rich deep orange and the corn is a high green fence on either side.

I walk fast, pumping my arms and fists for extra propulsion, sweat forming underneath my shirt, red dust rising up in an angry blur ahead of my sneakers. I go deeper and deeper into the cornfields, losing myself in the web of tractor paths, and in the bleating, rhythmic voices of the Thompson Twins singing "Hold Me Now." My breathing becomes raspy and labored as I struggle to keep up the near-running pace I perfected years ago with my mother on our road back home. A hard, sharp ache moves into my side and I grab it and try to knead it away so I won't have to break my stride. In another minute it grows insistent, a searing pain knifing through my ribs. I stop and bend over and grasp my side. It's hard to breathe. I sit down in the dirt and fold over on myself. The distinctive smell of iron-saturated earth stings my nose.

When at last I'm able to sit upright again, I notice something new in the cornfield: *corn*. Six or eight bright green, fat husks jutting out from every stalk I can see, some with silky tassels. Change was coming. I feel it in my bones and in my breath, the same way I felt it years ago on the cusp of starting my ninth-grade year in high school. It followed on the heels of one astoundingly perfect year, when my friend Bobbi and I rode our horses almost every day after school and all summer, galloping around the tiny pasture behind her house in tight circles and clearing low jumps bareback with our hands in the air. After we rode, we spent more happy hours mucking out stalls, sweeping the tack room, and scrubbing and refilling the water tub, all the while singing along to "Crocodile Rock" on the portable radio and talking about boys, other girls, and what life would be like the following school year.

One afternoon, we put our horses up early and climbed the hill overlooking the pasture. With summer's humidity gone, the air had thinned and the sky blazed a deep, suit-jacket blue. The grass had already turned brittle, and little leaf ponds of yellow and red and gold punctuated the ground. A light wind blew toward us, announcing itself first in the tall pines overhead. We sat down cross-legged in a clearing on a wide, flat rock and peeled the fat oranges we'd brought with us, licking at the juice that ran down our hands and made them sticky and cold. As we sat there eating our oranges and looking out over the little barn where our horses munched their hay, I felt a shift inside, an opening up, a deepening. In four days, Bobbi's father would have a stroke at the hospital where he was a physician, and the other doctors would not be able to save him. By the following summer, Bobbi would have sold her horse and moved with her mother and sisters to a new school across town, and I would see her only five more times in my life. I didn't know these things were coming, of course, but there was something unmistakable in the orange-scented air that felt irrevocable and frightening and new. Which is the feeling I have now, hugging myself deep in the bright, fruit-bearing cornfields. Like something is about to happen. Which it is, of course. My father's cancer was not detected early, and he would not be making any changes in his life.

* * *

"I ain't talking," Mr. Jenkins says on our way down the hall to Big Group. It is Monday morning, two weeks after my trip home, two weeks and one day after my fight with Linda at her trailer. We are not completely back on track. She still comes into my office in the mornings, but we are like bitter lovers, saying little and smoking in silence. I miss her. More accurately, she is my only friend in Tifton, and I need her.

On this particular day, I don't feel like going to group, much less helping to lead it. Linda and I sit next to each other, and Henriette sits across the room. Bridgeway has swelled to twenty-five residents, all of them restless and shifty with an itchy boredom that makes them cough and yawn and cross and uncross their legs. Within a few days, half of them will be gone. The thought of working hard to engage them in group just to have them leave mid-treatment saps my energy. More and more, this is how I feel: like recovery requires too much effort for most of our clients, and for me.

"You're just depressed," Linda says when I tell her this. She eyes me coolly, exhaling menthol smoke in a thin stream, her foot jiggling. She doesn't take it any further and neither do I. She knows about my father, though we don't talk about it. We haven't mentioned Joe since the night at her trailer.

Outside the group window, the air conditioning unit drones, a monotonous, rhythmic whirring as we wait for the group to gestate, to meld and become a thing, an entity larger than the separate members. Nobody speaks. My heart races. This is how it always begins.

After five minutes, Linda pokes a hole in the silence.

"Well?" she says. She looks from resident to resident. Henriette and I follow her gaze around the room. She lingers briefly on Joe. He looks at me, rolls his eyes nervously, and snorts. Linda pounces.

"What's funny, Joe?"

"Nothing, ma'am," says Joe.

"You laughed, something must be funny."

"I can't think of anything."

"You always laugh when things aren't funny?" Henriette says, leaning forward threateningly in her chair.

Joe looks helplessly at me. I feel for him but can't risk helping him out. Plus, I'm too tired.

"Can't hear you," says Linda.

"No, I don't always laugh when things aren't funny."

"Then what made you laugh this time?"

Joe exhales loudly. "I guess it was just funny to see everyone looking around, waiting to see who was gonna get fingered. I guess it's me." He snorts again.

"You were waiting to see who was gonna get fingered?" Linda

repeats. "Why is everybody sitting back waiting to get 'fingered,' instead of using group to their advantage? Aren't y'all here for a reason?"

I acknowledge silently that this is a great question.

"Yeah, people," Henriette says, emboldened by Linda. "This isn't about being fingered for something, it's about you working your program. I don't understand why everyone in here isn't *fighting* for group time." Again, a very good point. I can feel my energy begin to rally a bit.

The group goes silent again, all eyes on the floor. Feet jiggle, coffee is sipped. Down the hall in the kitchen I can hear Miss Hattie laughing on the phone. Outside, the steady drone of the air conditioner.

"I was thinking of leaving last week," Joe finally offers.

Linda stares at him but doesn't say anything.

"I decided to stay, though. Give it some more time."

He glances at me. I look away.

"So?" says Linda.

Joe looks at her, surprised. "So... what?"

"Exactly. So what? You're gonna give it more time. So? C'mon, Joe, give us something that means something."

Joe looks at the floor again. Helpless, at a complete loss for what Linda is looking for.

"Well..." he flounders, "It wasn't easy, deciding to stay. I'd already decided to go. Had a connection and everything."

The group starts to snicker. Henriette snaps back in her chair. "What are you people laughing at?" she demands. "Is this funny? One of yours was planning to quit the program, already had a *connection*, and you think it's *funny*?" Henriette looks from Linda to me for support for her rage. Linda shakes her head.

"Jesus, people," she says.

"Damn," I say.

I think about a counselor's comment to me three years earlier about giving up starvation. Hers was a simple, off-the-cuff remark, not the stuff of gurus or superheroes, or even moderately well-trained counselors. And yet, even a poorly aimed arrow sometimes hits its mark. *Nothing is easy*, she said.

Nothing is easy. I realized at the moment she said it that I'd been waiting for things to get easy for months. That I thought all I needed was a rolling push, and once I got that, recovery would be like a memory, fully in progress and its own driving force. *Not the case*, she was saying. Not long after she said this, I joined a support group for young anorexic women. Most of what they talked about was how, each time when their weight rose to an acceptable range and they were discharged from treatment, they started immediately to cut calories again, working to drive the number back down. They had learned only one thing: how to eat enough to merit discharge so that they could start losing weight again.

Back then, on the surface of it—if you looked at me and then looked at them—we looked the same. Underneath, however, I was beginning to grasp certain truths that most of them had yet to discover: about how we were looking for solutions in all the wrong places, the sad fact of wasted years, and the profound absurdity of it all, how we held fast to our weight loss venture even when it repeatedly failed to deliver us from banality, unhappiness, confusion, *ourselves*. Why I knew these things and others didn't, I wasn't sure. It occurred to me that perhaps these messages of burgeoning health were the language of the enemy, that insight was a ploy to fatten me up, throw me off course. That only the most dedicated survive the war of the flesh and that I was being weeded out, an unworthy representative of the triumph of will over hunger. With time however, as my weight began to stabilize at around ninety-five pounds, my brain seemed to right itself in small ways, moments of clarity falling into place like pictures in a slot machine: there I was, Too Thin, Too Thin, and Too Thin. It was beginning to make sense. I was beginning to see what my family and friends, my counselors and therapists, and the person on the street saw, and I had to ask myself whether this—illness, addiction, misery, war— was what I wanted for my life. I didn't know where I—or Joe—got the idea that recovering would get easier with time. I supposed it didn't matter.

I sit up in my chair and take a deep breath. My heart is pounding. "You can't just give it more time, Joe," I say. "You have to do real work. Time didn't make you an addict and time won't unmake you one. It's up to you to make yourself something else."

Joe is staring at me as if I have let him down, as if it were my job to support his half-assed efforts at treatment rather than hold him accountable in a real way to himself. He rolls his eyes and folds his arms across his chest. I don't care.

"You've been an addict for *five years*, Joe. Is this what you want for the rest of your life? To play around with your recovery, your time, the people who love you and are waiting to see if you're coming back?"

Joe is shaking his head, waving me off. "I know, okay? I know. I'll get serious about it." *Just shut up*, he is saying. But I don't shut up. "You'll get serious about it when? A *year* from now? *Two* years from now? A week from never? If not now, Joe, then *when?*"

My voice, which would ordinarily be quaking, is surprisingly calm. All of the residents are looking at me. Joe is looking at me. Linda and Henriette are looking at me. I look toward the one-way window behind which I know Mr. Jenkins is looking at me. But all I can see is myself looking back. *I am talking to myself.*

* * *

For the rest of group, Linda and Henriette talk specifics. A grocery list of to-do items for remaining sober: Get sober friends. Get a job in a sober environment. Start a savings account. Make amends. Eat plenty of fruits and vegetables. Get plenty of sleep. Go to therapy and AA. Get a sponsor. Joe nods. He won't do any of that, I surmise. But he does. Joes does all of that and more. Two years later, I will hear that Joe is Bridgeway's newest counselor.

After group, I implore Mr. Jenkins to put down his newspaper and talk to me, tell me how I did. It's the first time I have spoken in group to offer something, not just agree with something someone else has said. It was only a few sentences but to me it felt like a filibuster.

"You did good. I'm sure Joe is cured now."

"No, really, was what I said okay?"

"You made a valid point. Now, is your boy gonna stay and work the program?"

"—My boy?"

"Your sweetheart."

"My sweetheart?" From where we are sitting in the outer office, I can see Linda at her desk. She has stopped writing her chart note and looks up when she hears Mr. Jenkins say, "your sweetheart." She meets my eyes, covers her mouth, then makes a zipping motion with her fingers. I didn't tell him, it says.

My heart begins a slow but deliberate march into my throat. "He's not my sweetheart," I say.

"You sure about that?" Mr. Jenkins puts his paper down and leans back in his chair. My mouth opens but nothing comes out. I wonder if this is the moment of my firing. Ironic, I think, to be fired not for smoking dope or getting drunk but for loving somebody.

"You do know that if you cross a boundary once you'll do it again," he says.

My mind is reeling but I don't say anything.

"Well?"

"No, I didn't know that."

"That ain't the question. The question is, have you crossed a boundary?"

I look in Linda's office again but her head is down and she is pretending to write. Fast.

"No," I say. "I swear. Nothing has happened between Joe and me."

"Well, I seem to recall you making goo-goo eyes on the porch and hanging onto each other a few weeks ago."

In a rush, I remember standing on the porch with Joe the day I asked him to give it another week. Why had he waited so long to confront me?

"Nothing has happened," I say again. "Joe told me he was planning to leave. I just asked him to give it one more week. I guess—I maybe—grabbed his arm, that's all. I was just trying to help. I didn't want him to leave."

"For him or for you?" Mr. Jenkins asks.

"What?"

"Did you want him to stay and get treatment," Mr. Jenkins says, enunciating his words like I am a child, "Or did you want him to stay 'cause you gots the hots for him?"

The chill of the aluminum chair seeps through the seat of my pants and my butt bones begin to ache. The truth, I know, lies somewhere in between, in the cross-section between wanting what's best for Joe and wanting Joe himself.

Chapter 14

Rape of the Corn

M Y FATHER HAS HAD THE FIRST of his surgeries and is well into radiation and chemotherapy. But the reality of this simply doesn't get in until, on a rare visit home two months after my last visit, I see that he has lost his hair. And unlike *surgery*, unlike *radiation*, unlike *chemotherapy, shingles, vomiting,* or any of the words my mother has used to describe the hideous ongoing assaults of cancer, *bald* shouts out the news for the deafest of us to hear. It is the only voice in the choir loud enough to rise above the din of my unrelenting, nail-biting self-reflection. *Bald* screams, "Something is very, very wrong."

Along with the terror *bald* inserts into my already packed schedule of private worries, I am struck by how large and shiny my father's head is, how his eyes now seem to have been tacked on without regard to the overall composition of a face. They seem too high or too low suddenly—without the defining parameters of hair, it is hard to tell exactly what the problem is, but the fact that my father no longer looks the way he used to makes me tentative and shy around him, like a teen-aged candy striper visiting some strange, sick old man.

"Hi, Sweetie!" my father says, smiling, the edges of his lash-less, brow-less eyes crinkling just above his dimensionless, rubbery, pink cheeks. He is sitting at his desk in his study at home, and has swiveled his chair around to face me. "How's work?"

"It's good," I whisper, twisting my ring around on my finger and searching for some defining facial feature to remember him by. "How are you feeling?"

"Never better," my father says, smiling more broadly now.

His assertion depresses me for its bravado. My father, a lifelong hypochondriac, now seriously ill yet *never better?* What of the ever-present vague, indistinct symptoms that permeated our past, whose origins could never be pinned down? Symptoms for which, when one doctor said *It's just anxiety* and wouldn't prescribe medication, my father found another who would? What of the lifesaving assortment of pills, from the innocuous Tums to the warhorse Valium, forever rattling in his pocket, without which (and with which, for that matter) he takes to his bed or a soft chair in the darkened living room and with a grave and weighty selection of classical music on the stereo, nurses a crescendo of pain and sorrow that echoes the throbbing of his head and back, the burning sensation in his belly, the tingling of his sciatica, the roar of his pounding heart? Where are these agonies now, now that cancer is on the scene?

Of course, I think I know. After so many years of doubting his symptoms, because I watched the way he leapt to action if work demanded it or if there was a social occasion about which he was excited, I have come to believe that my father's shape-shifting illnesses and the subsequent slate of vague, undiagnosable symptoms was, like my anorexia, like my mother's food and exercise obsession, a kind of bleating of the soul, a wordless and indistinct cry for attention and love and support and sympathy, all of which he deserved, of course—all of which we *all* deserved—but couldn't seem to garner without pathology's leg-up. Now that cancer's army is nipping at his heels, and my father's world is filled with the indisputable evidence of pain and sickness, the burden of proof is gone from his mind. A lifetime of sickness and management, an incalculable madness that began as a benign thrumming in his chest and translated to the malignant rattle of pills in his pocket, ceases, with a profusion of tumors in his bladder, to exist. He seems, as I stand there in his doorway twisting my ring, to genuinely feel fine.

But cancer, like anorexia, is like an octopus, wrapping its poison-tipped tentacles around every single facet of your life. Cancer works from the inside, making its home in the dark recesses of the body's underground, undetectable in the beginning, a chameleon of sorts, its cells indistinguishable from other cells. At some point—weeks, maybe years later—cancer blows its cover, becoming something bulbous and dangerous and disrespectful of boundaries, blasting neighboring cells with tissue-invading enzymes, and riding the currents of the bloodstream or lymphatic system with an eye toward expanding its territory. In a fight to preserve itself, an octopus can lose an arm and it will regenerate. Tumors are like this, too. Heart attack, shingles, difficulty urinating, kidney failure, depression, terror, and our mounting fears and escalating denial—these are all the ways the long arm of cancer will wrap itself around not just my father, but my mother and brother and sister, too. How much about my father's health is disclosed to me at the time I don't recall exactly; I have the sense that what I knew I flung like something poisonous into a can and slammed the cover down tight, ignoring the rumblings, the warnings, that the beast was about to surge.

* * *

Five weeks after Linda and I had our fight, we are still not completely back on track. She still comes in my office every morning to smoke and tell me about her evenings, but I am aware of a red light that goes off the moment we start to feel too comfortable together. I tell myself it's because Linda no longer trusts me, but the truth, to which I have not yet awakened, is that I no longer trust her. In an effort to restore balance, I invite her and her husband DeWayne over for dinner on a Sunday night: broiled chicken (which I would never make just for myself) and salad. As I only have two plates, I have to go to Kmart to buy two more. And as I don't have a table, I filch a surprisingly sturdy coffee-table sized box from behind the grocery store.

"Okay, sure," Linda says. "I'll bring the hooch."

On the designated Sunday night, Linda knocks on the door and lets herself in.

"Hey, Bi-yatch!" She smiles broadly, walking into the living room, and hands me a bottle of tequila and a grocery bag with several limes, lemonade concentrate, and Doritos. "It's just us tonight," she says. "DeWayne couldn't make it." Which is okay by me, because for just a moment it feels like the old us. I hold up the tequila triumphantly.

"And Mr. Jenkins thinks I don't know what my needs are!"

"Jesus," Linda says, "That was fucked up!" She looks around the room. Her smile fades. "Dang girl, do you think maybe you need *furniture?*"

"I'll make us drinks," I say. I ease open the oven to the fragrant smell of Italian seasoning crusting nicely on three chicken thighs. It didn't occur to me to make an extra one, in case anyone wanted seconds.

"Where's your bed?" Linda calls from the bedroom. I close the oven and walk around the corner to where she is standing just inside my bedroom door.

"Right there," I say, pointing to a spot on the floor against the wall on which a rectangle of blanket is folded neatly. A pillow rests on top.

Linda just stands there looking at it. "You don't have a *bed?*"

"I like sleeping on the floor. It's better for my back."

"What's wrong with your back?"

"Nothing," I say. "See how the floor is helping?" I laugh.

Linda rolls her eyes. She looks at my clothes folded on the floor and my underwear and bras and socks tossed into a small cardboard box. "You keep your shit in *boxes?* You don't have a *dresser?*"

She walks across the bedroom and peeks into the bathroom. "Thank God a toilet came standard with the apartment."

"Very funny," I say. But I don't hear her, not in any real way. I don't register the look of alarm on her face, the draining of merriment that happened in the moment after she handed me the tequila and her eyes took a tour of the living room with its lone green recliner and box coffee table. I don't register any of it because I can't. I have lived in emptiness so long, I am blind to it.

"Let me show you the best thing about this apartment," I say. I tell

Linda to close her eyes and I lead her to the open sliding glass doors and out onto the porch. "Okay, open."

Linda opens her eyes slowly, like she is afraid of what she will see. Then she looks baffled, looking left, right, and down below the balcony.

"I give up," she says. "What am I looking at?"

"That," I say, pointing expansively toward the green sea of corn on which the eight o'clock sun is setting.

"That." Linda repeats flatly. I nod my head enthusiastically as Linda looks from me to the cornfields, then back to me. A thread of anxiety begins to wend its way through my chest as I sense that Linda and I are off-kilter again.

We eat our chicken thighs and salad hunched over the box. I don't mention Joe and, at least until we are finished, she doesn't mention furniture again. Afterward, I clear away the dishes, turn off the air conditioner, and open the sliding glass doors. I can hear my downstairs neighbor talking on the phone and dragging a chair out onto her patio to sit. The smell of grass and humidity creeps into the living room, the outside air overtaking the inside air like a slow moving cloud.

"So where was DeWayne tonight?" I ask, settling down on a pillow on the floor across from Linda. I have a fresh drink, a nice buzz, and am about to light a cigarette.

"He had to work late," Linda says. I start to ask doing what, and then I remember he hangs sheetrock. It seems strange that he would be working after dark, but just as I am about to question this, Linda leans forward from her spot in the floor and looks at me hard.

"Have you always lived like this?"

My hand with the lighter freezes mid-way to my cigarette. "Like what?"

Linda slices her hand, palm up, through the air. "This," she says. "Without basic furniture and real dishes and dressers and stuff. Hell, your momma drives a brand new Mitsubishi. I know you must have money."

"I have what I need," I say, feeling suddenly defensive.

* * *

At the time, I tell myself that Linda just doesn't understand, though admittedly I'm not sure exactly *what* she doesn't understand that I do. Perhaps it's something about simplicity, how something as elemental as a cornfield—looking at it, walking through it—could set your life right every single night. Or maybe she didn't understand how living with only what you absolutely must have keeps your mind uncluttered, your spirit somehow (I am not sure how) free. And I feel a flash of anger. Who is she to question how I live when she lives in a giant parking lot for houses? Sitting there with Linda in my little apartment, embraced by acres of agriculture and a silence that seems to echo my own wishful future of solitude, I am suddenly inflamed by what can only be my need to defend what I love combined with lingering shame from our confrontation a few weeks earlier. The upshot is that I want nothing more than for her to leave so I can do what I do best without having to explain myself: curl up in my green recliner and stare out at the cornfields. Linda has become a huge lump of human dross in my living room, someone whose presence is frivolous and makes me feel more alone than alone makes me feel. *Leave*, I think, and, as if in response, Linda lights a new cigarette and settles back against the recliner.

"You don't have to answer," she says. "I just think it's interesting."

"You act like I have a dirt floor and a cow sharing my living room."

"It just seems weird. It seems like you'd *want* more. Hell, I had more furniture in my dorm room than you have here." For a minute, Linda looks at me with an expression of genuine concern. Then, as if catching herself, she adds brightly, "But whatever gets you off." She drains her drink, sets the glass down on the box, and taps out her cigarette. "I have to go. DeWayne will be home soon and he'll throw a fit if I'm not there."

Before I can say anything, Linda is off the recliner and gathering up her pocketbook. I am glad she's leaving, but I know her sudden departure has more to do with me and my lack of belongings, and maybe even the cornfields, than it does with DeWayne.

"Thanks for dinner," she says. "It was yummy."

I listen to Linda's receding steps on the landing and then on the stairs leading down to the parking lot. I hear her car door slam, the engine turn over, and the lick of the tires on the pavement as she drives away.

In the quiet that is left behind, I lean against the living room wall and try to look at the apartment through Linda's eyes. On the box, now cleared of dishes, there is only an ashtray brimming with butts. My small black and white television set is too heavy for the cardboard box it rests on, and leans forward and to the right, something I have never noticed before. The green recliner faces the cornfields, its back to the room like an unfriendly guest. There is nothing else in the room—no knick-knacks, no family photographs, no bookshelves, no books. The walls are bare. The apartment looks unoccupied. Like the person who was going to live here was called away at the start of moving-in day and never came back. Or worse—it looks like I've been robbed.

I walk across the room and onto the deck. I inhale the rapidly cooling October air and look out toward the red dirt road that leads into the cornfields, a road I have walked hundreds of times since I moved here. I lean out over the deck railing and strain to see between the rows. With Linda gone, peering out at the corn like this, I feel my self return to me. Something—consciousness, thoughtfulness, fatigue—seeps into the length of my arms and legs, bringing with it a familiar weightiness I have come to recognize as the cost of inhabiting myself.

Silently I bid the cornfields good-night, and, not even bothering to wash the dishes, turn out the lights and go into the bedroom. I feel for the small reading light on the floor by the blanket and turn it on. Beside the dim circle of light I pull off my jeans and t-shirt. In the bathroom behind the door is an old, blue, button-down shirt of my father's that reaches to the middle of my thighs. I pull it on over my head, careful to avoid looking at my stomach, which bulges with dinner. I pull my hair back into a loose ponytail and brush my teeth. When I sit down to pee I look at the scale that is wedged in between the toilet and the shower and nose it out with my toe.

In the bedroom I unfold the blanket and shake it out to full length. Underneath it is another blanket folded into fourths, my mattress. It isn't like I am sleeping on a bare surface, although when I slide the length of my body between the two blankets, I can count each notch of my spine as it pushes into the floor. Most nights this discomfort gives me comfort. I pull the top blanket to my chin and stare up at the ceiling.

Linda's words roll around in my head. *It just seems like you would want* more. I remember running into Mr. Jenkins the day I was headed out for a walk wearing my Walkman, my sunglasses, and chewing a wad of gum.

"You look like the incarnation of *Tommy!*" he had said. "You got all your senses plugged!"

That day, I had walked out into the cornfields with a knot of shame growing in my belly, not knowing why, thinking it was because I was out to enjoy nature but was, in fact, as removed from it as I could be with my earphones, sunglasses, and mouthful of bubble gum. Now, as I lay on the floor, hands absently palpating the soft swell of my belly, I feel that same knot of shame take hold. I am not without needs. I am simply, for long stretches of time, deaf, dumb and blind to them.

I recall an afternoon from the hospital, sitting across from one of my counselors, Laurie, picking at the cornbread on my plate. I'd pulled the golden "cap" off and put the moist underside on my tray for disposal. I would eat the cap mixed in with a small amount of cottage cheese and six cherry tomatoes with their guts squeezed out. I was aware that Laurie was watching me work. A piece of the cornbread underside the size of a quarter fell into my cottage cheese bowl and I froze. I mentally calculated its calories as I tried to decide whether to leave it in or take it out. I picked it out. "Don't stare at me, Laurie," I said crossly.

Laurie clapped a hand over her eyes. I sighed. "And don't make fun of me." She put her hand down.

"Why are you angry?" she asked. It was the age-old question. Someone was always asking me why I was angry.

"I don't know," I said, "but I'm sick of being angry."

"What would you be if you weren't angry?" Laurie asked.

"I'd be *well*, probably," I said.

"So you think being angry is making you sick?"

"It makes me not want to eat," I said.

"That's a cop-out," Laurie said. "Anger doesn't make you not want to eat; not wanting to *deal* with your anger makes you not want to eat."

"Whatever," I said. "I'm just sick of sitting around talking about weight and eating when I don't *want* to talk about those things."

"Why does it bother you to talk about those things?" Laurie asked.

I thought. I wanted to say it was because I was more interested in the *real* issues, that food and eating weren't the point, that anyway, my eating habits weren't the bizarre spectacle everyone seemed to want to say they were. But as I stared down at my tray with the decapitated cornbread cap and eviscerated cherry tomatoes, I couldn't deny the evidence. I started to laugh in spite of myself. Laurie looked surprised, and then she too started to laugh.

"Why are we laughing?" she asked.

I could barely talk. I had both of my hands over my face and was laughing so hard I was afraid I might start crying. I pointed to the destroyed food parts with one hand while the other stayed over my face. Laurie looked at my tray. She pulled my napkin out of the way to better reveal the carefully dissected cornbread and deflated tomatoes.

"This?" she asked, smiling and leaning in close to me from across the table. "It *is* weird," she whispered. "It's almost like you have an *Eating Disorder.*"

* * *

I am wide awake and too hot between the blankets. I throw off the top one and roll over onto my left side, my hipbone and shoulder blade grinding into the floor. I draw my legs up to my stomach and feel the bones of my right knee dig into the bones of the knee underneath it. I feel like a pile of pick-up sticks. I flip over onto my stomach and wait for the ache that will move into my ribs. I can't get my conversation with Linda out of my head. No one had ever asked me before why I didn't want more for myself. I reach up and turn off the light, close my eyes, and try to focus on the sound of the crickets coming in through the open sliding glass doors in the living room.

I am asleep when the phone rings once, then stops. I turn on the little light and sit up, confused. It rings again. I struggle to get up off the floor and run into the kitchen, squinting at the clock on the oven. It is eleven-thirty. No one in my family would call me this late unless it is an emergency. *My father!* The phone rings again.

"Mom?!" I yell into the phone.

"I wanna come over an' blow my shit away."

"—What?" I fumble for the light switch.

"You heard me bitch, I wanna come over an' blow my shit away."

For a second I consider the possibility that I am dreaming. "Who is this?"

"You know who this is."

A procession of tiny needles works its way up the back of my neck as I struggle to place the voice.

"—*Joe?*"

I hear scuffling and the sound of the phone hitting the floor, then a dial tone. A blade of fear slices through me. I dial Linda's number. She answers the phone sleepily.

"Some guy just called and threatened me," I say, my voice shaking. I am both sweating and shivering.

"Who was it?" Her voice is calm.

"I don't know. It could've been Joe. I'm scared, Linda!"

"What did he say?"

"He's gonna come over and blow his shit away."

"Call the police," Linda says. "You're about to get raped."

"*What?? Holy shit, Linda!* Can you come back over here? Can you please come back over?" My whole body is shaking violently.

"Hell no, I'm stoned," Linda says calmly. "Call Mr. Jenkins. He'll come over. Call me later and let me know what happened." Linda hangs up the phone, the receiver rattling in the cradle for what seems like an eternity before the dial tone kicks in.

For several seconds, I just stand there shaking, elbows pressed against my sides, the receiver still at my ear. *Call me later and tell me what happened?*

I slam the receiver down and grab the phone book from under the cabinet. Jenkins, Jenkins... Rodney A. Jenkins? Rodney B. Jenkins? *Fuck!* There must be a hundred variations on the name Rodney

Jenkins!

I call Bridgeway. Mr. Bob answers the phone. I tell him I need Mr. Jenkins's number, that Joe has called and threatened me.

"Joe's sitting right here," Mr. Bob says sweetly. "You want to talk to him?"

"NO!" I yell. "Someone called and threatened me and I need Mr. Jenkins's number!"

"Ahh," says Mr. Bob, long, dangerous seconds ticking away as he considers the information. "You know Melissa left mad this afternoon because you wouldn't give her a pass to work last week. Could it have been a woman?"

"NO!" I yell again. "Please! His number!"

* * *

When at last Mr. Jenkins knocks on my door, I have gotten dressed and put away all evidence of the tequila. I don't want him to think I've been hallucinating. I open the door and pull him into the living room. He is wearing blue jeans and a wrinkled gray T-shirt and white socks but no shoes. I can tell I woke him up. It feels strange to see him half dressed.

"Someone threatened me," I say. My voice is still shaky, but I am not as scared now that Mr. Jenkins is in the apartment with me.

"You know who it was?" he asks, rubbing his face with both hands. He does not seem at all afraid for me.

"No. At first I though it might be Joe, but when I called Mr. Bob to get your number, Joe was sitting right there with him."

Mr. Jenkins nods his head as he looks around the living room.

"Any clients know where you live?"

I think a minute. "No," I say.

"Just someone trying to scare you," Mr. Jenkins says. He nods toward the sliding glass doors. "Lock your doors and close your blinds. Call me if you need me." He turns back to the door to leave.

"Why would anyone do that?"

Mr. Jenkins laughs softly and wags his head. "Desperate people do desperate things."

"I would never do that to someone."

"You ain't desperate." Mr. Jenkins opens the door and steps out.

"What if they call back?"

"Hang up!" Mr. Jenkins says, his face lighting up like he's just told a wonderful joke. Just before he shuts the door behind him he nods his head in the direction of my living room. "Your momma know you ain't got no furniture?"

* * *

I stare at the front door for several seconds after Mr. Jenkins leaves. Then, as if waking from a trance, I run into the living room and close the sliding glass doors, lock them, and pull the vertical blinds shut. Just before the last flaps fall into place over the door, I catch a glimpse of something that perplexes me, something that looks like lights in the cornfield. Again my mother's voice, warning of danger. I tell myself it is just a farmer checking his crops. My heart begins to slow. I sit down in the green recliner, light a cigarette, and stare hard into the blinds.

* * *

"I'm insulted," Joe says first thing Monday morning. I am rushing up the steps to the main office, twenty minutes late because it was two-thirty a.m. when I finally fell asleep in the green recliner, and then I overslept because the blinds were still drawn.

Joe is leaning with one hip against the railing at the top of the porch. He is wearing cut-off denim shorts and a half-shirt. His tanned stomach is taut and covered with a soft carpet of dark hair. He is smoking a cigarette and looking at the ground.

"I'm sorry. I was scared. I couldn't tell whose voice it was on the phone."

Joe looks at me then, his dark eyes round and questioning. "You think I'm so immature I'd call and *threaten* you? Is that what you think of me?"

"I said I'm sorry."

"Prove it." Joe takes a step toward me and leans in close to my face. I can feel the heat radiating off his bare stomach. I see where his razor missed a tiny field of stubble on his chin and I want to run my thumb across it. "Let me take you out to dinner," he says.

"Joe—"

"You owe me that."

"How do you figure?"

"One, for thinking I would call and *threaten* you. Two, for not supporting me in group last week."

"I *was* supporting you. I was trying to help you understand that you needed to put more effort in."

"That's not how it felt."

"I'm sorry."

"Then let me take you to dinner."

I can't help but smile at his persistence. "No."

Joe throws his head back, lets out an unintelligible growl, and kicks the railing. The porch rattles with the force of it. I hold my breath.

"Why not?" he demands, his voice a fierce whisper.

"You're *married*," I say.

"It's just *dinner*."

"You're a client."

"It's a *meal*."

"I know what dinner is."

Joe takes a step back and just stands there, looking at me. A tiny spire of fear pricks at my chest. In his eyes I see a rage that is carefully controlled, that is riding the current just below the surface of his frustration. Without another word he pushes the front door to the building so hard it bursts open, then slams closed again. If I couldn't see it before, I can now. Joe is fragile. I am fragile. A wave of exhaustion washes over me, and without even going inside, I walk back down the steps, get in my car, and go home.

I can't remember when I have been so tired. I park my car and struggle to roll up the window. I slam the door and consider the number of steps to the second landing. Joe's voice resonates in my head. *You think I'm so immature I'd call and threaten you?* I wish I had a dollar for everyone I've disappointed this year alone. There is my mother, because I moved away and left her alone with my father; my father, because I do not call every day to see how he's feeling; Keithan, because I left her behind; Joe, because I didn't defend his apathy; Linda, because I am not more normal; Mr. Jenkins, because he trusted me enough to hire me in spite of myself, and then I flung myself at a boundary with Joe.

And I am disappointed in myself. I remember driving to the interview with my mother, thoughts of friends and dating and eating normally playing out in my head. I thought I would be healing people left and right, or at the very least, making a difference in somebody's life. I climb the steps to my apartment, rattling off my disappointments stair by stair.

The apartment is dark and cool and I want nothing more than to light a cigarette and sit in my green recliner and stare out at the corn. I kick off my shoes, throw my pocketbook onto the floor, and remind myself I need to call in sick or Mr. Jenkins will think something really did happen to me last night. But first, I walk over to the sliding glass doors and yank on the nylon cord that opens the blinds. As the slats race neatly over to one side, sunlight floods the room, and my heart begins a slow, methodical pounding.

* * *

It is hard, if not impossible, to pinpoint the exact moment when your life changes course. Life is fluid and arguably changes minute by minute, making everything you do novel for the simple reason that you have never done it before at exactly the moment you are doing it. Most of the minutes of our lives are seamless and small and hard to catalog. When I look back over my time in Tifton, I see millions of such minutes, all of them drifting into other minutes, becoming still others. Life rides on the wide back of time, whose footprints are shallow and shifting and hard to follow.

Change is like this too. You can't see it at the moment it happens, unless it is something big, unmistakable, a death or a birth, a fire or a sickness. But in its wake you inevitably find that another sort of lifetime has passed, and later, maybe years later, you discover in yourself a wide open field, in which you can see clearly all the places your new self intersects with your old. As I stand at the sliding glass doors, the blinds still clattering from their race to one side, I know that this is one of those minutes that will not slide seamlessly, unaccounted for, into another. I sit down hard on the edge of the green recliner. Outside, acres of cornstalks lay flat in the morning sun, and in the distance, ahead of a tractor I cannot hear, other stalks are falling.

Chapter 15

The One That Went Away

I KNEW, OF COURSE, from the moment I moved to Tifton, that the cornfields behind my apartment would be harvested. But I didn't know when and I didn't ask because I didn't want to know. Every morning, gazing out over the corn from my deck, and every night, walking the dirt path between rows, I was comforted by the presence of something larger, something strong and life-affirming and seemingly permanent. When summer came and went, and then early fall, I let myself believe—tentatively at first, and then with increasing conviction—that the fields behind my apartment had been happily overlooked, that the farmers had too many other fields to worry about (wasn't there corn lining the highway all the way to Atlanta?).

Which was why, when the tractors came, I watched with disbelief as they did their ugly work, stripping ears from stalks and leaving nothing but short, broken sticks studding the fields. While I have the sense that I must have moved during that terrible afternoon six months ago—gotten up to go to the bathroom, to eat, eventually to go to bed—all I remember is long, sorrowful hours watching the tractors cut and gather, the noise of their threshing muted by the sliding glass doors, chaff floating in swirling eddies like snow.

* * *

A year after starting the job at Bridgeway, what I know is this: my already rocky friendship with Linda ended the night I received the threatening phone call, and Mr. Jenkins, not she, came over to calm me. The cornfields lay barren all fall and winter, and while I continued to watch them from my green recliner and to weave my way through their dirt paths every night, their embrace was cold and my thoughts were no longer expansive. Soon I was thinking only about getting through my walk, getting back to my apartment, being inside.

My father continued chemo and had more surgeries. My mother settled in for "the duration," meaning she would stay without complaint until he died. I gained six pounds, which I attributed to finally letting myself eat Miss Hattie's weekly banana pudding and to "having a little fun." And two months after Joe was released from Bridgeway, we went out to Red Lobster, where I'd gone with Scott. I wore my long blue and white ruffled skirt and blouse, despite swearing it off on the way to my interview. Joe loved it. After dinner, at which I ate broiled fish and a salad (and yes, picked out the croutons) Joe drove me back to his apartment where my car was. We kissed—heavily, deeply, sloppily. We groped. And then I got into my car and went home, after which we never saw each other again.

"Once a client, always a client," Mr. Jenkins had said, and while I argued, silently (was I still nothing but a client to the counselors who had helped me years earlier? I wanted to think not, but probably the answer was yes), I was also relieved. Joe, for all his good looks and the way he made me feel desirable, wasn't going to spend hours on my sofa with me, talking about psychology and books and dogs. We would always have the specter of our uneven relationship between us, and it was this that I understood Mr. Jenkins to be talking about more than anything, to say nothing of his family, the wife and children who still needed him, the addictive illness we shared that would have only made things more complicated. Mr. Jenkins, and even Linda (though I hated to admit it) knew what I would only later come to understand, which was that Joe's rightful place must be in my past.

But perhaps the most important thing that I know now, a year after starting at Bridgeway, is this: psychological superheroes aren't born. They're made. And the longer I worked at Bridgeway, the more apparent it became to my idealized self that I was no psychological superhero.

I blamed it on a lack of training. I was quickly aware that, despite how moving and stellar were the insights and gems of wisdom I shared with clients in my fantasies, in reality, I more often than not did not know what to say or how to proceed with therapy. Having had no hands-on counseling training, and no guidance beyond watching Mr. Jenkins work with clients in Big Group and asking a few questions afterwards (which were usually met with laughter and reassurances that therapy was "an art" and that I would "get there"), I was left wondering, for example, how to talk to the parents of a resident (the resident himself ten years older than me) who arrived at Bridgeway for family therapy. In a three-hour session that should have been one hour, I went over and over the only point of which I was certain, which was that their son had no sense of personal responsibility.

"And why do you suppose that is?" asked the father, a lawyer, arms folded across his chest as his pretty wife shredded a tissue.

I supposed it was because the parents (most likely the mother) let him get away with all manner of big and small infractions, but I couldn't bring myself to actually say this, terrified as I was by the lawyer-father and already siding with the mother, whom I assumed had been bullied all marriage-long by him. And so what I said was that their son blamed everyone but himself for his addiction. It was this true but innocuous and mostly unhelpful point I made, multiple times over, in lieu of anything else I knew to say, until we all emerged from my smoke-filled office (I smoked, they did not) in a kind of draw: they agreed to see things my way in exchange for being allowed to leave.

I was also uncomfortable handling confrontation in my Split Group. And while I had no trouble getting the residents to open up or even to cry (something I discovered simply listening in silence will often do), I wasn't exactly sure how to proceed after that. But it wasn't until almost ten months after I started at Bridgeway that I decided to talk seriously to Mr. Jenkins about it.

"Can I ask you about something?" I said. We were sitting in the main office after Big Group, waiting for lunch. Linda was in her office, talking softly on the telephone. Henriette and Margery were already downstairs.

"Yup." Mr. Jenkins didn't look up from his paper. I sat down in my interview chair by the desk.

"I'm pretty good at getting the clients to open up to me. But I don't always know where to go with what they tell me."

"You go wherever it takes you." Mr. Jenkins was matter-of-fact, like it was the most obvious thing in the world.

"But how do you know which threads to follow?"

"Which *threads?*" Mr. Jenkins put down the paper and squinted at me. He looked mystified, as if I had used some funny sounding, nonsense word.

"Which things to follow up on," I said. "Some things they talk about are just side issues. Dead end roads."

Mr. Jenkins laughed softly. "No they ain't. They're all a part of the big story. They all take you where you need to go. You're just too impatient, Slim."

I thought about this the following night and all of the next day. I was impatient, that much I knew. But the idea that you could take *anything* someone told you and use it as a door into their psyche was a revelation, even though I'd often marveled at how Mr. Jenkins seemed to be able to (as Linda called it, half insultingly, half admiringly) "make something out of nothing." (Here I remember my father saying to our therapist, "Everything means something to you, doesn't it?" as if this were a problem of the therapists rather than a finely honed skill.) I'd been amazed at how Mr. Jenkins could pick up on Eli's or Joe's seemingly innocuous comment in group ("I'm tired, I'm bored, I'm cold") and ten minutes later we would be discussing how that client brought no energy to his recovery and expected everyone to do the hard work for him, or how they had turned a blind eye, a cold shoulder, to the friends and family who had tried to get them into treatment before now. I thought about Linda and Henriette and how they interacted in Big Group, and while they were confrontational and often supportive, it was clear they couldn't do what Mr. Jenkins could do, get a bead on the heart *and* the head of a person, rather than just one or the other. I supposed it was possible that Mr. Jenkins' abilities were unschooled, so completely organic that it was impossible for him to hold his gift to the light for others to emulate. But if that was the case, then I didn't know how I was going to get any better at finding and opening the doors to hearts and minds.

* * *

Two days after our talk, Mr. Jenkins called me outside to the porch. It was late winter, but unseasonably warm. Spring, it seemed, wasn't far off. *Almost corn planting season.*

"You know anything about fishing?" He was sitting in one of the rocking chairs, staring straight ahead. I sat down in the rocker next to him.

"Fishing? You mean like *fishing* fishing?"

"Yup."

I thought a minute. "Well, my parents took us once when I was about nine." I smiled as I remembered the story. "My brother and I each caught two fish. We took them home in a cooler filled with lake water and transferred them to a tiny pond we made for them in our back yard. By the next day, two of them were dead." I rolled my eyes. "My brother insisted they were my two. Of course I cried. Two days later the other two fish died. I said, 'Now we're even.' And he goes, 'No, I realized the first two were really mine, so the two that just died were yours!'" I laughed. "He was so mean."

Mr. Jenkins was still staring straight ahead. "You know that when you fish, there's a size requirement on the ones you can keep. If they're too small, you throw them back."

"Who's there to see you?" I asked. "Does someone check your take-home fish when you leave the lake?"

"It's self-policing," Mr. Jenkins said.

"I bet a lot of people don't throw them back."

"If you don't throw them back, they can't grow up and make other fish. Then there aren't enough fish to eat the algae, which leads to too many mosquitoes, which eventually leads to no more fishermen.

Everyone benefits from throwing the little fish back."

I considered this. "I'm pretty sure the fish we got were full grown," I said.

Mr. Jenkins looked at me at last. "Sweetheart," he said. "*You are the little fish.*"

* * *

It took a while for his meaning to sink in. I had come to Bridgeway young, inexperienced. I had a lot of ambition but no skills, which ultimately hurt my confidence. I could keep doing what I was doing— no one was going to fire me just because I had the same limitations many counselors have their entire career—or I could make another choice, one that would benefit not just me, but future clients as well. I could get back in the water. I could go back to school and get a graduate degree and return to counseling once I had a few tools under my belt, not to mention a handle on my own impatience.

I fought Mr. Jenkins' insight. I held tightly to my life as I'd come to know it, pushing away what he'd said the same way I'd pushed away the understanding that corn is planted in the spring and harvested in the fall. But when my client's lawyer-father and beaten-down mother returned for their son's discharge planning and we faced off in my tiny office once again, the idea of school came barreling back to me. One month after our fish talk, I wrote to Augusta College for graduate school information. And just like that, my day-to-day interactions took on a kind of retrospective blurring, as if they were already behind me.

Chapter 16

A Jew with a Dog

Y MOTHER LETS A PEA-SIZED amount of cream fall into her coffee. She considers it for a moment, then stirs it in. We are at a Denny's restaurant in Augusta, Georgia, looking at the classifieds. I've only been gone from Tifton two weeks, but it feels like two years, and everyone—Linda, Mr. Jenkins, Joe—are like actors in a silent film, still moving around in my mind, but muted by the distance I've put between us.

At the time, it is hard to believe I've left there for good. But I have always moved forward with great hesitation, as if an errant look around could send me careening astray from my desired path, the facts of my new situation slipping ever so slowly into place, until they become at last familiar, a part of what I already know about myself.

The waitress approaches with her pot of coffee and gestures toward my mother. *More?* My mother shakes her head.

"So what have you found?" my mother nods toward the classifieds.

I push the newspaper to the middle of the table. What I've found is that my rental options are limited. After I crossed out the ads that said NO PETS and CHRISTIAN PERSONS ONLY, there were just two houses in the three hundred dollar range. Augusta, it turns out, is a very small town, and I am, unfortunately, a Jew with a dog.

"There's a quadruplex in a 'quiet neighborhood' for two-seventy-five a month. And there's a house with a fenced yard in an 'up and coming neighborhood.'"

"'Up and coming' is a euphemism for 'down and out,' my mother says.

"You don't know that. It says it's two hundred twenty-five dollars per month, or sixty-five per week."

"The only thing worse than renting by the week is renting by the hour," my mother says. "Call the other one."

When we get to the property, a dark green van is already parked in the gravel driveway and the front door of the quadruplex is standing open. "Quadruplex" is something of a misnomer; the house is actually a duplex, and there is another duplex behind it. Both are powder blue with a concrete slab for a front step. Mine faces the road, the other one faces the woods. They sit below the road as if in a pit; directly across the street, a brick church sits high on a hill, like a bland god staring down at two lone parishioners.

The property is a dump. The driveway is rutted with standing water and the front yard is weedy and mushy-looking. Someone has kicked a green plastic flowerpot with a dead plant into the middle of it and, next to that, a muddy, pink tricycle lies on its side. There is a single, thin tree in the yard with a few green buds. There are no cornfields, nothing that suggests expansiveness. At the time this is reassuring; it means there will be no silent, unbearable harvest, no winter-wide sleep during which I will walk a grid of borderless dirt roads, waiting while the ground dreams luscious, invisible dreams, readying itself for a spring I will be too aggrieved to appreciate.

My mother is looking hard at my profile, imploring me not to get out of the car. *We don't live like this,* her look says, but I don't look over. Many years later, she will see a photograph of the quadruplex and not remember it at all, but for now it is the worst thing she can think of, and she is hoping that the era of this house will end in the driveway, that this brush with destitution will slide quietly, unobstructed, into the wastebasket of our past.

* * *

The reasons my mother can only stare wordlessly into my profile (i.e., why she does not grab me by the arm right there in the driveway, and whisper hoarsely, *don't you dare get out* before throwing the car into reverse, spraying gravel in our hasty get-away) I can only conjecture later. When she was fifteen, her own mother died of complications from diabetes. For the next three years, before she went off to college, my mother and her father lived quiet, inward lives inside their Manhattan high-rise, eating their meals in restaurants too fine for everyday, rarely speaking, oceans apart in thought, in their lives.

"This," my sister likes to point out, "is the reason Mom never hugged us and didn't bring me a casserole when I had a miscarriage. She can't mother because she wasn't mothered."

I get out of the car. Just inside the door to the quadruplex is a man wearing a one-piece coverall, rubber boots, and a black ten-gallon hat—*like a lumberjack who collided with a rodeo clown* is how I will later describe him to a friend. *Darrin Johnson Tool and Die* is written in script inches above the gradual summit of his enormous girth. Just as I am about to introduce myself, my mother steps gingerly through the door, and I watch as a look of surprise crosses Darrin Johnson's broad, sweaty face. If I am put off by his looks, he is alarmed and intrigued by hers. My mother is wearing skin-tight blue jeans tucked into black boots studded with rhinestones, and a tiny denim shirt unbuttoned to reveal the frilly, satin seam of a tank top. Around her neck is a small diamond hanging from a short gold chain, and on her left hand is a collection of diamonds in a setting that looks like a queen's crown. Her hair is so black it's almost blue, razor-cut, and barely reaches her ears. She looks like something slightly unreal, standing in the doorway of the powder-blue house, backlit by the sun.

"DJ," says Mr. Johnson, extending his hand to my mother. He can't take his eyes off her.

"Phyllis," my mother says, taking his hand, although it obviously pains her to do so.

DJ informs us that the rent is three hundred seventy-five a month.

"But the ad said *two* seventy-five!" I say.

"Misprint," DJ says to the frilly seam of my mother's tank top.

My mother seems not to have heard about the rent hike. She is taking in the dingy, discolored walls, and rubbing the toe of her boot across the nap of the brown shag carpet, which is so stiff it practically does not flatten under her weight.

We walk through the empty unit, the carpet making a loud *shush shush* sound. The small living room has one square window that looks out onto the tree and the church. There is one bedroom, a tiny, dark bathroom, and a kitchen with a linoleum floor whose shine has long ago been walked off. There is a window next to the stove, which looks out onto the back of the parallel duplex and the muddy swath of ground that the sun never hits long enough to completely dry out. The whole place smells dusty and ancient. I feel like I have been here before, and then I remember my sister's apartment.

In 1976, when I was fourteen and my sister was just out of college, she rented an apartment fifteen minutes from our house. I visited her on weekends, happy to be away from our parents, proud to be in the company of my grown-up sister. I even liked her roommate Katie, who had a cat named Lucy which, immediately after moving in, had kittens. But after a few weeks, the smells of kitty litter and sour milk and animal dander permeated the air, and soon after that, there were other smells: of trash not taken out regularly, soiled carpet, decaying food in the refrigerator, mildew in the bathroom. I remember spending many weekends there, making pizzas and watching *Mary Hartman, Mary Hartman* and talking about boys and men and sex, fun weekends full of dire warnings and titillating language, the stuff of growing up under the generous tutelage of an older, experienced sister. But most of all I remember how she seemed not to notice the smells, even though they hit us like a force field when we opened the refrigerator or front door. I remember how she laughed when she reached for the mozzarella cheese and pulled out a black hairy block that looked and smelled like a small, decomposing animal. How she stood it, I didn't know, and when I would ask her she would brush it off, as if the stench and the crud and the moldering food were minor irritations, not strange and dangerous ways to live. Later, after I'd gotten my psychology degree, I'd attribute her lack of concern to a kind of sensory blindness layered over by narcissism: a basic inability to see how truly bad things had become because it had happened gradually, coupled with a defensive view of chaos as the expression of an authentic self. Standing in the kitchen of the quadruplex, smelling the smells of dust and neglect, a little wiggle of insecurity twists its way through my belly. On one hand, I admired my sister's flagrant dismissal of the facts, her explanation (that chaos expressed, rather than defined you) that seemed, at least on some level, plausible. But I also suspected she had lost sight of the real problem. *Mildew could make you sick. Black cheese would kill you. Bacteria teemed in the soiled carpet, waiting for an open sore.* Still, I march forward into my first disaster of a house by telling myself that, while things look bad, my sister might be right: perhaps authenticity does emerge from the jaws of chaos.

* * *

I turn back to the landlord. "I have a dog," I say. "She's housetrained," I add, although, as I look around, I wonder if it even matters.

"It can't run loose," DJ says.

"You know, Keithan is fine with us," my mother says. "You don't *have* to get a house."

DJ looks at his watch. "I got another girl comin' to see it this afternoon."

I am flattened between the opposing wills of the landlord and my mother. Suddenly the (albeit unlikely) possibility exists that there is another girl, and that she too has a dog, and that she has already looked at the other house and been talked out of it by her mother.

"I'll take it," I say. A prickle of disbelief goes through me, but I hide it, knowing that if I show any outward hesitation, my mother will move in with her infinite reservoir of certainty: *Don't make a decision right now. You don't need a house. Keithan is perfectly happy where she is.*

Darrin Johnson tucks his toothpick back into his breast pocket and claps his hands together. "Maintenance man lives right next door. Anything breaks, Robby'll be right over and fix it. Rent's due first of every month."

I pull out my checkbook and write Darrin Johnson a check for three hundred seventy-five dollars. I sign it, and then, in the lower left-hand corner where it says *For,* I write, "Keithan." I am happy, because although I should know from my sister's example that squalor, like debt, is easy to accumulate but hard to shake, I don't.

Twenty-five years later, standing in the spare bedroom of the farmhouse I share with my husband, my mother will see a picture of the quadruplex and shake her head. "How in the world did I let you live there?"

Chapter 17

The It Baby

MONDALE AND FERRARO lose their bid for the presidency. Granted, it is a weak ticket in a country that is unprepared for a female Vice President. Although I happen to like both candidates—Mondale is nice looking (at twenty-two, this is, for me, half the battle)—and I am excited about a woman on the ticket, I have never voted. Instead, I do as I have always done: stand silently by as things I am fervent about (equal pay for equal work, the right to an abortion, animal cruelty laws) float around aimlessly in my head along with things I only care mildly about (pottery mugs being superior to porcelain for drinking coffee, for example, and cotton sheets over polyester). I don't vote, and I still don't buy myself things I want but don't need, and it will be years before I understand that my disengagement is actually denial arising from a singular impulse: to hide from myself the fact that, in my opinion, my voice is insignificant, my desires undeserved.

* * *

Five people—four adults and one baby—occupy the four units that comprise the quadruplex on East Avenue. I am the only graduate student. Robby, the maintenance man, lives in the unit next to me. A man named Ulie, who works at a nursing home, lives in one of the back units, and Patti, a single mother, lives in the other with her newborn son. For a while, I think of us as a family, my new Linda and Henriette and Mr. Jenkins, although the only time I see Ulie is through the front window when he gets home from work in the afternoons, and I've only spoken to Patti twice: once out our kitchen doors, and once at the grocery store. Soon, however, I realize that there is nothing family-like about us. We are as separate as we can be, unmeddling, and, for the most part, uninterested in the lives of one another, with the exception of Robby the maintenance man, who harbors a not-so-secret anger toward Patti.

"You know Patti?" Robby asks me one day about a week after I've moved in. He is hunched over my stove, trying to figure out why the pilot light keeps going out. Keithan is locked in the bedroom, barking and clawing at the door. I don't even worry that she's scratching the paint off. After only a week, I have aligned myself with Darrin Johnson's code of order: broken and/or dirty is standard fare at 442 East Avenue. There is no way not to bring the mud from the yard into the house with me, in spite of an outdoor welcome mat and rigorous foot-wiping. Dust filters in from unseen openings, coating my stove and coffee table, and something—I suppose it is the carpet, perpetually damp at the door and trampled over by Keithan's muddy feet after a walk—smells like musty old clothes.

"Does Patti have trouble with her pilot light, too?" I ask.

"Naw," Robby says. He straightens up to wipe his face with his t-shirt. He is wiry thin and his flat, narrow stomach is pale and hairless. His jeans sit low on his hips, revealing the top band of his underwear. He lets his T-shirt fall back down over his torso and leans in close to me. He smells like perspiration and cigarette smoke.

"She just had a baby," he whispers. "She ain't married and she don't work. Who d'ya think is payin' for that baby?"

I think a minute. "Her mom?"

Robby points a long, dirty finger at my chest. "You an' me, sister. You and me're payin' for that baby, and for her to sit on her ass all day and watch soaps. While we're slavin' away, she's back there livin' it up."

I glance out my kitchen window toward Patti's unit. Two large bras and several baby bibs and sleepers hang on the laundry line that runs from her kitchen door to a tree about ten feet away. Under the tree, a blue, two-door Datsun sits waiting for someone to bring it a front tire. I look back at Robby.

"She's over there havin' the time of her life while the rest of us have to *work*," he says. "The trouble with the government is it's payin' for people like her to have babies. I ain't gettin' no free ride. You gettin' a free ride?" Robby fishes for a lighter in his pocket and pokes it down between the burners on my stovetop.

I think about the fact that my parents paid for my college education, and a deceased cousin on my mother's side is now paying for my graduate school. Rides hardly come any freer, but I sense that I should keep this to myself.

There is a soft *pop* and my pilot light flickers to life. "You're all set," Robby says, wiping his hands on his thighs. Suddenly he steps back as if he's seeing me for the first time. "Damn, girl! You're skinnier than me! Do you even know *how* to cook?"

"I cook a little," I say, uncertain what I will say if he asks *what* I cook. Air-popped popcorn sprinkled with water to hold the salt on? Green beans and bullion? Toast, for eating their crusts? It all sounds like what you would serve your enemy in prison, to slowly starve him to death. But I needn't have worried, as Robby is already headed out of my kitchen door, uninterested in my recipes. Which is fine with me. Like the whole Rudy Milsaps debacle with the flaming vodka, there is the familiar remove. In part, it comes from pushing people away, feeling as I do that their presence is a barrier to the version of me I carry around in my head, *my authentic self,* is how I think of it, while *the obstacle of the forced interaction,* is how I think of the presence of other people and the requirement that I converse with them about things that are seemingly relevant on the surface but that I couldn't care less about. Like Patti and her baby. When I really think about it, in fact, most of my interactions feel forced and fake, like I and the other person are two dolls tottering side to side in front of one another in a comic but unreal enactment of conversation.

* * *

Later that night, Keithan and I are curled up on a blanket on the floor watching television when there is a knock on my door. Keithan bursts out of sleep and rushes for it, barking wildly. I open it a crack. Patti is standing about a foot from the door with her arms crossed. Although it is cool out, her hair is damp and she is wearing a robe and slippers.

"Can you help me move something?" she asks.

Keithan is snarling, trying to wedge her nose into the crack. I restrain her with one leg as I hop out of the door backwards on the other, then follow Patti around back to her unit, careful to dodge the clothes line with its perpetual display of bras and bibs, even at night.

"How's the baby?"

"Oh, it's fine," she says.

I have never actually heard anyone refer to their own baby as "it." The callousness of it jars me. Even Keithan is always a "she."

Patti pushes her kitchen door open and goes in ahead of me. "It's a mess in here, sorry," she says.

The florid smells of dirty diapers and sour milk collide with my face. I inhale sharply and look around. A tower of dishes rises from the sink, pizza boxes are piled beside the trash can, and the oven door is standing open, revealing something that was recently cooked but is no longer identifiable. On the kitchen counter, a dirty hairbrush sits in a little puddle of water, and I suppress the urge to gag. There is something of my sister's old apartment in the chaos of it. The only difference is that Patti has apologized, suggesting not a disturbed sense of creative freedom, but embarrassment over an admittedly mismanaged household. Eventually I will wonder whether the effects of one over the other are preferable in a house with an impressionable baby, but for now, I am at least minimally comforted that she knows the difference. Patti calls me out of the kitchen and into the bathroom.

"This here," she says.

We move a yellow, four-drawer chest out of the bathroom and into the bedroom, where the baby is asleep in the middle of the bed amidst mounds of towels and baby blankets and underwear.

"Things was getting damp with the shower and all," Patti says.

I nod. I don't ask her why there was a dresser in the bathroom in the first place. I just want to leave. "Is that it?"

"Do you want to hold it?" Patti points toward the middle of the bed.

"—The baby?"

Patti digs down into the mountain of laundry and scoops up the sleeping lump, at which time my heart begins to pound.

When I am older, I will be less prickly, but in my twenties, I am not a fan of babies: the wobbly heads, the wordless sobbing, the ever-present cloud of sweet-smelling powder which barely masks the dark, fusty scent of a dirty diaper.

"You just don't like yourself," my mother would say, when I was thirteen and complaining bitterly that the neighbors had asked me to babysit.

But whether my youthful anti-baby stance was the result of projected self-hate or something else, the fact is, I have never been comfortable with or particularly interested in babies. I am not moved to buy calendars featuring bald-headed, fat-cheeked infants, or to coo in a restaurant at a swaddled one, or even to lay my hand on an expectant mother's swollen belly. Whenever I have actually held babies in my arms, their tiny bodies always rebelled, always arched in protest against mine. By the time I am forty, I will have never held a baby that gave in to my embrace. Naturally, I begin to think it is because they know I how feel about them. That if a dog can sense fear in a person, a baby can sense ambivalence. Certainly, I sensed early on that my own mother had more interesting things to do than fawn over me.

Patti holds the baby out to me. I do not reach for it.

"Oh, is she cute!" I say, in a voice I recognize as my mother's. I cradle my face with my hands, miming astonished admiration.

"His name is Charlie William Armstrong Hedges. CW for short."

"Well, he is *really* cute," I repeat. I wave furiously at the sleeping baby as I begin backing away. "Bye- bye, CW!"

Patti ignores my movements toward the door and lays CW back

down in the center of the bed surrounded by the tornado of laundry.

"So, you in school?" she asks, teasing out a group of tiny washcloths which she begins to fold.

Patti's movements are practiced and seamless, so that there is no moment uncluttered with words or actions during which I can escape.

"I register next week."

"Mmm," she says thoughtfully, as if there is more to what I am saying and she needs extra time to consider it. She bundles together a couplet of teeny socks.

"You real smart?" she asks.

Her question, which seems to have a core of longing to it, saddens me. I ponder the parameters of Patti's disarray—the dank, dirty, two-room unit she shares with a baby she calls "it" and corrals in a fence of linens and underwear. Patti's tragedy is not my sister's. There is no desperate lunge for authenticity here, only a heartbreaking and complicated landslide of unmet needs, something I know a world about.

"I better go," I say.

Chapter 18

A Body Apart

KEITHAN IS HAPPY. For the first time since living on my own, I feel complete. In the apartment in Tifton, I was just a single girl living alone with a cat (which I gave to Rose when I left), but with Keithan, I feel like the head of a small family. Before classes start, I find a vet's office and register her so she will have a record in case of emergency. And at the grocery store, I buy a box of dog biscuits, four rawhide bones, and enough canned food to feed three dogs for a month. As the cashier is ringing up my purchases, I think about Patti taking care of a baby by herself, and I wonder if she feels what I feel: not just the sense of responsibility, but the incredible gratitude, the certainty that there is no life that matters as much as the one that I alone sustain.

* * *

The Goodwill store in downtown Augusta, Georgia, sits between a wig shop and a defunct Sears outlet store. In the window, a bone-white female manikin leans provocatively to one side, her abdomen thrust outward, and one hand-less arm perched on her hip. She is a body in three parts: there is a dividing line where her head and neck attach to her shoulders, and another line where her bottom half attaches to her torso. She has no facial features or feet. She is like a grown-up version of Mr. Potato-head: instead of a silly face assembled from a variety of cartoonish features, her mature female body is assembled from a cartoonish assortment of incomplete parts. She reminds me that, when I was a teenager, I fantasized about fashioning my own body from a collage of bodies I saw in fashion magazines, on television, and on other women. The re-tooled me would still be Jewish, but my trademark long, wavy hair would be stick-straight and yellow. Instead of my shapeless long nose I would have an adorable, upturned one. I would be female, but with the sharp, narrow hips of a young boy. Tall as a basketball player, but without any of the heft required to support height. My assemblage—illogically thin and imperceptibly ethnic—was, to me, a winning goal.

I am at Goodwill for a sofa and desk.

"Help you, baby?"

A very large woman moves toward me, pushing a cart piled high with curtains and bedding. The effort of pushing the cart seems almost too much for her, and she leans into it heavily, like it is a walker. When she comes to a stop in front of me, she is panting, and I can see a line of sweat across her brow. Her name tag rides an enormous breast. It says, "Carline."

"Furniture?" I say.

Carline waves toward the back of the store. "Back there, baby," she says, still breathing hard. She produces a damp handkerchief from between her breasts and wipes her face with it. "Lordy, lordy," she says, before moving on, and I watch her go, her short dark hair slicked back into a tight ponytail, her broad shoulders listing left and right with the task of propelling her forward.

I walk toward the back of the store, past crowded racks of clothes and a huge, multi-tiered display of misshapen shoes and boots. The whole area smells of worn leather and dirty feet. *Who would buy these?* I wonder as I hurry past.

Suddenly, I catch sight of a pair of black, fur-lined clogs. I pull them off the shelf, glance around to make sure no one is watching me, then examine the insides. They are 7½, exactly my size. I turn them over and inspect the wooden undersides. Scuffed, but not chipped. With one hand holding onto the display rack, I twist my right foot free of my sneaker and slip into the clog's warm embrace. Just then, I hear a girl's agitated voice on the other side of the display. "Why are you so judgmental?"

I peek between the rows of shoes. A girl of about sixteen is standing in front of a mirror wearing one trampy, high-heeled ankle boot and one sneaker. Behind her in the mirror is a woman I gather is her mother.

"I'm not being judgmental," the older woman says to the girl's reflection. "The shoes are molded by someone whose movement is not the same as yours, and that's just asking for problems. You should never wear someone else's shoes."

The girl's mouth drops open and she wheels around to face her mother. "You're wearing *my* shoes right now!" she blurts out. "*God!*"

In the mirror, the older woman's face falls. I recall my mother's face falling in exactly the same way when I announced that I despised the new ruffled blouse she had bought me and that I would never wear it again. Standing in front of the six-story tier of depleted footwear, a dark well blooms in the pit of my stomach. I lay the furry clogs back up on the rack. I have always fought my mother with an intensity I later regretted, an intensity that, owing to her quiet concessions, the fact that she never speaks back harshly, makes my treatment of her seem, in retrospect, ferocious and hurtful.

Suddenly, I miss her. Suddenly, I want to apologize for all the ways I've been petulant and arrogant and unkind, all the times I made her worry, or didn't appreciate her help. She didn't have a mother to help her navigate the scary things, no one to show her how to help a daughter move away from home. She has no information about how to grieve this particular kind of loss. As I walk through Goodwill, I feel a deepening sorrow, and after that, an explosive forgiveness. I decide I will call my mother when I get home and tell her about my new furniture. And then I will apologize, in general, for everything.

Later that afternoon, the Goodwill truck parks at the top of the driveway and two men spill out. The back wall of the truck descends to form a ramp, and my two-part, L-shaped sofa leads the way out. Robby emerges, shirtless, from his unit, and sits down in a metal chair by his front door, peeling a tiny apple with a pocket knife.

"About time you got some furniture," he says.

My new things fill up the living room. The tan sofas fit neatly against the living room walls. One coffee table fits nicely in front of it, and a matching smaller one fits along the other wall and holds my stereo. The desk is an old oak teacher's desk, massively heavy, with two pull-out writing boards and six deep drawers.

With great effort, I push the desk into the corner of the living room facing the window. I line up my new, unopened textbooks along the back edge of the desk and plunk a mug of pens down on the windowsill. Then I call my mother.

"*Two* sofas?" she says.

"It's an L-shape. They go together."

"That seems extravagant," she says.

Which is when I realize that our disputes are not about apartments or weight or furniture. They are not about whether I can take care of a dog or what I should eat or how I should live. Rather they are, and have always been, about the kind of growth that leads the way from one home to another. Something in me is groping toward a larger awareness that has to do with my mother and my mother's mother, with the kinds of loss that pull us up and away, out of the warm lake of childhood and into the dry, cool lap of a world we won't fully understand until we are older.

"It is extravagant," I say, and we both laugh. This is my apology.

Chapter 19

Ethics for Psychologists

I T IS THE FIRST DAY of my very first graduate Psychology class and I can hardly believe who is there. I stare in disbelief at the broad back that is like a bearing wall, the short, straight dark hair fastened at a fatty roll of the neck. I lean forward. "Car*line*?"

The woman in the desk in front of me turns around. "Moira."

I'm taken aback. From the front the woman looks nothing like large, lurching Carline from Goodwill. Moira has the well-defined features of a woman who has always been pampered, someone who would never be caught—working *or* shopping—at Goodwill and who, although she is large, would never, ever lurch.

"Sorry," I say. "I thought you were someone else."

Moira smiles. "I often wish I were."

I am so surprised and pleased by her easy self-effacement that I actually slap her shoulder and we laugh, wide, open-mouthed laughs that will become our trademark interaction, no matter how hard the territory of what we are discussing.

At the front of the room, the professor has planted himself at a small podium in front of a chalkboard on which is scrawled Ethics 101.

"Ethics is the most important class you will take in your graduate career," he says by way of introduction. He seems to be looking specifically at Moira and me. "Do you know why? Besides, of course, that I'm teaching it?" He smiles.

Dr. Singleton is in his late fifties, tall, with a profusion of gray-streaked hair shooting from his head like flames. When he talks, he seems to be perpetually on the edge of a fabulous joke, his eyes and mouth all stretched sideways into narrow grins. He is wearing dark khakis and a sleeveless, brown sweater-vest over a black, button-down shirt. He looks like a box turtle. No one is answering his question.

"Let's try this again," Dr. Singleton says. "*Why* is there is an ethical code for psychologists?" He looks around the room hopefully.

"To set a standard of behavior for licensing," Moira says confidently. Her neck jiggles when she talks.

Dr. Singleton smirks and his eyes stretch out. "I am a firm believer that psychologists should never be allowed to drive," he says.

Moira cackles. "Then how could they take their patients out on dates?"

"Touché," says Singleton, smiling more broadly, his eyes disappearing into his head.

After Ethics class, there is Statistics, for which I will require the concerted efforts of a dedicated tutor to pass, and then Introduction to Personality Disorders, where, professor Woods tells us, we will learn the proper diagnostic nomenclature for everyone in our families, including ourselves, which is, as we all know, the real reason most of us are in Psychology in the first place.

At noon, I leave campus and drive the eight miles home. I am so hungry I think I might faint before I turn onto my street. Although I can barely stand to walk Keithan before I eat, I do, up the two blocks to the stop sign and back, letting her sniff each empty beer bottle, tossed out fast food wrapper, and something that looks like a mud-encrusted sock. The walk takes about fifteen minutes but feels like an hour. Back in my kitchen, lightheaded and shaky, I open a small can of water-packed tuna, drain it, and mix it with a teaspoon of sweet relish. I fold the mixture into a flaccid iceberg lettuce leaf and eat the whole thing standing over my stove, savoring every dry, fishy bite. Afterwards my stomach feels watery and full, like I used to feel when I ate only bullion and green beans, and then, like a thought that exists apart from my thinking it, I wish I had eaten only half of the tuna. It is a thought that defies true parameters: after I eat, always wish I'd eaten half of whatever it was, because then I'd be half as full. After years of this kind of thinking, I know that when I *do* eat half of whatever I've prepared, then I just wish I'd eaten half of that. At some point, I realize that "half" is like "up and coming": a euphemism for something that, on the surface, holds promise, but on further inspection, only delivers you deeper into trouble.

* * *

"So who would you be?" I ask Moira.

It's the end of our first week of classes and we are having drinks at a bar called Adam's. I am surprised to find myself out with her, since it took me almost a month before I'd agreed to socialize with Linda. Moira laughs when I tell her this. "You might not make friends easily, but I do," she says.

Adam's is just down the street from the Augusta National Golf Course, home to the Master's tournament. The wallpaper, napkins, tableware, and wall art are all Green Jacket green and golf-themed. Like its name, it is a male-centric establishment, with opulently stocked liquor shelves that are illuminated from behind and throw a warm glow on the faces of the businessmen crowding the half-moon bar. Tall, heavy, wooden tables and deeply, darkly cushioned chairs surround a large dance floor with an overhead revolving silver ball, not yet a cliché in 1983. The dance floor thrums with the glittery, monotonous up-beat of Madonna and Diana Ross and Gloria Estefan and Wham, irresistible disco music that causes people to glide onto the pulsating floor seemingly without thought.

Because I had only another half-can of tuna and two Saltines for dinner (after which I wished I'd eaten a fourth of the can and only one Saltine), my rum and Tab drops a veil of woozy comfort over me almost immediately.

"What was the question?" Moira yells over the music.

I lean in and repeat it. "You said in class you wish you were someone else. Who do you wish you were?"

"Not who," she says. "*What.*" She stirs her bright red drink with the middle finger of her left hand, then pops it into her mouth.

"Okay, *what?*"

She twists her finger dry in a napkin bearing Jack Nicklaus's face. "Not fat!" she says. She upturns the palm of her hand as if to say, "Isn't it obvious?"

I stare at her, uncertain how to respond. In high school when someone complained about being fat, you automatically waved her off and disagreed with her assessment. But Moira is so big, her rear end spills off both sides of her bar chair, and she can't cross her legs. It would be absurd to deny the obvious. She scribbles a number on a napkin and slides it under my nose like an opening bid. *225.*

"It's the most I've ever weighed," she says, watching my face for my reaction.

I stare at her. Moira is beautiful in a studied, stylized way: she shaves off her eyebrows in order to reinvent their shape. She ignores the true borders of her mouth, creating two wide, juicy red swaths of lip that quiver seductively when she is otherwise still. She wears tailored clothes that are not too tight, and that show off the feature she is most proud of: enormous breasts that are, on this night, glitter-dusted and a third of the way exposed to the air. So although she is large like Carline, Moira is sexy, even graceful; by the time we have had two drinks, she has been asked to dance three times. (I've been asked once, but declined.) And, unlike Carline, huffing and lurching through Goodwill's narrow aisles, Moira's movements on the dance floor are fluid and confident, reflecting an understanding, even when her eyes are closed, of where her body is in relation to others on the dance floor. Watching Moira, I can feel all the places where I am stiff and rigid. While I used to believe that once I was thin I would be graceful, what I discovered was that grace, like the worth of a human, was independent of size. I am thin but awkward, like the pieced-together manikin in the Goodwill window. I am a collection of flailing boards, a rickety house always on the verge of coming apart.

Only I don't know this, or I only know it in condensed moments, like now, or at my Bridgeway interview, when the importance of appearing healthy wakes me from my comfortable dream of normalcy and forces my perceptions of myself into alignment with the perceptions of those around me. One afternoon, about a month after I was admitted to the hospital, eighty-eight pounds and still denying anything was wrong with me, my parents took me to Madison, Georgia for a day out. As I wandered the grounds, I came across a chest-high stone wall.

"Take my picture up here!" I called to my father. He aimed the camera just as I put my hands on the wall to hoist myself up, but my arms, whose muscles had been starved away, didn't catch, and I fell back to the ground, stunned. My father lowered the camera. I hadn't known my muscles were gone until that moment when they failed me, and later would wonder what else was gone, what other seemingly simple act of living I might have lost to starving.

"Have you always been... big?" I ask when Moira comes back to the table. I can't say the word fat; it sounds too mean.

"Since I was eight," Moira says. "I'd diet and lose weight, but then I'd gain it back, plus thirty or forty more."

This last statement horrifies me. "*Pounds?*"

Moira rolls her eyes. "I don't measure my weight in grams like you do. Yes, *pounds.*" She takes a long sip of her sugary drink, then pats her lips with a napkin and rearranges herself in her seat. "So what about you?"

"What about me what?"

"How long have you been anorexic?"

The rum in my stomach churns suddenly, and a dark, bitter taste crawls up my throat. I haven't told Moira anything about myself.

"I'm not—" I begin, but even as my line of defense starts to arrange itself, a simultaneous wall of safety built of rum and loud music rises up around me. I look into Moira's bright, kind eyes. I would lay my secrets here, at the feet of my new friendship. Moira had already shown me how.

"Three years ago, I went from a hundred and thirty pounds to about eighty in eight months. But I'm not anorexic anymore, I'm okay now."

Moira's mouth falls open. "*Fifty* pounds in eight months?"

I nod.

"What do you weigh now?" she asks.

I cringe, remembering my therapist's admonition to my parents about whoever owns the weight owns the girl. But Moira, as far as I can tell, is not looking to control my weight or have a hand in my eating. What's at stake is not my right to self-government, but something else that is deeply personal and highly confessional and that I sense will be binding. I pick up Moira's pen and scribble *115* on the napkin below her *225* and slide it back across the table.

"I'd like to be a hundred thirty," I say. "But I'm kind of stuck for now."

It is a double lie. In addition to adding twelve pounds to my actual weight, I have said that I am "stuck," when, in fact, I am only stuck in the sense that I continue to refuse, meal after meal, day after day, to eat enough calories to gain any more weight. And although I know this—that my refusal is what keeps my weight at a hundred and three—there is a part of me that believes, despite therapy, despite my year counseling addicts at Bridgeway, that the decision to become *unstuck* is something that will happen *to* me, a force that will impose itself on me from outside my own mind, reasoning me to a healthy weight without any real input from me. At that point, the final piece of my recovery will click into place, like the *pop* of a pilot light igniting, and I will go forward with my indisputably healthy body (defined as a body about which my perceptions align perfectly with the perceptions of others), at the helm of which will be an indisputably healthy mind. This I still believe, despite the wisdom of the cornfields, which showed me that mental and physical health were inexact constructs on a grid, occupying only points of approximation. *Stuck*, no. *Sticking*, yes.

To my relief, Moira's expression is compassionate, and not at all judgmental. She nods her head thoughtfully and her eyes arch into a waiting question. But before she can ask it, a husky Latino man in a crispy pressed shirt unbuttoned to reveal a simple gold chain stops at our table. He nods at me, then places his hand lightly on Moira's broad back. Moira smiles up at him, winks at me, and maneuvers herself out of her tall chair. Just before she heads off to the dance floor, she leans in over the table, squeezes my shoulder and smiles.

"A hundred fifteen, my fat ass," she says.

I down my drink quickly. As I watch Moira undulate to Tina Turner's "What's Love Got to Do With It?" I review my options. There are three, as I see it: I can insist I really do weigh a hundred fifteen so I don't look as unrecovered as a hundred three sounds; I can admit I lied and that I weigh a hundred three and see where it leads; or I can do a little of both: admit I lied, but tell her I weigh a hundred ten. This last, bumping my weight up by seven meager pounds, as if this spells all the difference between sick and well, feels, even at the time, like typical anorexic thinking: short-sighted about tiny things, like dousing a match in the ashtray in front of you while, behind you, your house is burning.

And the prospect of lying on top of lying sobers me. I recall that, in order to earn the right to go to Madison with my parents in the first place, I had to show a weight gain of half a pound, and so on the morning of my weigh-in, I stuffed my robe pockets with mixed nuts. I left the hospital giddy, but quickly felt guilty about having lied. An hour into the trip north I felt lightheaded, almost airborne, with a sick feeling in my stomach. By the time I tried to jump on the stone wall and couldn't, I'd already had what I only later recognized as a glimmering of insight, a kind of *if not now, then when?* realization, that getting on with my life meant gaining weight and returning to school and to work and to friends and the future, not playing games with my weight and marking time on a psych unit and at small historical towns with my parents.

I thrum my fingertips on the table. If I tell Moira the truth about my weight, it's possible she will confront me, and throw evidence of ongoing illness in my face. I turn in my chair to look at her on the dance floor. She is swiveling her enormous hips, arms out to her sides like helicopter blades. A small voice in my head pipes up: *so what if she does?* And this, the same glimmering I had in Madison, moves me forward. *Nothing was going to happen if I didn't let something happen.* In my chair, looking out over the swirling colors of the dance floor, I make my decision. A little thrill darts through me as I realize I've made a friend who just might see through me to *me*, who has already shown she will bulldoze over niceties and compulsive lies and witless conjecture in favor of calling a spade a spade. Or, in my case, an anorexic an anorexic.

Now I can hardly wait for Moira to come back to the table, only she and her partner aren't coming back and instead are slow dancing to Madonna's "Two by Two," their arms lightly encircling each another. Moira's partner's arms don't even begin to make it around her, but Moira is smiling like she's the most beautiful woman on earth. In my mind there is no room for the possibility that you could be obese and still feel attractive, yet the evidence is there in front of me. Likewise there was something oddly unemotional, almost removed, about the way Moira said she gained "fifty or sixty pounds" as if she were saying "five or six"; it seemed to me almost cavalier, Moira gathering flesh as if it were nothing more permanent or burdensome than a bushel of extra tomatoes she could toss out later.

I want to know how it happened: did the weight sneak up on her, and by the time she realized it, she was a hundred pounds overweight? Or did she watch it happening with a kind of casual indifference, disconnected from her own slowing gait, expanding waistline, and the sheer commitment it took to eat enough to keep on growing?

As for me, not long after the "you used to be cute" comment from Randy Russell in the school lunchroom, followed by the fat ugly pig incident in the parking lot with my mother, I came to believe my life would be fundamentally different were I smaller, cuter, less piggish: were I "*not fat.*" My presence in the world would be fundamentally changed.

"If I pulled the fire alarm," I told a girlfriend at school one day when I was in the ninth grade, "No one would leave the building." We laughed. Hysterically. It was the encapsulation of my belief at how "fat" had rendered me so worthless that the actions I brought to bear, real though they were, were cancelled out by virtue of having come from me. In other words, the impact I had on the world actually *defied the laws of physics.*

It would be years—decades—before I learned that my body was not the problem. Before the synthesis of hundreds of hours of therapy and conversations with close friends and journal entries and confrontations with family members and clawing my way down the scale and then back up again would deposit me at the threshold of something other than *fat*, something I could actually use, something *real*, to explain my feelings of invisibility and inconsequence. Something that seemed to begin with *fat ugly pig* but wasn't *fat ugly pig*, that convinced me, erroneously, that the worth of a human being was dependent on her size. Something that was itself a synthesis of all the other somethings I felt to be wrong about my life but that I couldn't do anything about: my father, passionate about his work but seemingly blind to me, my unhappy mother, my sister losing herself in a web of dangerous authenticity, my brother's name-calling and hitting. *All the cost of living inside a family. All practice for life on the outside,* I told myself, as if *family* were a prison and turning eighteen were parole.

But along the way, I had an awakening. People liked to tell me, when I was anorexic, that I was the same person on the inside no matter what I looked like on the outside, that the fundamental truths about me wouldn't change with size. But the fact is, they did change. As I began, ever so carefully, to regain the weight I'd lost, I began to see myself differently, which ushered in, for the first time ever, the realization that I *could* see myself differently. As I re-approached a healthy weight, I was finally able to see that my childhood wish to be "not fat" had been misguided, my journey toward a coveted size really a fundamental desire for a life that felt large enough to matter.

The arrival at this realization was like taking a sledgehammer and cracking the ice on a pond that had been frozen for twenty years. Only then did I see what I'd never seen before: that a graspable, *inhabitable* life teemed just below the surface of that which had always barred my way: the myth of my inconsequence, the story I'd told myself about myself that was never true.

* * *

Moira sits down, breathless from dancing, and radiant. She takes a long sip of her drink, lights a cigarette, and pats the shelf of her breasts with a napkin. When she can talk normally again, she says, "Whew! He wants to see me next time he's in town. He's a pharmaceutical rep."

"He's kind of old, isn't he?"

Moira cackles. "The older ones can hold out longer."

"But he's like, *forty!* At some point doesn't the pendulum start to swing the other way?"

"He's forty-six," Moira says. "And even if they can't hold out, there are other *skills* they've had time to master, if you know what I mean. And they aren't queasy about using them, either."

So Moira is not even queasy about sex. *All those skills having to find their way around all that flesh.* While I don't even like to roll over on my side during sex because my stomach pools onto the bed. (*"Skin,"* a boyfriend will tell me. "It's your *skin* and it has to be flexible!") I toy with the remnants of our conversation. I have the sense that Moira, as a friend, has things to teach me. I reach for our little slip of confessional paper. Moira watches as I scribble out my *115* and write *103*. I slide it back to her. To my surprise, she picks up the pen, scribbles out *225*, and writes *250*.

Chapter 20

Assess Thyself

T HE DESIRE TO SELF-DIAGNOSE accounts for fifty percent of all
admissions to graduate school. The desire to diagnose our
families accounts for the other fifty percent. We laugh when
Dr. Singleton tell us this, but scramble to line up the telltale markers.
According to the Diagnostic and Statistical Manual (DSM), Moira has
a dysthymic disorder, and lays the blame at the feet of her mother, who
might have had schizophrenic tendencies. Her father, a dependent
personality disorder, kept her perpetually distraught about her weight,
telling her no one would ever love her as long as she was fat. I'm a
recovering anorexic with an underlying dysthymic disorder, the
daughter of an exercise bulimic/severe food restrictor mother and a
workaholic father with an anxiety disorder and Valium addiction. I am
also now fairly certain that I meet the criteria for borderline personality
disorder, which includes impulsivity in sex. The reason is this: two
weeks into graduate school, and the second time Moira and I meet at
Adam's for drinks, I meet the CEO of a land management company
named Mitch who is thirty, blonde haired, green-eyed, and weight-
lifter fit, and because he has a habit of cocking his head to one side and
half-closing his dreamy eyes when I say something that pleases him, a
gesture which feels somehow terribly intimate, I sleep with him on our

first date. Of course, I know my history. If I try to read the future in his handsome face—whether with each sexual encounter there will be a concomitant shove out to sea, or whether we will go and go and go and never find the edge of my longing—I can't do it.

*　*　*

On our first night together, Mitch and I have both been drinking. Because of this, I am slightly numbed to my own self-consciousness, and the sex is passionate, comfortable, and fun. *This could last,* I remember thinking, and for a while, it does. For awhile—about four months, in fact—our relationship functions the way I think a relationship should: we go out to dinner, go to parties (mostly my graduate school functions), and return to the quadruplex to walk Keithan and have sex. On weekends we go for long walks in the woods, walks that imbue us with a kind of earthy vigor and make us horny. Mitch is kind but masculine and makes me feel beautiful. On hikes, I wear my long wavy hair down rather than in some athletic ponytail, and I keep my nails polished, something I've never done before. We talk—my family, his family, work, school— though not deeply, and this I chalk up to my idea that, for very masculine men, sex *is* talk. I tell myself our lack of deep conversation does not bother me. I tell myself that sex is paramount, that, at least for now, it is most important that we keep having it, that our relationship will find its conversational footing in time. Four months later, however, we are sleeping together less and less, and our conversations have become more about that.

Mitch says, "It's been two weeks since we did it."
I say, "I just don't feel like it right now."
I say, "Tomorrow, I promise."
I say, "I have exams."
At the time, I can't say for sure which apathy is in effect, the apathy that comes with growing tired of your partner for all the right reasons (you don't converse well or easily, you don't enjoy the same movies or parties or foods, and there is no sense that, beneath the scrim

of sex and dinners and walking the dog, your relationship is going anywhere profound). Or whether this apathy is the re-emergence of my sexual reversal left over from Neil days, when I rendered myself nearly genderless and completely asexual beneath the strain of diet and neurotic guilt. In the case of Mitch and me, I will later suspect apathy of head begot apathy of heart and vagina; however, when I mention it to Moira, she says she's never had that problem. Because I am not ready to admit defeat, I ask Mitch to bear with me while I "work on the problem."

"I really care about you," I tell him (though I don't, not really). "I want to get better." (Better, I only flimsily understand, means that I want to be a sexual automaton like Moira, able and willing to have sex at the drop of a hat. I do not understand that my notion of "better" is the equivalent of handing my body on a serving platter to Mitch, that it means taking no account of my real, explorable feelings about sex, or my role in it, or how much sex I actually even need—or want—for that matter.)

And as I am considering—or more accurately, not considering—the limits and functions and preferences of my sexual self—I should say, *as I am shutting my eyes to what I did and did not learn from my experience with Neil and my mother's rage over my sexuality and my father's admonitions and censure and closed-mindedness around sex*—a new suitor appears on the scene. I don't immediately know he's a suitor because he is thirty-five, is my supervisor at the research hospital where I have just started a new job gathering data on depression in sick children, and because he is older and in a position of authority, I do not consider him boyfriend material. By the time he calls me at home, Dr. Ansley and I have spoken in his office a few times, where he gave me an overview of the research tools and we discussed, very briefly, me: where I was from, what my psychology training had been, how I was liking Augusta. Was I married? The last question slotted in so seamlessly I barely notice it, even as I answer it.

"No," I say. "I have a boyfriend, Mitch."

Late one Friday night, I am lying on the sofa making a bridge with my hands across the canyon created by my hipbones and eyeing the space underneath when Dr. Ansley calls. I am afraid I've done something wrong at work and I jump up and put a pillow against my chest to quiet my pounding heart.

"Yes, sir," I say, when he asks if I can stop by his office in the morning to pick up some new data sheets.

"Call me Forrest," he says. Then he asks why I am alone on a Friday night.

The question takes me by surprise and I am not sure how to answer. I am alone because Mitch is mad at me because we haven't had sex in a week.

"It's a long story," I say, although it really isn't any longer than *sex.*

"Tell it to me sometime," Dr. Ansley says. "Maybe I can help."

Which is when I suddenly know Dr. Ansley is a suitor. And that I am about to go from sleeping with Mitch (such as it is) to sleeping with Forrest Ansley without actually leaving Mitch first, so that I can go back to Mitch in case things don't go well with Forrest. Which is also when the Diagnostic and Statistical Manual falls open in my head to the page which delineates borderline personality disorder in all its embarrassing glory, not just the sexual impulsivity but the other shameful criteria as well: the *fear of abandonment* and the *shaky self-image* and the *rapidly shifting allegiances.* Especially the rapidly shifting allegiances, for didn't I just ask Mitch not to leave me, to give me more time to work on my sex problem? Did I mean with somebody else?

When I go by Dr. Ansley's office later that morning, it turns out he has forgotten to bring in the Likert Scales he is so eager to have me introduce into the research. If Mitch doesn't mind, he will run them by my house later.

That evening I open the door before Forrest can knock. I am wearing my tightest blue jeans and a long red sweater belted at the waist. Forrest is wearing jeans and a long-sleeved, button-down white shirt neatly tucked in, a brown belt, and brown-and-white boat shoes. His stick-straight, blonde hair is neatly side-parted and combed. His angular face is freshly scrubbed, and he smells like a new car. He smiles his boyish, kooky smile revealing the tiniest gap between his front two teeth. A whoosh of attraction flies through me.

"I brought the scales," he says, stepping inside.

A moment passes, and then I start to laugh. "For a minute I

thought you meant to weigh me," I say.

Forrest laughs. "Do all your dates do that?" The word "date" rings in the air like a high, clear bell.

"Is this a date?"

Forrest looks slightly uncomfortable.

"No," he says. "It's not." Then he smiles his kooky smile again and his eyes light up. "But I could come back Friday without the paperwork."

* * *

Forrest comes over twice more in the next two weeks before making a move to sleep with me. During that time, Mitch and I continue to see each other, and we have sex twice, mainly while I conjure Forrest's blond hair and angular, Norwegian face. By the time Forrest and I have sex I have imagined it from start to finish, but the real thing is nothing like my imagining. We are sitting on my sofa talking when there is the sudden entangling of legs and arms and mouths. The suddenness, the urgency of it, ignites me. I don't even have time to worry about what my body looks like, whether my belly is jiggling unattractively. As soon as Forrest, leaves I pine for him. We see each other every other weekend or so, during which time I continue to see Mitch, although I don't look forward to my dates with Mitch like I do with Forrest. Once, I even leave Mitch in the middle of a date and call Forrest, who happens to be free, and so I spend the rest of the evening with him.

But I am not without guilt.

"You're not a borderline," Dr. Singleton says when I tell him my fears. "If you were, you wouldn't know it. And if you knew it, you wouldn't care."

As with Mitch, there is no real relationship underpinning my time with Forrest. Years later, I will read in my journal that we went to this or that place for dinner, saw this or that movie, but I won't remember being anywhere with Forrest except in his office or in bed, and I won't remember doing anything except talking about sex and having it. I will come across a card he gave me for my twenty-third birthday, a tasteless, dirty greeting card which he signed *Love, Forrest,* and will remember staring hopefully at the sentiment for a very long time, thinking, "Really? *Love?*" Within three months, I leave Mitch and devote myself entirely to Forrest, elated that my sexual appetite remains strong.

* * *

In addition to playing boyfriend musical chairs, juggling the demands of a full schedule of classes, and trying to walk a miserable tightrope between eating enough while not adding an ounce of flesh to my body, there is, of course, the issue of my father's bladder cancer, which is playing a sinister game of hide and seek with my father's doctors. There is talk of remission followed by hideous sickness, more tests, and the discovery of more tumors. I go home to visit and am confronted again by the baldness and the strangeness of my father's moon-like face and my mother's quiet resignation.

"Major depression," I tell Dr. Singleton the Monday following one of my trips home, and I list my symptoms confidently.

One: Feelings of worthlessness and guilt. (I did not stay the extra day at my parents' even though my father begged me to.) "I have my own house now," I'd said, parroting what my sister used to say when our father begged her to stay over. But the assertion, made to my sick father, came out sounding not like independence, but like selfishness, which it was: I could not bear to stare at his bald head one minute longer, and so I had to leave.

Two: disrupted sleep patterns. (I am having nightmares.)

Three: loss of interest in formerly pleasurable things. (I hardly feel like going to Adam's with Moira anymore, and I enjoy walking Keithan less and less.)

And *four:* a depressed mood with symptoms having been present for at least two weeks. "It's been longer than two weeks," I say. "More like *years.* I'm thinking maybe I need medication."

Dr. Singleton just shakes his head. "The DSM is like a twenty-four hour diner. There are hundreds of options to choose from, all of which seem appealing when you're feeling bad."

* * *

After we have been dating four months, Forrest invites me to his apartment for the very first time.

"Like chicken soup?" he asks. The way he says it makes it sound licentious, the way Linda made banana pudding sound somehow dirty. I can't wait to finish eating so we can have sex.

Forrest pulls bowls from the cabinet and sets napkins and spoons on the table. It is in watching these simple acts of domesticity that I feel, unbidden, the stirring of something new in my chest, a feeling that, at the time, I attribute to succumbing physically and emotionally and spiritually to another human being. It is different from the way I felt about Neil, whom I loved but did not feel my soul *welded* to.

Taped to Forrest's refrigerator is a picture of him with his parents and sister, and although I know it is a risk, know it is a leap to feel and certainly to confess that I think our relationship might just be going somewhere, I say, "I hope to meet your sister and your parents someday, Forrest."

Forrest looks up at me and then at the refrigerator and back at me. He hesitates, then sets the ladle down carefully on the counter.

"That's not my sister," he says. "That's my fiancée."

* * *

At home in the quadruplex over the next two weeks, I spend increasing amounts of time lying on the sofa with Keithan. My life has reached a level of bleakness beyond what I even believed possible. Moira is busy with a new boyfriend, and between him and school, has little time for me. Mitch hasn't tried to win me back. The pilot light on my stove has gone out again, and so I am eating canned tuna for both lunch and dinner. At my lowest point, I telepathically *will* Forrest to call me, which actually works. But he isn't leaving his fiancée, and so there is nothing else to talk about. I think about calling my mother, but know she's busy with my father, and I don't want to talk about my father. I stare at the ceiling for hours. As if in response, nickel-sized pieces of plaster loosen themselves from an overhead seam every few minutes and flutter down like snowflakes. I watch them fall and join the other plaster snowflakes that have been drifting down for weeks, and which cover the brown carpet like a dusting of snow since I don't have the energy to clean. I am here, lying on my back on the sofa two weeks after Forrest's revelation when my father calls with the news that my mother has been hit by a car. She has a fractured pelvis and extensive bruising. She's in tremendous pain. She'll be in a wheelchair for six weeks.

"But," my father says, "at least she's alive."

* * *

According to the Diagnostic and Statistical Manual, anxiety disorders are characterized by a state of heightened arousal and a feeling of impending doom, often described by patients as a feeling that "the sky is about to fall in."

There is no getting around the fact that I am anxious, and I don't even take my concerns to Dr. Singleton this time. I am a garden of disorder, harvested from all of the things I am striving to have and do and be, including love and sex and good grades and friendship, none of which come easily to me, or naturally. More and more between classes and in the evenings, I sit alone in the middle of my living room, surrounded by bits of plaster and dust, and rub Keithan's face.

Later, I will forgive myself. Later, I will understand that I could not have ministered to my father's epic need for empathy, or re-route the car that hit my mother, or stop the forces that were at work against the two of them from the very beginning of their lives together. I will understand that I could not have foreseen what would happen with Forrest, that since he didn't wear a ring, and I had yet to meet his friends or family, there was no context by which to really know him.

But for now, I am awash in a sea of sadness and anxiety and guilt, none of which I know what to do with anymore, and so I just store it away and tell myself I will figure it all out later, when I am feeling better.

* * *

It turns out that houses, like people, have diseases, and their own diagnostic manuals to parse them. A good builder can diagnose a house the way a good psychiatrist diagnoses a patient, but what exactly is wrong with my quadruplex, since I don't know the terminology, I can't say. More plaster and soon paint seem to be falling from the joints where the ceiling and walls meet, and every now and then, I hear a faint cracking noise like I used to hear in my parents' house, a settling of the foundation they said, a slight shifting of the ground.

Looking back, if I had to call it something, I would say my house had a nervous breakdown. If emotions are combustible, which I think they are, then I would say the quadruplex simply couldn't stand the pressure anymore. Late one night, when I am studying for an Assessment exam, I hear the cracking noise again, this time louder than usual and coming from behind the wall in the kitchen. Keithan sits up suddenly, her ears pricked forward. I put down my book and listen. *This is what impending doom feels like,* I think, and no sooner is the thought fully formed than the roof over my kitchen collapses. Keithan jumps up and races around the corner toward the noise. I jump off of the sofa and run after her, yelling for her to stop, but she can't hear me over the din of sheetrock and plywood raining down. The scene in my kitchen is dreamlike and strange. Keithan, wild-eyed, is standing on a pile of broken rafters, barking, dust mushrooming up around her like a nuclear cloud.

And over my stove, the moon is full and bright.

Chapter 21

There Goes the Neighborhood

THE QUADRUPLEX, with its collapsed roof, is uninhabitable. While I think of it as a freak accident, Mitch, with his land management background and who stayed at the quadruplex many nights prior to our break-up, is not surprised by the news.

"It lasted longer than I thought it would," he says.

"You never told me you thought it was unsafe."

Mitch shakes his head. "I told you a hundred times."

Darrin Johnson says he will put me up in a hotel for a few days while he gets the roof fixed. He suggests we keep the incident between ourselves, meaning that I not tell my mother. Believing that this is his way of validating my independent spirit, I wholeheartedly agree. It does not occur to me that he is afraid of a lawsuit.

Meanwhile, Mitch explains that shoring up a roof requires extensive work. He uses words like trusses and cat beams and pitch and leveraging, and says that if Darrin Johnson scrimps on the repair, the whole thing could collapse again in another year.

"I'll be finished with my coursework in a year," I say. "It would be easy enough to move then."

Mitch stares at me. "Are you not listening? A year is just a guess. It could be sooner than a year. It could collapse in six months."

Suddenly I am nineteen years old and sixty pounds underweight, sitting on my bed at Georgia Baptist Hospital as my doctor issues a stern warning. *If you do not add three pounds by next Wednesday, I will stick a tube in your heart and feed you that way.* I recall that I nodded gravely, but I also recall that the challenge, as I saw it, was how to gain the three pounds without going over by an ounce. It was a fundamental refusal to see the larger, more complex picture. Three pounds by Wednesday? *Three pounds by Wednesday.* The roof will fall in a year? *I'll move in a year.*

"Okay," I tell Mitch. "I'll look for a new place."

After two weeks of scouring the classifieds and feverishly driving the neighborhoods of Augusta, I discover, tucked behind a long, brown ranch house, what amounts to a house on stilts: a two-room dwelling built high over a garage, with a steep flight of wooden steps leading to the door. The neighborhood is racially mixed and an economic disaster, but this is not what I see the afternoon I navigate the hilly road with its shiny beer cans glinting in the gullies, its weedy front yards littered with bright toys, and people leaning on parked cars, smoking and chatting like they have no better place to be. How I don't notice the litter or the poverty or the aimlessness I later chalk up to the kind of blindness that afflicts dreamers, the same blindness that guided my supposed love for Joe. The fact is, unless I am a social worker or a probation officer, I have no business being in this neighborhood. Unaware of this fact, I move in.

Even now I can see what attracted me about the house. It had a large, shady yard which was completely enclosed by a badly misshapen but functional wire fence, perfect for Keithan. The house felt like a fortress, sitting high up over the garage and surrounded by trees. It had an open floor plan, meaning the tiny kitchen opened into the slightly larger living room, where there were five enormous windows. And the rent was only a hundred thirty a month, more than two hundred dollars less than what I was paying at the quadruplex. These were the seductive things, the winning qualities that made me feel, when I called my mother to tell her about the house, that I'd exceeded even my own expectations.

But there were a few things I didn't tell my mother about the house. Even though she was healing quickly—she had begun walking up and down the hallway just two weeks after her accident—there was still the issue of my father, in remission but not out of the woods, and I didn't want to give them anything extra to worry about. Which they might, if I told them, for example, about the enormous in-ground swimming pool in the dog yard with the crumbling walls and ten years' worth of dead leaves lining it. Or about the fifteen steep, rickety steps leading up to the porch, the majority of which was roped off because there was, dead center, a gaping hole the size of a human being. Several broken floor planks dangled from the mouth of the hole, along with a large nest of pine needles, a sight which gave even me pause, but the implications of which (i.e., that the house was already beginning to fall apart) I refused to see. I did this by telling myself that, unlike the predatory Darrin Johnson, who raised my rent the minute he saw the diamond on my mother's finger, my new landlord, quiet, lisping Mr. Sowells, had morals, and would never rent out a house that posed a danger. Hadn't he, after all, taken the time to rope off the rotten parts?

After I've moved in, I am examining the house with characteristic indiscriminant forgiveness, noting how the stovetop, kitchen sink, and oven are each built onto a wooden platform and teeter on a single, thin stilt, when a tiny flame of recognition sputters to life inside me. I get a glimpse, though no more than a glimpse at this point, that there might be something more than blindness or forgiveness at work in me when I consider a house and a neighborhood. That there is a certain condition of class and comfort, and maybe even safety that, at the time, I believe I do not need, but will later say I could not *allow myself* to inhabit.

When I am older, I will see the wretchedness of my choices. I will understand the thinking that led to them, will see that I inhabited poverty, not in defiance, but because I was somehow *forbidden*—and this is the best word for it—to live otherwise. I will see again how anorexia was like an octopus, its tentacles encircling all my thoughts and feelings and ideals, curling them back in on the beast until it was impossible for me to distinguish between my right impulses and those that had become corrupted.

But for now, as usual, I don't see the whole picture. I don't get how, with the actively rotting stilt house, and, before this, the seedy quadruplex, and, before that, the apartment devoid of furniture, my choices speak volumes about the way I feel about myself. I don't understand, even with my father's comment years earlier that I have to punish myself to reward myself, that selective discomfort is my modus operandi. The glimmering of insight I have upon moving to the stilt house and its ne'er-do-well neighborhood, that this move is part of a pattern of divestment, is not enough to steer me away from it. Instead, my powers of denial seem, in retrospect, to have just kicked in harder. So that what I see, for example, is not a twisted, mangled, pieced-together wire fence suggesting a pattern of neighborhood trespassing, but a secure yard for Keithan to roam and play. I see not heavy appliances teetering on thin stilts in my kitchen—fire hazards and plumbing disasters awaiting their big moment—but quirky styling and interesting configurations.

* * *

Moira and her boyfriend the drug rep break up. Because she is devastated, and because I have cried on her shoulder many times about Forrest, I vow to take care of her in her time of need.

"All you'll do is think about Bill if you stay in your apartment," I say. "Come stay with me in the new place for a few days. It'll be fun. We'll just hang out." I practically plead with her to let me do this small act of caring. She doesn't want to leave the comfort of her own apartment, but she agrees she'll just obsess. She packs an overnight bag of clothes and, still sniffling, gets in her car and follows me to the stilt house. Twenty minutes later we are standing at the gate to my dog yard. Keithan is barking non-stop and rushing up and down the steep steps, which Moira is staring at with red-rimmed eyes.

"You're kidding, right?" she says, thrusting her chin out at the steps and up at my house in the trees. She looks as if she is going to start weeping again. It hadn't occurred to me that two-hundred plus-pound Moira might have trouble getting up my steps. Or that my steps, many actively rotting, might not hold her up.

"There are only fifteen of them," I say brightly. "Endorphins will kick in around ten and the last five will be a blur."

Moira shuttles her giant pocketbook off her shoulder and lets it fall to the ground. I hoist it onto my own shoulder, and watch as she scans the outside of the house, her eyes skipping from detail to detail: the leaf-filled pool, the pile of broken concrete blocks pushed up against the house and partially covered with a torn, black tarp, the ratty wire fence, the black curtains over the windows that make the house look like a giant smile with missing teeth. With a sigh and a heave, Moira lurches toward the first step. Minutes later, breathing hard at the top, Moira spies the roped-off section of porch and her mouth falls open.

"Do you have something against houses *without* holes?" she says.

"Those are a dime a dozen," I say. "I had to really hunt for this."

I lead the way into the kitchen, past the stilt-legged appliances and into the living room with the five large windows hung with black cloth to keep the heat out. Moira stops abruptly.

"Are your curtains *nailed* up?"

"There were no curtain rods."

Moira rolls her eyes. "I just want to lie down. Are your sheets nailed to your bed or can I just crawl in? And turn on some air, please."

Of course the stilt house does not have air conditioning. And while the blackout curtains help, they can only keep things so cool. While Moira estimates that it is "ninety-five fucking degrees" in the house, I assure her it probably isn't over eighty. But the worst is yet to come, worse than Moira's shocking realization that there is no air conditioning, worse than having to haul her body up fifteen steep, iffy steps and navigate past a human chute dead center of the porch. There is still the matter of my bedroom.

The bedroom is long and narrow with cheap wood paneling and a ceiling so low I unconsciously duck when I enter. At one end of the room is my desk littered with books and papers and coffee mugs, and at the other is my bed, which is really just a mattress on the floor. In between the desk and the bed is what is left of the blue shag carpeting that I attempted to pull up when I first moved in. The glue was stronger than I'd expected, and after an hour or so of clawing at the looser spots, I ran out of interest in the project, leaving islands of carpet dotting the subflooring. I meant to get a rug to cover it all up but never did. Moira's eyes dart from the paneling, the ceiling, the carpet, and finally to the bed which rests like a partially deflated life raft on the patchy floor. She turns on me like a wild animal.

"Are you fucking *kidding* me? I can't get down there!" She glances around the room some more as if by some miracle she'll discover her own bed, sitting high off the unsightly floor, ringed with an eyelet dust-ruffle and fluffy with pillows and down.

* * *

In my memory, Moira withheld further commentary. I assume it was because she was in too much pain, that she simply did not have the energy for it. It would not have been for lack of understanding, for I am certain that she already knew what I was only just coming to, that what I dismissed as the cost of living with a dog, the cost of independence, the cost of living only with what you needed, was, when you added up the anorexia and the caved-in quadruplex and this actively rotting stilt house, nothing more or less than the flagrant flaunting of my self-denial.

Or perhaps there is a fault of memory here and she did address it. Perhaps, were I to call her today and say, "Why didn't you tell me my houses were a metaphor for how I felt about myself?" she would simply say, as Mitch had, "I told you a hundred times." The fact is, while I was just beginning to see my choices for what they were, true insight was still years away, and it wouldn't have mattered if Moira had laid out in eloquent detail all she knew to be true: how my rejection of my physical body in the form of self-starvation dovetailed perfectly with the way I embraced derelict structures, like a trade-off: one bad, uninhabitable body for another. It wouldn't have mattered because I wasn't ready to listen.

"Take me home," Moira says. "I can take care of myself."

Chapter 22

You're Number Three

I LIVE IN THE STILT HOUSE until I finish my graduate school coursework, which is a year and a-half. My father goes back into remission, and my mother executes her three-mile walks with even more conviction than before she was hit by a car. More and more, without the distractions of parents and illness and fear, I wake to my own misgivings about the house: it seems to have a slight sway when the wind blows, and the stilt appliances have begun to make me nervous, as if a chicken not perfectly centered in the oven might topple the whole thing. When I finally tell my mother about the appliances on stilts and my worries about upending the oven, she wants to know what I'm serving with the chicken.

During this time, Mitch calls to see how I am doing in the new place. We talk for a long time. At the end of the conversation, he says, "Do you want to try dating again?"

Why he would want to try again I can't imagine, as our first round of dating ground to a sexless halt after only four months. Why I would want to try again I also don't know; I suspect it was a combination of loneliness and a belief that I couldn't "work on" my sex problems in the absence of a partner.

"Okay," I say.

By the time Mitch arrives a week later for our second "first date," I have talked myself into giving him a real chance. This requires me to ignore the feeling this is just a stop-gap measure, human filler to pass the time, to make us feel we are not alone. In preparation for the beginning of our Real Chance, I have showered, downed two tall rum-and-Tabs, and now stand naked and steaming in front of my full-length mirror, modeling everything in my closet in order to find an outfit that will prove my relationship worthiness.

It's a challenging job. Weight is still the primary gauge for how I feel and think about myself, and because I have opened the food gates to allow broiled chicken in place of tuna fish dinners, and sandwiches for lunch in place of salads, I am up to a hundred ten pounds. The area that presently concerns me is the narrow strip of terrain between my navel and my crotch, the gentle female swell whose existence I have always believed I must nullify in order to be found praiseworthy and desirable. I have, at various times, left the house with hair I have forgotten to brush, my shirt buttoned wrong, and once got as far as my car in my slippers, because I was too busy deconstructing and camouflaging this middle section of my belly to notice the rest of my body. After an hour of drinking, fighting back tears, and putting on and ripping off successive outfits, I settle on a black knit miniskirt, black sweater, pink tights, and the little Chinese slippers from Bridgeway House days. Thirty minutes later, Mitch bursts through the door. His hair is freshly washed and shiny, and he is dressed in a dark flannel shirt and down vest. He smells like a campfire and looks like a lumberjack, a restless combination of earthy exterior and masculine energy. And he is horny.

"You look great," I say, and in response Mitch shoves me up against the stilt-sink and lunges hungrily for my mouth.

I laughingly push him away. "We have to get to the party!"

And with that, the dance begins anew. Why Mitch doesn't back away from the stilt-sink right then and leave, I don't know, though later I will know it's because he'd decided to dedicate one full night to this, our second go-round. Until such moment as we are or are not resting in my patchy-floored bedroom, our breath entwined in sex-sated sleep, this, our Real Chance, isn't over.

"Can you read a map?" Mitch asks in the car.

"Of course!" I say, working not to slur my words as I turn the directions in a circle in front of my face. The party is at a fellow grad student's house. I have been there one other time for a party, but don't trust myself to be able to find it without directions, especially after two drinks.

Mitch jerks the map away from me. "Who is this Andrew guy anyway?"

"Just a friend from school," I say. "You'll like him. He's very easy going."

"What, like a pansy?"

I look over at Mitch. His face is an eerie pale green from the glow of the dashboard.

"Like nice," I say. "Like easy to get along with."

"I hate parties where I don't know anyone," Mitch says.

My chest flutters. I can feel that something is wrong between us but I do not connect it to the scene in the kitchen, to the fact that, thirty seconds into our Real Chance, I was already pushing Mitch away again.

"You'll know me," I say brightly. "Oh, and you'll remember Moira from the bar that first night we met."

"Oh, Jeez," Mitch says. "The *cow*? Why do you even hang around her? She's disgusting."

A little alarm goes off in my head and I press down with my foot on an imaginary brake.

"She's *fat* Mitch," I say, using Moira's own word and speaking calmly, some more mature, sober woman having slid into my place in the car. "That doesn't make her disgusting. How can you judge her like that when you don't even know her?"

"Oh, please," Mitch says. "Is this what you and your friends do, sit around and psychoanalyze everyone?"

"No, just the ones who need it," I say bitterly. At that moment the rum elevator that has been delivering bliss to my brain stops abruptly. The fuzzy veil over my consciousness lifts like a sunrise, and a little invisible box tumbles out of the ether and into my lap. Inside the box is a tiny bird. Because I am now so clear-minded, I remember that this is the way understanding always comes to me: like a bird falling out of the sky. On the heels of Mitch calling Moira a cow and Andrew a pansy, which follows the innumerable times he pushed for sex when we were dating that I said *no, not now, tomorrow*, I realize that although I find him attractive and want him to find me attractive, even convincing myself that we might have a Real Chance, I, in fact, do not even like him. This is such a basic realization that I ignore it. I close the lid over the tiny, preening bird in my lap, and I do not open it again. Then, because I do not want to fight anymore, especially outside Andrew's house with a party going on, I decide to patch things up as best I can. I get on my knees in my seat and wrap my arms around Mitch's neck.

"Hey," I say, "Let's not fight."

Mitch softens. "You're right," he says. "I'm sorry." Then he grabs my head and pulls me hard into his mouth, so hard his teeth cut into my upper lip. He gnashes at my mouth and jams his tongue into every corner, holding the back of my head so I can't pull away. The kiss is painful, a punishment, and we both know it. When he finally lets go, my eyes are stung with tears. I fall back into my seat and for a minute we just sit there in the dark of the car, breathing hard and wiping our mouths. And then, as if something ugly and intangible hasn't just passed between us, we get out and go into the party.

Andrew's house is lit up inside and Fleetwood Mac is blasting on the stereo. Moira is sitting on a piano bench with another grad student I don't know well, a pretty, blonde girl named Alexandra. They are both smoking and laughing hard at something. About twenty-five other grad students are milling around, most of whom I have only spoken to in class. The music is too loud and the smoke is already thick in the room. I wave at Moira and Alexandra.

"Where's Andrew?" I yell.

Alexandra juts her head in the direction of the kitchen. "Getting a beer," she yells. She points her cigarette at Mitch, who has stationed himself in front of a table with chips and dip. "Who's the hunk?"

"Mitch," I yell.

"Rich?"

"MITCH!"

Mitch looks up from the chip table and saunters over. "You call me?"

I introduce Mitch to Alexandra and remind him that he met Moira a few months before, at Adam's. *Be nice*, I think to myself.

"Hi, Moira! Nice to see you again!" yells Mitch. Then he does something I cannot believe. He leans down and kisses her on the cheek. Moira looks surprised but delighted and smiles approvingly up at me.

I rub Mitch's arm and he leans in and kisses me on the mouth, gently this time. The tension in my chest releases.

"Sit here, handsome," Alexandra says to Mitch in a smoky voice, patting the bench next to her. "I wanna talk to you."

Mitch sits down and Alexandra puts her hand on his knee, and the sight of the two of them, leaning in talking to each other, stirs a little pot of jealousy in my stomach, for which I am glad. *I must really like him*, it tells me, on the heels of our car confrontation that told me exactly otherwise.

"Andrew?" I push the open the swinging kitchen door but don't see anyone. The counters are lined with huge bags of open chips, dip cups, empty beer bottles, a huge bottle of Jack Daniel's, and a stack of plastic cups. It looks like a party has been going on for days.

"Down here!"

I lean further into the doorway and scan the floor where the voice came from. Andrew is on his stomach, peering behind the refrigerator. I let the door fall shut behind me and the music is instantly several decibels lower.

"That's a strange place to keep your beer," I say.

Andrew laughs in short choppy gusts and turns over onto his side to see who I am.

"Oh, hi! Oh, hey! Hello!" he says. He seems genuinely thrilled to see me.

"Don't get up," I say. Andrew smiles a broad smile and flips back over onto his stomach and reaches behind the refrigerator.

"Just let me... just give me... oh... there... got ya!" He draws his arm back out. There is a tiny black kitten in his hand. "Can you...?"

"Oh, my gosh!" I say, rushing forward to take it from him. "Where did it come from?"

"A larger female cat," Andrew says, smiling, getting up from the floor and dusting off the front of his jeans and white sweater. Andrew is thin but solid with a round face and dark blue eyes that lighten when he smiles. We have been on a couple of group outings together, for pizza and, once, to a golf course. He has asked me out a few times. Although I once thought I heard the high, clear trill of the bird telling me to let Andrew in, I've always been involved with someone else.

He nods at my pink tights. "Nice socks." He opens the refrigerator, pulls out a beer and hands it to me. "Congratulations are in order."

"For my socks?"

"Finals," he says. "I graded exams for Singleton. You're number three in the class, right behind Moira and Greg!"

For a minute I just stand there and stare at Andrew, my hand with the beer frozen over the kitten's head. I've never been number three at anything; only once was I ever in the upper percentage of anything, and that was back in my high school English class.

"So congratulations!" Andrew retrieves a thin silver flask from the back pocket of his jeans, raises it toward me in a toast and takes a quick pull. Then without warning, he leans in and places his large, soft lips over mine. The remnants of whiskey sting my lips where Mitch's teeth cut into them just minutes earlier. Andrew straightens back up and we stare at each other without saying anything. I put my fingers to my lips where they burn, and try to contain a smile.

"Mitch is out there," I say, nodding toward the main room.

"Okay, I'll behave," Andrew says. "So how's it going?"

I feel an unexpected lurch of emotion. "It's a long story," I say, remembering that this is exactly what I told Forrest when Mitch and I were having problems the first time around.

"It usually is," Andrew says. "Well, anyway, you did good on exams. Let me know if you want to celebrate sometime."

* * *

The stilt house is cold when Mitch and I get home from Andrew's party. Keithan is asleep in the kitchen but wakes quickly, butting happily against us with her torso, wanting to be petted. On the sofa, the pile of clothes is a depressing reminder of how much effort I put into getting dressed, and on the counter, my empty rum-and-Tab glass tells the rest of the story: I needed alcohol to numb the anxiety of clothing myself, of seeing Mitch again, of worrying about sex, of going to a party where there would be plenty of fattening food; in short, I needed to drink in order to numb the anxiety of being myself. All of a sudden, Mitch's arms encircle me from behind. He buries his face into my hair and neck and takes a deep breath. The campfire smell is gone from his vest, replaced by the smell of ordinary cigarette smoke.

"You smell good," he says.

You don't, I think.

Mitch pulls my body back against his. Even through the soft baffles of his down vest I can feel the quivering in his chest. His embrace feels like a straightjacket. I know this energy. This is not an energy I can say *not now* to, *tomorrow I promise,* or even *I'm not quite ready.* This is the energy that says there won't be a tomorrow for us if there's a *not now* today. It is the energy that leads to the sex you have not because you want to, and not because there is anything sexual or loving about it, but because it is required; this is end-of-the-line sex, the kind you know is the only thing that stands between you and your relationship's end.

I turn around to face Mitch. He smiles and takes me by the hand and leads me into the bedroom. I'm tired and cold and my mouth and throat are dry and scratchy from smoking and talking all night. With the downing of two more rum drinks, I found myself blindly eating potato chips and dip, only sketchily aware of what I was doing, and now that some of the alcohol has worn off, I am acutely sensitive to the uncomfortable feel of my full belly. Lastly, I want to spend some time with Keithan, but Mitch doesn't want her in the bedroom. Having sex is so far down on my list of what I would like to do at this moment that it would appear below "finish removing sticky carpet glue from floor."

Mitch lifts my skirt with one hand and pulls down my tights and underwear with the other. Without so much as a peck on the cheek, he forces himself into me. My eyes water and I hold my breath to keep the pain from traveling through me, to keep it down between my legs where I don't have to reckon with it in any meaningful way. The last thing I want to do is take the deep breath that will usher the pain up from my mindless vagina and into my heart where it would become something bigger and sadder and harder to disengage from. In my vagina, sex that hurts is just a bad lover. But in my heart, sex that hurts is all the people who have let me down, including Linda and Forrest, and now Mitch. It is the last time I saw Joe, the neighbor's dog never coming home from the vet, the fourth grade teacher who punished me unfairly, the horse that threw me in the middle of a street when I was twelve. It is my parents, sick, struggling, and working to hide their own grief. It is the original refusal of food at the trailhead of anorexia. In my heart, sex that hurts is an intensely solitary sadness, the loneliness of which is so unbearable that, at its culmination, there is the paradoxical gratitude toward the person who delivered me there, who afterwards, if I lie in his arms, can make me feel visible again.

"That was great," Mitch says, pecking me on the cheek and getting up to go to the bathroom. When he comes back in the room his shirt is neatly tucked in and he has wet his hair and combed it into place. "I can't stay," he says.

"What? Why?" My voice is tired and squeaky. It is two a.m. I pull the covers over my exposed torso and raise up on my elbows, squinting through my dry, filmy contacts.

"I have some things I need to take care of," he says.

"Now? Tonight?"

"First thing tomorrow. I'll call you later in the day."

I scoot down into the bed and pull the covers up to my nose. A current of warmth that begins as a chill shoots through me. I turn over onto my stomach and close my eyes.

"Let Keithan back into the bedroom on your way out," I say into the pillow, and I am asleep before the kitchen door announces Mitch's departure.

* * *

If anorexia is like an octopus, it is also like a parasite. Its numbing bite endows its host with endlessly mutating rounds of magical thinking, which feel, at first, like a gift. With magical thinking comes a claim to insight with no basis in fact, a clarity so fine that reality cannot touch it. So clear is anorexia on issues of cause and effect (*if I gain weight I will feel bad; if I lose weight I will feel better*) that it is like having your own personal theory of physics and religion distilled down to a simple, divided highway of explanation that detangles the complex intangibles of living, just as the successful camouflaging of the gentle female swell smoothes and nullifies whatever rocky realities might be giving you pause.

The morning after Andrew's party, I stagger into the kitchen, my mouth a cottony replay of potato chips and rum. Semen is plastered to my inner thighs. As I begin to stitch together disconcerting memories of the previous evening—fight in car, Andrew's kiss, the unwanted, painful sex—my magical brain moves in with spin.

I've been letting myself go lately, it begins, *which is why my life is so out of control.* "Letting myself go" refers to gaining the pounds that have the needle on the scale hovering anxiously at one hundred ten, poised to go higher if I'm not careful, as I wasn't the previous evening. The result of "letting myself go" is a panoply of mismanaged emotions like those of the previous evening, some leading to fight, some to illicit kissing, some to regrettable sex. The solution—what will lasso my life and drag it back into submission—is a rededication to weight management. If there is any part of me, four years post-hospitalization, to whom this refrain sounds depressingly familiar or like a bad idea, she is absent from my kitchen.

Then, as if nothing has just happened, as if I have not just flung open the door to a killing army and waved the flag of allegiance, I measure out two teaspoons of instant coffee and hot water into a mug, forgoing the skim milk that makes it drinkable. I also forgo breakfast. I lean against the stove and let the fading burner heat warm my back as I sip. I do not think about how funny it is or how ironic that inside this precarious house on stilts is a microcosm stilt-world, everything balanced high on spindly legs, everything unstable, including and especially me. Or maybe—just maybe it *does* occur to me on some healthy but unconscious level how wobbly things have become, and perhaps this is exactly how the next thought gets formed: *I need support.* And how as a result—not because I want him back (which I do, but deny), but because I just want to hear his voice—I pick up the phone and call Forrest.

"I'll always be there to support you, regardless," he told me, after I'd found out about his fiancée.

"All that means," Moira had said, "Is that it's fine with *him* if you keep sleeping together."

At the time, I'd agreed with her interpretation. But now, standing in my stilt kitchen surrounded by emblems of my unsteady interior, I decide that wasn't Forrest's motive at all. I decide that he meant he would always be available to talk. Even though Forrest and I had never talked, beyond the kind of conversing couples do on the edges of sex.

I dial slowly and walk out onto the porch with the phone.

"Yes?" Forrest says. This is how he always answers.

"It's me." My heart is slamming against my chest, though I don't know why, since I only want to talk.

There is silence on the line and then Forrest says softly, "Claire is here."

I start to shake. "I just needed to talk," I say, my voice quaking. I push the phone in harder against my ear, already feeling the gush of tears starting behind my eyes. I feel like I might throw up. "Will you call me later?"

There is a beat as if he is considering this. And then he says, "You have the wrong number."

There is a click that I know was swift and soft but that, in my mind, is like a bomb blast ricocheting through a metal corridor. Then the dial tone explodes into my ear. Every bit of the rage and helplessness and pain from the night before comes back to me in a rush, and I draw my arm back and hurl the phone, baseball style, from the top of the porch. It sails end over end like a slow-motion movie clip. So mesmerized am I by the phone's trajectory, by how it seems to float, far, far out over the yard, that when at last it loses momentum, landing with a quiet splash in the dry leaves in the deep end of the swimming pool, I almost don't hear it ringing.

I race down the porch steps in my socked feet, jump down into the shallow end of the pool and half-run, half wade through the cushion of leaves to the deep end, where the phone lies trilling.

"Forrest?!" Out of breath and off balance in the soft leaf bed, I plop down cross-legged.

"No, not *Forrest*," Mitch says.

"Oh, hey. Forrest was supposed to call me about work," I lie.

Mitch grunts. "What are you doing?"

"Well actually, I'm in the swimming pool." I laugh, a sound that, because I have been crying, comes out as a half-gurgle.

Mitch doesn't ask me why I am in the swimming pool.

"Listen," he says, and with the utterance of that simple word, I know that this, our Real Chance, is over. And even though I knew it was over the minute Mitch shoved me up against the sink and I said no, even though I fully *got* last night how not-nice Mitch can be, even though I know this *needs* to end, I am beside myself with panic. Some great tectonic shelf of emotion is shifting dangerously under my feet. Without Mitch, I feel like I am falling through space. Our relationship is difficult and painful and sad, and there is little respect for my physical boundaries, for what I want or even what hurts, but it is precisely this that connects me to a world with which I am familiar, so familiar that the thought of losing it is like losing my very center.

I hold my breath and push the receiver hard into my ear as Mitch goes on saying everything I already know to be true: that nothing has changed since the last time we dated, that it isn't fun anymore, *I'm not fun*, that there's no reason to keep trying to make it work.

"I want to get married sometime, you know?" he says finally. "You're not even thinking that way."

Hot tears create a waterfall from my chin.

"Are you still there?" Mitch says.

I nod and pull my other hand up out of the leaves to wipe my nose. Which is when the stench of dog shit hits me. I look around, and, with horror, realize I am sitting in what has been, for an entire year, Keithan's toilet.

Chapter 23

The Happiness Problem

B Y THE TIME SPRING COMES to the house on stilts, I have taken two very important steps and am on the verge of a third: I have replaced the blackout curtains with vinyl blinds that I can open and close. I have gotten a second dog, a solid black puppy named Jesse. And I am about to live with a man again for the first time since college.

Replacing the curtains with blinds was such a simple task, I wonder why I didn't do it before. But then I remember. "Before"—that categorical shorthand for "the time period predating insight"—I simply didn't see the difference between one window treatment and another. But, more importantly, *before* points a knowing finger at my own personal antiquity, a past which calls up the naïve and Spartan-like time when I relied on nailed-up blackout curtains to send a message of unavailability to the world outside my door. During the especially bad month after my final break-up with Mitch, in which I returned to a punishing regimen of tuna fish and sit-ups, I never peeled back the curtains at all and hardly went out except for school.

But that was before I found an ad for free puppies in the newspaper and went to look, not knowing that it is impossible to gaze upon an assembly of puppies and not drive off with one of them (the largest of the litter, in this case) cowering under your seat. It was before I knew how satisfying the *swish-swap* of plastic blinds could be, the way they snap from open to shut and back again with a simple, two-fingered twirl of a plastic rod. Before I knew how simple it could be to draw healthy, effective boundaries between yourself and the world outside your window.

"How does it look?" I asked Andrew when I'd screwed the last of the blinds into place. I was standing on the back of the sofa, arms outstretched like I'd just nailed a complicated gymnastics landing.

"A little more padding in the ass and it would be perfect," he said, laughing in his characteristically quiet way: shoulders shaking, one hand cupped in front of his mouth.

At the time I yank out the nailed-up blackout curtains and hang the blinds, Andrew and I have been dating for six weeks. It is too soon to be talking about living together, of course, but I tell myself that, because of my newfound skill at erecting fluid but working boundaries, I will be fine. After all, Andrew, unlike Mitch, is a soft, kind presence who never pushes me beyond my comfort level, in sex or anything else. And unlike Forrest, he would never harbor hurtful secrets. But most of all, as third-highest performing in my graduate Psychology class, I need to believe that my studies are making me not just book-smart, but life-smart.

While I am admittedly smitten by the new blinds and their rich metaphorical implications, the truth is I bought them because of Andrew. The blackout curtains, he said, were starting to depress him. (Amazingly, this is the only thing he complained about in the stilt house.)

"Depress you," I said. "Depress *you*."

In our three months of near-constant togetherness, I had never seen him so much as weary, much less dispirited. Andrew at twenty-five was one of the most carefree and irrepressible people I had ever met.

"Andrew could flip a penny and find a quarter on the other side," I tell Moira, and twenty-five years later this is still the way I think of him.

"I *can* get depressed, you know," Andrew had said, sounding almost defensive. "I just choose not to."

How Andrew chooses not to get depressed is hard for me to understand, but I decide it's his deliciously happy upbringing that gives him this "choice." The third child of six children, and oldest of three boys, Andrew's description of his family and the family-owned bakery—where all the kids, when they were old enough, ran the mixers and ovens, waited on customers, and delivered cakes—puts me in mind of a crowd of friends perpetually in the midst of a party, which, when we visit his family, is exactly how it will seem. Siblings coming and going at all hours of the day and evening without anyone passing judgment (no "You're leaving *now*? You're going *where*?"). Five different conversations happening at once, not one of them angry. Laughter erupting in the kitchen, which, when I investigate, I will see is coming from Andrew's mother, with whom Andrew is posing for a photo with a case of beer under his arm, a puffed up chest, and a crazed smile.

"We were just always talking," Andrew says. "That's how we worked things out."

"By *talking*?" I repeat the word like it is gibberish. The idea that as a family you might talk flies in the face of what I have always believed: that family is built on a foundation of acrimony and ill will. We didn't talk so much as we traded witty repartees, sarcastic rejoinders meant to make the butt of the joke laugh embarrassedly at him- or herself. ("You want to talk? Go ahead, I'll be in the other room watching TV.") The worse you felt, the more they proclaimed you just didn't have a good sense of humor. (My sister once asked loudly, at a festive family dinner party with twenty-five other people in attendance, "So how's your crumbling relationship with Mitch?" When I was angry and moved to tears by this, she looked truly stunned.)

Andrew nods. "We talked all the time. And besides, it was impossible to stay mad when everything smelled like cake."

It is obvious that Andrew carries this sweet current of optimism forward into his life. He asked me out for months on end, never discouraged when I said no, I was involved with Forrest, or trying to get re-involved with Mitch.

"Is that why you kept pursuing me?" I ask. "You have no construct for disappointment?"

"I just knew you'd come around," he says airily.

And either in spite of, or because of, Andrew's unrelenting and seemingly indigenous cheeriness, he tolerates what is unrelenting and seemingly indigenous to me: the bitter current of pessimism that threads through me like a cord, powering my life. The trifecta of self-doubt, self-loathing, and emotional blindness that propels me toward flawed houses, that etches away at my sex drive, that situates me for long hours on the porch, my arms wrapped around Keithan's neck, bemoaning all the ways I am not guiding my life purposefully toward maturity, like Moira who has just been accepted to a PhD program.

While it doesn't occur to me to wonder *why* a happy man like Andrew pushes for over a year to pair off with an unhappy woman like me, I am aware, early on, of his attempt to change me, to coerce me into seeing the world his way. Which, far from altering the way I see the world, just entrenches me more. One night, out with Moira, I try to put into words what it is about Andrew's unfailing cheerfulness that bothers me.

He's *too* happy," I say. "It's like there's no fundamental processing ability moderating him. He should be more *realistic*."

Moira watches me carefully. "You mean more depressed. Like you."

"No," I say. "I mean there should be something that makes him see that life isn't all cake and ice cream. That there's crappy stuff everywhere. That you can't just go around ignoring the bad stuff just because you don't want to deal with it." What I mean, but cannot say, is that, just as I believe that acrimony defines a family, so do I also believe that a certain measured unhappiness about the right things defines intelligence. Andrew's cocoon of bliss is not just as a failure of reason, but a failure of intellect.

"It's easy to be happy," my sister always said. "It's people with brains who see the darker side of life." According to my sister, "brains" was the consolation prize for a lifetime of conscription in depression's army.

"You're kidding yourself," Moira says. "The problem isn't that Andrew is happy; it's that you're *not*. You don't want him to move in and you know it. His happiness problem is just a distraction."

I open my mouth to argue, although I don't have an argument lined up. As usual, Moira is two steps ahead of me. The waitress arrives with drink refills and we pay. As I am tucking my change back into my wallet I remember to tell Moira that, after two anxious weeks, I found my misplaced driver's license.

"It was in Andrew's car the whole time," I say. "In the glove compartment."

There is a beat of silence, after which Moira says, "WOW."

"What?"

Moira smiles the huge smile she gets when she has information someone else doesn't have and is relishing the moment of the telling. She chases her straw around her glass with her tongue, then takes a long drink, never taking her eyes off me.

"In the glove compartment," she says finally.

"I must've stuck it in there one day when we were going somewhere and I didn't want to take my purse. Why? *What?*"

"Oh, come on," she says, exasperated. "*Think!* You stuffed your *identity* away. You *hid it* from yourself by *giving it to Andrew!*"

* * *

There are moments of memory that stay with you in captivating detail, like the singular outline of pond grasses frozen under a sheet of ice. The moments are frozen there, not just because of what they mean for you at the time, but because of what they will mean for you in the future. It is as if your brain knows that what you don't fully understand in the moment, you will revisit, and so it holds the thoughts for you undisturbed, as pristine as when they first arrived, so that decades later, you can dissect them anew.

At the time, Moira's comment stops me cold. How often do I structure my day, my *self*, not around what I want, but around what someone else wants? Go for a hike instead of studying. Go to a movie instead of playing poker with friends. Have sex instead of not. Agree with Andrew that we should live together in spite of the fact that I am quite happy living alone.

The following night at The Green Jacket steakhouse, I pounce.

"Moira thinks you're stealing my identity," I say to Andrew, "and I think I agree." (In fact Moira said I *hid it from myself* but I like the sound of this better, probably because it absolves me of the responsibility for setting the boundaries I believe I've gotten so good at setting.)

"*What?*" Andrew's beer screeches to a stop halfway to his lips.

"Me sticking my license in your glove compartment. She thinks it's symbolic of my lost identity."

Andrew puts down his beer and leans forward in his chair.

"Moira is telling you you've lost your identity? Why would she say that?"

"She sees the way I let people take over my life."

Andrew sighs. "Did it occur to you that Moira might be jealous of you? Of *us?*"

I assure Andrew that Moira isn't jealous.

"All right then," he says. His bright blue eyes have darkened and there is a hint of sadness in them, a new, interesting dimension. "How is it I'm stealing your identity? Or taking over your life?"

He asks nicely, as if he truly wants to understand. There is none of the sarcasm I constantly expect from people I am close to. ("Stealing your identity? Won't I give it back when I see what it is?") Instead he searches my face for meaning, and it is this lack of derision, this openness, that reminds me what draws me to him.

I tell him I go along with a lot of things that I don't really want to do, like hiking and movies. I don't say *like letting you move in.*

"You always tell me to make the plans, you don't care what we do."

"I know," I say miserably. "It's more... like an *internal* encroachment. It's like you invade my thoughts." Even as the word *invade* leaves my mouth I am already embarrassed for how picayune it sounds, and at the same time how dramatic.

"You invade my thoughts all the time," Andrew says, smiling. "But I *like* thinking about you."

"It's not that I don't like thinking *about* you," I say, wishing Moira was here to help me explain myself. "It's that I can't think clearly *around* you. It's like your huge, happy thoughts crowd out my serious thoughts, and then I can't think as deeply." None of which, of course makes sense. I can't think deeply because I am anxious about Andrew moving in with me, but I can't tell Andrew this because I am afraid it would hurt him and then he won't move in. *Which is exactly what Moira means by tucking my identity away from myself.*

Andrew looks perplexed.

"I find that, when I'm with you, I avoid thinking about certain things just because they're unpleasant," I say.

"Yes!" Andrew says. "That's the point! Why entertain negative thoughts?"

"Because they're a part of life!"

Andrew looks at me earnestly. "Hon, there's no rule that says you have to latch onto every thought that comes your way. I think it's good that you're thinking less about negative things. You seem happier."

"I don't want to be happier!" I practically yell. A woman looks up from the table beside us. "I don't want to be happier," I whisper. *"I want to be exactly who I am!"*

Andrew sits back in his chair. He looks stunned and confused. "Maybe I shouldn't move in," he says.

Surprise and then relief floods my chest. Then, unbelievably, I begin to backpedal. "No," I say.

"No, what," Andrew says, staring down at his plate. "If you're feeling this unsettled before I even move in, then maybe we should wait."

Of course, we should wait. I have the wisdom of the blinds on my side, telling me that I am now in charge of who gains entrance to my world. That I am the sole guardian of my self-hood. That I am no more the floodplain I felt myself to be at the hands of my family, formless and without boundaries, pieces of me chipped away by sarcasm and mockery and fighting and the wet, black cloud of anger that hung inside our house. I own my destiny. I have the right to say yes or no to things I do or do not want to happen. In fact, I have the obligation. I *owe* it to myself.

But I can't hurt sweet, unfettered Andrew.

"No, it'll be fine," I say. Later I will tell Moira I had Andrew exactly where I wanted him but that I caved in. "He wasn't going to move in," I will tell her. "I talked him back into it. It was like—" I will pause as the image comes to me. "It was like leading a horse to water and watching it drink and then prying its mouth open and shaking the water back out."

Andrew's face softens. "Don't worry, this is gonna be great," he says. "You'll see." He reaches for my hand, eyes shining.

Chapter 24

I Don't

I F I CLOSE MY EYES, my neighborhood sounds like any other
neighborhood in the summer: parents call out, children call back,
dogs bark, lawn mowers drone. At the top of my porch steps, I sit
and run my hands through the long, soft fur of Keithan's neck. It is a
curiously free feeling to be through with classes and to have only my
internship at the women's shelter to complete and comprehensive
exams left to take. Andrew has gotten a job as a social worker at a
nearby prison, and for the next two months, our lives follow a
predictable pattern: I go to the shelter three days a week, grocery shop,
take care of the house and dogs, and make dinner. Andrew goes to
work at eight and comes home at five-thirty. At six-thirty we sit on the
L-shaped sofa in the den and eat chicken and salad in front of the TV.
After dinner we take Keithan and Jesse for a walk, then we read or
study or watch TV again until bedtime. It is a domesticity that on some
days I inhabit with awed gratitude, for how easy and how reassuring it
can be to simply co-exist with another. Other days, I feel strangely
removed from my own life, like I am watching it from above, the way
people sometimes talk about seeing their own body in a car wreck.

* * *

I chose my internship carefully. As with my search for a job that eventually led me to Bridgeway, I was interested in a very specific mental health population. I did not want to intern in a hospital with sick people, or in a nursing home with old people. I did not want to work in a residential setting with children, and never, ever had I wanted to work in a setting with the developmentally disabled. I wanted to work with healthy adults of average intelligence whose circumstances were regrettable but not permanent. I wanted to be somewhere where I had a real chance at making a difference.

"Women?" Dr. Singleton asked one afternoon as we pondered possibilities. "Do you have anything against women?"

"Women *where?*" I asked. "What kind of women?"

Which is how I ended up interning at the Light House, where women fleeing abusive partners went for counseling and all-important life-restructuring. For safety reasons, the true mission of the shelter was kept a secret from the community at large, so there was a certain mystique, an excitement surrounding the idea of "being on the inside," and it was the double opportunity here—not just to counsel, but to counsel under mysterious circumstances—that made me leap at the position. Not to mention it was the first of its kind to be offered by Augusta College. Which gave me a third dimension: pioneer.

There is much to be done for the women on the inside, and I approach the prospect with reverence and bravado. I know that what I will see will be disturbing, as I have read accounts of women in abusive relationships who have suffered grave injury at the hands of their partners. I am well aware that, along with taking detailed intake histories, scheduling doctors appointments, documenting injuries with photographs, arranging new housing in new cities and new schools for the children, there will be the larger, more personally demanding (and rewarding) task of bestowing immense amounts of emotional support to women who have become so isolated by physical and emotional abuse that strangers in a government facility are their best and only friends.

What I actually *do,* however, is sit in a cavernous office with a metal desk and an empty bookshelf and read and re-read the two-page intake forms that are filled out by someone else. Some days there are two intake forms, some days there are none. I am allowed no face-to-face contact with the women, who come and go in secrecy in a downstairs location, and their files, with the exception of the intake form, is off-limits to me as well. Which means that, three days a week, instead of offering myself and my newfound counseling skills up as a lifeline to hope, I sit in my cold, barren office, chain-sipping V8 juice from cans and struggling to stay awake. I wonder what it might be like to actually *see* the things I am reading about on the intake forms—"nose broken in three places," "shattered cheekbone," "exploded eye socket"—and imagine they are devastating when you attach them to a real human being sitting in front of you. But they are for me, alone in my upstairs office, nothing but words on a page, bad things happening to flat characters playing bit parts in the dramalessness of my internship.

It does not occur to me to go to Dr. Singleton after a week of this brain-rattling tedium and explain how I am reading forms until my eyes rock in my head. Nor does it occur to me, after two weeks, to tell him that I still am not even allowed to lay eyes on the women. I suppose that I expected to be ushered into the private, terrible world of domestic abuse once I had put in my time doing nothing, but incredibly, the entire semester goes by before I completely wake to the seriousness of my predicament, which is that I have done nothing, learned nothing, and been afforded no counseling experience. After holding out for an internship that would not make me feel anonymous, I had managed to find one in which I was completely invisible.

* * *

Internship aside, cohabitation with cheerful, even-tempered Andrew makes me content, and, at times, happy. Andrew is attentive and playful and publicly affectionate. My friends, including Moira, like his sweet, quiet nature and the silly way he sometimes cracks himself up with his own jokes. Andrew and I play volleyball, hike with the dogs, and take weekend car trips to Hilton Head. From one trip, he comes home horribly sunburned but doesn't complain; he just lies naked on the bed under a cool, damp towel that I re-wet every twenty minutes, grinning weakly as I snap pictures of his unfortunate and yet somehow hilarious predicament. Our sex life suffers from the same ennui to which I have become accustomed, which is to say that, once Andrew and I settle into a routine—once all illusion of newness and conquest has worn off—I am less and less interested in having it. But even about this, Andrew doesn't complain. Things being mostly good, I ponder why exactly I was so worried, what made me buy so readily into Moira's neat assessment that I was losing my identity to Andrew. *What*, I wonder, *was the big deal?*

In March, my sister has a fifty-ninth birthday party for my father at her house in Atlanta. Andrew spends an entire afternoon in our tiny stilt house kitchen baking a "book cake" in preparation: a wide, chocolate sheet cake that is carved and decorated to look like an open book, with the title "Dad: A Celebration" (after my father's book, *Atlanta: A Celebration*) written in blue icing across the top. There is a green icing "bookmark" down the center, and "Page 59" is written in icing in the lower right-hand corner. It is the most creative thing anyone in my family has ever done for my father, and I feel a surge of warmth for Andrew at the moment of the cake-cutting, even though the cake is barely acknowledged by my family.

My father's head is fuzzy with new hair and my mother is exercising with gusto, like she hadn't had a near-crippling run-in with a car just a few months earlier. In my sister's kitchen, as we are cleaning up, she asks how Andrew and I are doing. Only she asks as a statement, the way she and my father have always asked after information they don't really want.

"We're good," I say.

I don't tell her how in the beginning I struggled with fears of losing my identity, nor do I tell her that I sometimes feel like I am watching my body from above. My mother's concern is not for my internal struggles so much as for the fact that Andrew and I seem, from outward appearances (the personalized cake meant to win over my father, and smooth over the issue of our cohabitation) to be barreling toward something they—meaning she and my father—do not want for me: marriage to a non-Jew. A few weeks later, visiting them without Andrew, the conversation continues, this time at the dinner table. I am working to pull the skin of my chicken away from the leg quarter, then patting the leg dry of grease with my napkin, when I become aware that my father is eating noisily but saying nothing. His eyes are large behind his glasses, and he breathes loudly, not looking at my mother or me until he is finished. Finally, he drains the last of his iced tea and puts down his glass.

"What will Andrew do when he's through with school." The question is heavy with fatigue.

I feel a prickle of alarm. My father's question-as-statement, on the heels of my mother's just a few weeks earlier, gives me the uncomfortable feeling that I'm in line for an intervention. I half expect my brother and sister, and maybe even my mother's maid, to burst from the pantry with their own Andrew-inspired question-statements.

What will you do for the holidays.

How will you raise the children.

What do we tell the rabbi.

"Work?" My answer to my father's statement comes out as a question. "Maybe stay on at the prison if he can?"

Weariness lengthens in my father's face like an afternoon shadow. "Dana," he says. "Why Andrew. What if there were someone else— someone Jewish—who came knocking on your door."

A twist of anger snakes through me. My father's habit of waiting until I've chosen a path—a dog, an undergraduate college, a graduate school, a boyfriend—and then swooping in with his weary opposition and dire warnings, is not new.

"A grown dog? Don't you want a puppy?" my father asks after I've picked out Keithan at the Humane Society.

"Bard College is too expensive! You can't stay there," after I have one semester under my belt.

"Graduate school in Augusta? The paper mills stink!"

"Andrew? You should hold out for a Jew."

My father pushes his plate away and my mother carries it, and our plates, to the sink.

"Do something for me," my father says settling back in his chair. "Pretend you're a therapist. Your patient is devastated because his daughter is dating a non-Jew. What do you say to him?"

"I'd ask if the non-Jew was good to his daughter," I say, a simple, ignorant anger igniting at the base of my neck.

Because I don't have the years of counseling under my belt that will later lead me to revisit the conversation in my head, I do not grasp the real struggle behind my father's question. Because I am young and self-focused, I don't fully understand how his life of imagined illness has degraded him, holding him back from any number of plausible paths, so that, in the end, he would consider himself a failure for not having earned the medical degree his father wanted him to earn. I don't take into account the fact that he has one daughter struggling with anorexia and another with depression, or that his marriage, while enduring, is demoralizing and discomforting. Because I don't understand these things yet, I don't know that every course of action I choose that disappoints him is a beacon leading straight to the heart of his own savaged potential. While my father, not so much a devout Jew as a dutiful one, would be upset were I to marry a non-Jew, this, the reckoning of my religious soul and its alleged misalignment with his, is not the proper focus of therapy. The proper focus of therapy is his own devastation.

My father says nothing more, and that night I write in my journal that we had a "meaningful conversation." That I held up this short, impersonal banter as relevant and meaningful only highlights our lack of substantive discourse. There was not, nor would there ever be, dialogue that sought to reach beyond the injunction to marry Jewish, no investigation, or shared contemplation, about the wholly individual and unquantifiable human heart that might lead one to make a different decision. While perhaps not unusual—none of my friends talked about having serious discussions with their parents, after all—I suppose I still longed for something more. Many nights when I was young, I could hear my parents talking to my siblings in the den after I went to bed, the drone of their voices reaching me through a haze of sleepiness. I imagined these were briefings in matters crucial to living and loving, and that I would be privy to the same wisdom when I was old enough. Now, plenty old enough, what I discover is a one-size-fits-all spiritual expectation that leads me no closer to my parents' generation of expectations, or my own.

* * *

Life with Andrew, it turns out, is neither one thing nor another. It is neither good nor bad, loving nor hateful, something I could see myself staying in nor ever imagine leaving. It is a vast white space of neither-hood, slow to take hold and so lackluster that I will not even recognize it as full-blown misery for many weeks. When I do finally wake to it, I will tell myself it doesn't count. I will tell myself that it was a seed planted by my parents. I will tell myself that my upcoming job interview three hundred miles away in the north Georgia mountains, that I've yet to mention to Andrew, doesn't mean a thing about us.

But regardless of where it came from or how much I pretend it doesn't count, the fact is that I have reached a platform of discontent that is as average and uninspired as my daily routine has become. By the time my pointless internship limps to a close, I am forced to view it against the backdrop of my larger life with Andrew, to see it not as the tedious, unfortunate thing I mistakenly slotted into an otherwise full and interesting schedule, but as the tedious and unfortunate thing that was a mirror of my life in the stilt house with Andrew: the same trips to the same beach in Hilton Head. Watching Jeopardy and Moonlighting. Chicken and salad. Friday night poker and beer.

But worse than the repetition, which breeds a day-to-day surface boredom, there is a deeper, more insidious kind of *soul* boredom, the growing sense that, safe in the presence of Andrew, I am shrinking. And it is here that my conversation with Moira comes back to me, the night I told her Andrew was too happy, that he lacked the fundamental processing ability which would allow him to modulate cheerfulness with reality. The same conversation in which I told her I had finally found my driver's license in Andrew's glove compartment, after which she accused me of hiding my identity from myself. My problem with Andrew's happiness, she said, was just my way of distracting myself from the real issue at hand, which was that I did not want him to move in. Which was true. What was also true, and which I do not see until my discontent swells to such a size that I can't ignore it any longer, is that I have made the classic, if tired, psychological error of gathering up my issues and foisting them upon an entirely separate human being, fully convinced they are his. What I am fighting for is not a less optimistic, more realistic, more emotionally relevant Andrew; what I am fighting for—and always have been—is a more fully realized, uncompromised *me*, whose wishes and fears and needs I do not hide under compulsions to starve, refusals to have sex, rejections of emotional attachment, and biting assumptions about my parents' failures as parents.

And then, astoundingly, I force this newfound insight under the scrim of consciousness and agree to accompany Andrew on a twelve hundred mile drive to Kansas to see his family. I can only presume I do this to delay the need for action. What I tell myself however is that, because Andrew met my parents, I should meet his, should at least lay eyes on the famous family bakery that has catered every happy and sad occasion in the tiny town's history for thirty years, not to mention that set the stage for Andrew's pristine mental health.

* * *

By the time we head west, Andrew and I have been living together six months and we have finished school. My interview in North Georgia, which I finally told him about, has come and gone.

"If you get it," Andrew says, "I am going to ask you to marry me. If you don't say yes, I'm not moving with you."

I recall the day I ripped down the blackout curtains and hung the blinds, marveling at the sudden realization that it is deftness, not force, that sets a truly effective boundary: porous enough to let in the light of day, yet unbroken enough to afford solitude. This is the gift of Andrew's proclamation. It precludes the need for a battle, or for weeks of unhappy anger, terse discussions assigning fault and blame, even tears. I have only to do this simple thing—decline Andrew's hand in marriage—to set myself free. I am indebted to him, at the same time I feel sad for him, for making it so easy; for making it so that, by the time we cross the Georgia border into Tennessee, and long before the Kansas plain unspools in a monotonous ribbon outside our windows, I am already gone from Andrew's life. He will be wearing mirrored sunglasses, each lens reflecting a tiny white sun. *How fitting*, I will think, *that Andrew has the biggest star of all in his eyes.*

Andrew places his hand on my thigh and smiles. I smile back. It has always been so easy, so safe and so comfortable just to be with him, and it is this that drew me in, then convinced me to stay. If my own family was unavailable and unhappy, if Mitch and Forrest were demanding and untrustworthy, then Andrew was a warm summer day, lush and soft and bright. No sooner do I have this thought than something—a luxuriant thrill that is, paradoxically, freedom from the safety—wends its way through the lower half of my body, a profound want, a yearning. I unbuckle my seatbelt and wriggle out of my shorts, and then out of my underwear. The worn seat leather is scratchy on my bare rear end. Andrew watches me with a funny look until comprehension spreads across his face and then, without speaking or slowing the car, unzips his fly and slides his seat back. I straddle his lap, facing the back windshield. For a moment, I watch where we've been recede. Then I reach down between my thighs and guide him into me, and we hurtle through the Kansas landscape banded together like ill-fated june bugs.

Chapter 25

Ways to Die

THE YEAR I TURNED TEN, I started to have nightmares. I woke, several times a week, writhing from the imagined pain of bullets in my back, knives in my groin, bones broken in falls—hideous scenes of mayhem that varied from dream to dream, but whose end was always the same: I died. One night, I had a particularly disturbing dream about being hit by a bolt of lightning that followed me down the street on legs. I told my mother about it the next day.

"Did you 'bolt' upright in bed?" she asked, laughing.

That night, I, too, tried to see the humor. "Wouldn't it be funny if I dreamed about the lightning bolt again?" I said to myself. I didn't. Over the next several nights, I added other nightmares. "Wouldn't it be funny if I dreamed about being shot? Stabbed? Drowned?"

I quickly saw that naming my fears had the curious effect of, if not dispelling them, at least ensuring I would not dream about them. Soon I was engaged in a nightly, twenty-minute recitation of possible ways my life could end, which, at ten years old, which was surprisingly creative and went something like this: *Wouldn't it be funny if I was thrown in a lake with a concrete block tied to my ankle? Wouldn't it be funny if I fell from a balcony onto a freeway? Wouldn't it be funny if I was strangled to death by my Sunday School teacher? If my head was hacked off with a machete? If I got hit by a driverless car rolling mysteriously down the street? If I was attacked by Hitchcock's birds? If I was stung to death by killer bees? Stabbed to death by steak tongs? Burned to death in my school? Was trampled to death by my own horse? Wouldn't it be funny if I suffocated in outer space?*

My nightmares stopped. In their place, a belief in magical thinking took hold, the idea, not yet articulated, that thought could control outcome.

* * *

Andrew watches me pack. I move quickly, throwing away notebooks and magazines I might otherwise keep, packing chipped mugs and threadbare sweaters I might otherwise throw away. Clothes, books, and dishes all go into boxes together, making each one overly heavy, and the items inside at risk of breakage. It is a frenzy of activity meant to keep my emotions at bay.

Immediately after our return from Kansas, I told Andrew I was taking the job in North Georgia, and that I didn't want to get married.

"Not right now," I said, although it was clear that I meant not ever.

And as easy as that, all of the questions I had harbored over the previous six months fell away, about whether I (or any woman really), having discovered an unfailingly kind and credible man, should ignore the voice inside her that said *it's not enough.* The voice was with me in my quiet moments, hovering over me as I watched TV or brushed Keithan on the porch, floating about the car on my way to the grocery store, echoing back to me in the *thur-ump thur-ump* of the clothes dryer as I sat waiting for our jeans to dry at the Wash-n-Go: *not enough, not enough.* By the time we left for Kansas, the voice had become a noisy chorus chanting in my head in a constant loop, like the Marvin Gaye cassette *(I heard it through the grapevine/no longer would you be mine...)* that finally strangled itself in my tape deck: *not enough, not enough! Not enough, not enough!*

Still, now that moving day is here, the relief I feel is mingled with a sadness I don't want to feel. Mirrored in the boxes that I struggle to carry down the long stilt house steps to the waiting rental truck is a scary but wonderful weight: the gravity of permanently unhooking my future from Andrew's. But reflected in Keithan and Jesse's eyes is the innate canine understanding of how boxes and silence translate to a leaving, and it is there that the residue of uncertainty and guilt and sorrow resides. I am taking the dogs away from Andrew. I am taking Andrew away from the dogs. Never again will they race the shore of the Savannah River together, playing fetch-the-stick in the cold, muddy water; never again will we picnic on the cliff overlooking the river's edge, Andrew tearing away pieces of his turkey-ham and bread crust and tossing them, underhanded, to the two wet, adoring dogs at his feet. No more mornings will they wake, the three of them, into this singularly happy family.

And it is this separation—of Andrew and the dogs, not Andrew and me—on which I focus, a tearing apart what is happening, all because of something that is new in me: a perceived inalienable right to something better that I believe is in my future, that I don't even have words for. With that belief, however, a decades-old shame settles around me. *Who are you to follow your dreams?* is the message implicit in it. *Why are* your *dreams worth destroying someone else's?*

"Who is saying this?" my therapist asks, during one of the last sessions we will have together. I assign the voice to my mother.

"Yes," she says quietly. "You have to learn to hear in a new way. Even though your mother never spoke those exact words, the message was there, in the choices she made for herself."

She means, of course, that in spite of her unhappiness, my mother never left my father.

"Where would you be without your horse?" my mother asked me the summer I was fourteen (if she left my father, I would have to sell my horse). I considered the toll this loss would take on me—to be robbed of the primary thing in my life that, as a gloomy, inward kid, gave me comfort—not my father, but my horse—and I told her that I would be fine, because I thought that, if she was happy, I would be too, and the loss would have been for something.

But she pushed the desire to leave underground, where it lay fallow or festering, reappearing every year thereafter like a trusty perennial. *I want to move out,* she would say one year; *I want YOU to move out,* she would say to my father in another year. In the end, she buried her dreams of freedom, not only because she was afraid to be alone, but because, she would tell me later, she didn't want to leave pain in her wake. Eight years later, when my father would grow a tumor in his bladder, she would say, "I can't leave now that he's sick," and I understood then that there are many ways to lose things: some are taken from you, and some you give away, and it is important to understand the difference.

I am giving Andrew away.

Andrew carries the biggest boxes down the steps as I squat down in the kitchen and put my arms around Keithan and Jesse's necks.

"I'm sorry we have to go," I whisper, and they look back at me quizzically, tails thumping. This, I tell myself, is a message from their heavy hearts. *Maybe you'll change your mind,* they're thinking. *Maybe we could stay.*

"That's all your stuff," Andrew says from the doorway. I look up at him from where I am squatting and I see emotion in his eyes, too. But we have already been through this, the cautious hope that I'll change my mind, the ever-optimistic air that envelops Andrew like a sweet cloud, and through which he reaches out for faintest possibilities. If he has any more hope left of a last-minute stay, it isn't visible from where I am.

"Good luck, you," he says.

We hug goodbye, standing for a long time in the kitchen. It is already unfamiliar, this embrace, and while I don't understand why it should be this way, because Andrew and I hug this way almost every day, later I will know: it was because I had been gone for months.

Backing out of the driveway, I look at the stilt house one more time. The blinds are all the way up to let the late-September sun warm the living room, and I can see Andrew's pained face swim up to the window. The yard is weedy, the pool practically obscured by ivy and cattails. The wire fence looks alarmingly misshapen, and I wonder how it ever contained two energetic dogs constantly lunging and pawing at its perimeter. Here, too, as with the embrace, there is already a strangeness, an unmistakable reserve that, even before I have left, is saying *I no longer know you.*

* * *

It is 1986. While on one hand, nothing more than a piece of paper in a frame, my diploma, which boasts "Master of Science," is my proof that, no matter how intellectually inferior I might feel on my bad days, I am at least capable of this, a graduate degree. This is no small thing for me. If I could somehow wear my degree out into the world, I would. I think about Carline at Goodwill, her name tag riding out ahead of her on the leading edge of her gigantic breast. In similar fashion, I would like for my Master's degree to announce me to a room ahead of my arrival.

My weight, that all-encompassing gauge of how I am really doing, is one hundred thirteen at the time my classes come to an end. I have a small collection of foods I have brought under the banner of "safe" (i.e., won't make me feel fat) to choose from on a daily basis. This includes the occasional palm-sized piece of steak and baked potato half, as well as pretzels and peanut-butter sandwiches.

Still, at times, when I feel frightened or overcome by sadness, my emotions translate so seamlessly into the familiar—boring, even—compulsion to lose weight that it feels like true recovery is years away. Immediately after moving away from Andrew, for example, when my psyche's monotonous lament (*not enough, not enough)* was supplanted by the endlessly repeating vision of his grief-stricken face swimming up to the stilt house window, I quite predictably found myself "not hungry," a psychological, not physical, sensation which led to fingers feeling for my stomach in the mornings even before my eyes opened, a blind hunt for malleable, fleshy rolls that signified I needed to cut back on calories. Then came the palpating of the flesh that padded my hipbones and masked their sharpness, then the flat-palmed measuring of the blank space between the rise of my hips and the valley of my belly, and lastly, there came the weighing, not just once but hundreds of times throughout the day, monitoring the progress of my stomach as it swelled from pre-breakfast flat to post-dinner rounded and back again.

This resurgence of weight-focused measuring and monitoring is the price on the head of taking back my identity, I tell myself, what I must pay for leaving Andrew and causing him pain. Really, though, it is just an old story whose underlying themes never change. And even though I am able to step back, to watch myself grope for swells and belly rolls and anxiously monitor the needle on the scale, it can take me several weeks to wake from the magical dream that is weight loss. This time around, my weight dips to a hundred five before I surface back to the place where I am in control of my thoughts.

* * *

Chickamauga, Georgia, is a tiny, Civil War town, twenty miles south of Chattanooga, Tennessee, my father's birthplace. When I call to tell my parents I'm looking at a house for rent on the outskirts of town, my father tells me he spent many boyhood afternoons at the historic battlefield park, playing on the cannons.

"You know, the bloodiest battle of the Civil War took place there," he says. "In fact, the word Chickamauga means 'river of blood.' "

Instead of hearing this for what it is, an avid historian imparting information that is fascinating to him, I am reminded of his many weary injunctions not to do exactly as I am already doing.

"Well, I can't help what happened a million years ago," I say.

There is a moment of silence on the line and then my father says gently, "The Civil War was a hundred years ago, Sweetie, not a million. All I'm saying is, Chickamauga has a rich history."

Which, it turns out, *is* all he was saying. Along with a rich history, told in park monuments and a Visitor's Center, there is an unspeakable beauty which flies in the face of its gory past. Beyond the ShopRite grocery store, with its perpetually rotting produce smell, the Civil War clothing store that is never open, a dime store, and an ice cream parlor, there are, stretched out flat like an emerald sea, countless farms and meadows where cows, horses, and even goats and alpacas, graze and sleep in the sun. There are red-slatted barns and little white houses and big, fluffy clouds, and a softly undulating mountain chain that encircles the valley on three sides that, as opposed to the weedy yard of the stilt house with which I was instantly unfamiliar on the day I left, make me feel at home right away, the same way I felt driving through the cornfields to get to Tifton three years earlier. These are the foothills of the Appalachian mountain chain, and somewhere in this curvy maze of twisty roads and bluish mountains and endless valleys, there is, I see by my newspaper, an older home for rent with a thirty-foot garden spot on a road called Rollercoaster.

"Do you allow dogs?" I ask the landlord on the phone. This is always my first question now.

"What do you have?" he asks.

I tell him I have a little shepherd mix and a black lab. "Good dogs," I say. "Well behaved."

"Well I got me a great little hunting dog," says the landlord. "Softest mouth you ever saw, can carry a quail a mile without making a dent and drop it still twitching right at your feet."

At first I think he is telling me this to spook me, to have fun at my expense, but he goes on to say he can meet me at the house in an hour, which is when I realize he is simply making conversation. Two days later, my first client at my new job will ask whether my brother squirrel hunts. *My brother's a journalist*, I will say, and my client will sit in the chair beside my desk worrying his cap, not understanding this answer. When I've been here awhile, I will discover that hunting is to rural people what shopping is to city people: a pasttime, a food-gathering mission, a social occasion. Before I understand this, however, the image of the twitching quail, and the moral dilemma it causes to percolate in me (can I rent from someone who kills defenseless animals for sport?) almost keeps me from my appointment to see the house. In the end, because it is getting harder and harder to rent with dogs, I go.

I dress carefully for our meeting. I want to appear neat and professional enough for Mr. Blevins to trust me, but not so polished that he will raise the rent the minute we meet, like Darrin Johnson. To this end, I eschew my usual jeans and sweatshirt for black leggings, a long, purple shirt belted at the waist with a wide scarf, and silver-and-turquoise Israeli coin earrings that hang down to my shoulders and make a satisfying tinkling noise when I walk. I dress it all down a bit

225

with pink high-top sneakers.

The red house at the end of Rollercoaster Road is sturdy-looking, not rickety like the stilt house, or boxy and cheap like the quadruplex. The red wood siding has few buckles, and the chimney has lost some of its bricks around the lip, but other than these telltale signs of age, the house looks strong and capable, and somehow masculine. Tall pine trees tower over it protectively on three sides, obscuring the house from the road and lending it a cabin-like feel. The property backs up to a long, winding, dead-end road that has been cleared for a subdivision on both sides, but whose financing, Mr. Blevins tells me, has fallen through. Rather than calling the eroding expanse of naked plots the eyesore it is, however, he suggests that the lack of homes lends a special kind of privacy that you don't have when your yard backs right up to someone else's. (I nod in agreement.) And thirty yards from the driveway, an area the size of a large living room that was once tilled for a garden lies rocky and dry under the cool October sky. I am, unsurprisingly, smitten by the whole feel of the place, by the camp-like setting and the strangely empty subdivision and the rock-filled garden spot that I will try, unsuccessfully, to hoe clean one afternoon. And although I should know better by now, because I am older and because of all the ways blind certainty has led me to irredeemable houses, I decide, before I even walk inside this one, that it is where I want to live.

What is behind my blind certainty is, of course, a decades-old faith in magic, that I can, simply by believing it, make harmless a neighborhood that is dangerous, make sound a house that is not. It is the natural outgrowth of my conviction, born of the "Ways to Die" list that I compiled as a child to stop my nightmares, that I can think the world safe, innocent, repaired. This idea that things can be made well if I *think them well* means I need never see homes or neighborhoods—or even landlords—for what they really are.

"Let's go in," says Mr. Blevins. He explains that the tenants are home but won't mind if we take a walk-through. Before I can ask questions—*Where are they going? Why are they leaving?*—he pushes open the mudroom door without knocking, and then the door to the kitchen. The sweet smell of pancakes and bacon and wood smoke hits us in the face. A woman standing at the sink spins around.

"Mornin', Diane," he says. "This young lady's here to see the house."

The woman stands wide-eyed, unblinking, her tiny body pushed up against the sink into which water continues to gush. Her hand fumbles behind her for the faucet. She looks at me. I am flushed with embarrassment, for, of course, she did not know we were coming, or she wouldn't be standing in her housedress, hair in a net, hands submerged in a sink full of dirty dishes. I have my first inkling that something untoward is unfolding and that I should leave, but I am unable to move, paralyzed by the need not to offend Mr. Blevins, and also by unabashed curiosity: *I want to see the rest of the house.* Mr. Blevins reaches around Diane, his face within inches of hers, and shuts off the faucet. Without the gushing of the water, the room feels dangerously quiet.

"Don't mind us," he says into Diane's ear. He squeezes her arm, then motions me to follow him. I look down at the cracked linoleum floor with intense interest as I walk past her, my coin earrings jingling with every step.

In the poorly lit living room, the sweet smells of pancakes and bacon give way to the stale odor of cigarettes and old carpet. Smoke hangs in the air like a low, dirty cloud. A man in a gray sweatshirt with the sleeves cut off is pushed up against a table, his back to us, his long, narrow torso hunched over the metal parts of what I guess to be a disassembled tire jack. Next to him is a plate of half-eaten bacon with syrup drizzled over it and a cigarette extinguished in it. In front of him is a long sofa, like a boat, on which two young boys are stretched out in pajamas, watching cartoons. And on the other wall is a big black metal box from which a wavy wall of heat emanates, filling the room with a feverish warmth that is seductive and alarming, making the walls seem to bow in on themselves from the pressure of trapped heat.

"I'm showing the house, Jay," Mr. Blevins says.

Jay whirls around in his chair. The boys on the sofa sit up. I stand rigid so as to keep my earrings quiet while Jay's hard eyes take in the landlord and then me: my face, my giant purple shirt, my pink ankle sneakers. From the TV set comes the silly *meep-meep!* of Roadrunner's never-ending flight from danger. I glance nervously around the room for an escape should one become necessary. My eyes land on the door that leads to the front porch, but where a knob should be, there is only a nail. Anxiety swirls at the base of my spine. Unlike in the kitchen, where my impulse to leave was overcome by my desire to see the rest of the house, I really do want to leave now, but I understand that I can't, that I am hostage to this unseemly and perilous situation and that, if I turn to go, it will only make things explosive, just as walking away from a vicious dog can make it attack. I hold my breath.

Jay jumps up from the table with such force his chair falls over backwards. He grabs a piece of the jack and stuffs it in the waistband of his jeans. Then he bends over and jams his bare feet into a pair of heavily mudded work boots. When he straightens back up, the tire jack in his waistband has shifted slightly; I start to shake and my earrings to tinkle even before my brain fully registers that it is a gun. My heart hammers so hard against my chest that I imagine the outline of it is visible, like a frightened cartoon character's heart pushing out its shirt with every thump. I glance at the landlord for a cue, knowing that no matter what he tells me to do, I will be unable to move. But Mr. Blevins' face is pasty and inexpressive and I realize, with uncompromised clarity, that there is no concern for me here, that I am nothing more than a prop for his act of eviction, and that, like the hunting dog of which he is allegedly so fond, I matter only in that I continue to do my job—which, in this case, is to stand there. *Wouldn't it be funny*, my brain begins, *if I were shot to death in a rental house?*

"You coulda given me some damn time," Jay says thickly, then brushes past us and out of the room. The kitchen door slams first, then there is the muffled slam of the mudroom door, and then the roar of a truck engine coming to life.

"Are you gonna rent the place?" Diane asks from the doorway.

I'd almost forgotten she was in the house, and her soft voice startles me.

"When are you moving?" I ask, knowing that it is a ridiculous question, that Diane and Jay might be in the midst of a lot of things, but moving is not one of them.

Diane looks at the landlord. Mr. Blevins says the house will be available in one week. Her face collapses.

"I got to have some rent, Diane," he says, not unkindly.

This is when I begin to pit Diane's heartrending life story against the shiny story of my own life: Diane and her husband, obviously poor and probably unemployed, with two school-age children, facing eviction from a house that, by the looks of things, they have lived in for quite some time. I, on the other hand, have a good job, no children, and the financial means to live anywhere, but due to an imperative that builds in me when I lay eyes on a derelict house, its mismatched furniture rife with the nicks and scratches of careless, bankrupt living, I am driven to take it from them. If at the time I feel ashamed of my role in this unhappy braiding of our stories inside the Rollercoaster Road house or whether this comes to me later, I no longer remember. What I do remember is that despite, or more likely because of, the awkwardness and the fear and the sorrow—all of the pain building inside that house as I stood there beside Mr. Blevins, awaiting the right to move in—there was an unmistakable quickening of my heart, the same lure I felt toward young, self-destructive Richie Deiner, and coke-addicted, brooding Joe: irrevocably drawn to a core of despair that I clearly saw, but did not know, was my own.

Chapter 26

My Slippery Brain

I T IS FANTASTICAL NOT TO KNOW a thing but to trick yourself into believing you do. In high school, I often skimmed over reading that was crucial to passing a History or Science exam, knowing I hadn't taken in a single word but believing that the information would be miraculously made available to me at the time of the test. I believed fully in the duality of my own mind, that while half of my brain was absorbing necessary facts for an upcoming exam, the other was free to roam the thought-corridors of my social life, ponder the calories of my next meal, relive an argument I'd had with a friend, puzzle out a dream from the night before. While I invariably did poorly on exams, I never stopped believing that my brain could segregate, could glean necessary facts while at the same time immersing itself in a rich emotional sea.

It is another version of blind certainty at work. Like my belief that shoddy construction could be healed by refusing to see it—a denial of facts—the belief in my brain's duality, that one part can fact-hunt while the other tracks endlessly looping thought-trails, is also a conviction of faith. I fully believed that, at the moment I needed them to, the two halves of my brain would unite, and the outcome would be, like hunter and dog, a prized collaboration of intellect and instinct.

Over the years, blind faith in my brain's miraculous abilities would play out in other ways: I would drive toward a destination I hadn't mapped, believing in an innate ability to get there. I would open my mouth to defend a point, with no argument in mind and none on the way. I would compete for a job I did not want, confident that once I got it, it would be something else.

"Believing you are fat doesn't make it so," a therapist once pointed out to me. It was a fact so basic I could feel my consciousness peel away on the spot and head doggedly down the trail of what not to eat for lunch.

Of course, belief doesn't make something so. I am sure I nodded my head in agreement with the therapist. But her argument was cluttered. At a time in my life when fear made a list of creatively horrific ways to die, faith assured me that naming my fears would tame them, which it did. So while I understood her point—that my beliefs and the world's reality were not the same thing and that it was dangerous to equate the two—what I couldn't explain at the time was that, just as a dog doesn't know he's a dog, neither does blind certainty know it is blind. Blind certainty believes, utterly and wholly, in itself.

* * *

The Help Wanted ad for the Behavioral Specialist position at Northwest Georgia Mental Health Center in Fort Oglethorpe, Georgia, clearly stated that the job was working with developmentally disabled adults. These are people over the age of eighteen whose IQ falls somewhere between approximately thirty and sixty-nine points. They can't complete a regular course of high school, although those at the higher end of the IQ spectrum are able to care for themselves, and some can even live alone with help paying bills and grocery shopping. Those at the lower end of the spectrum can do very little, and usually have trouble toileting and dressing themselves.

When I interviewed for the position, I discussed, in graduate school terminology, the theories of behavior management in the intellectually challenged. I listened—carefully, I thought—as the director of the developmental disabilities program and the staff psychologist painted a comprehensive verbal picture of my duties. I would be working partly in a sheltered workshop setting, where higher functioning clients earn a pittance doing rote manual labor such as packaging sample-sized tubes of sunscreen in tiny boxes, and where lower functioning clients sort screws and bolts for the purely educational purpose of learning to distinguish similar from dissimilar. My job would be to consult with case managers and workshop leaders, and to compose, in exquisite detail, behavior management plans designed to either strengthen desirable work and social behaviors (remaining on task, shaking someone's hand when first meeting) or extinguish undesirable ones (these might range from pants-soiling to slapping others to inappropriate hugging or touching). I would test the IQs of new referrals to the center. I would make certain that all current clients had been re-tested within the past three years. I would make home visits to clients too physically disabled to be managed in the center, for the purpose of assessing behavioral management needs with the parents. I would assess, on a regular basis, whether the behavior plans I'd drawn up were working, and make adjustments as needed so that clients could be either more productive or less disruptive.

But I was not listening to my own interview. Not to the director, the psychologist, or even myself. I can only surmise that while half of my brain was in the oblivious presence of the job description, the other half was skating down the hallway in search of my new office, barking excitedly into the phone to Moira about my new job as a therapist, or arguing with the image of Andrew's face, still stubbornly swimming up to the window of the stilt house in search of closure. As usual, I did not know that the crucial information wasn't getting in, until my first day on the job when I discover that I have *not*, as I'd led myself to believe, been hired as a therapist to work with high functioning adults. It is with horrific mounting clarity that I come to understand that my caseload is made up not of depressed or anxious but potentially curable individuals who are wrangling with issues of existential importance, but of people for whom my greatest accomplishment will be to quell their outbursts and update their files. This, the job for which I have attained a Master's degree, left Andrew, moved five hours away, gotten a haircut and bought a new wardrobe, is my new life.

* * *

In the house on Rollercoaster Road, things are also not shaping up exactly as planned. I am struck by how different the house feels from when I first saw it, when it was furnished and warm and smelled of pancakes and echoed with cartoons. Now it is an empty, chilly shell with only the odor of stale wood smoke caught in the wool of the carpet. The living room floor is littered with scraps of paper, and the curtains are gone from the windows. The wood stove, from which a wall of heat emanated that first day, is a cold metal box. In the bedroom where I will sleep, there are crayon scribbles all over the walls that were not there a week ago. The shower curtain in the bathroom has been sliced, a sight which makes me shudder, and the plastic tube that holds the toilet paper roll has been stomped and broken. In the other bedroom, there is a fist-sized hole in the plaster through which I can see the wiring. It is like looking at somebody's exposed blood vessels.

I am sickened by the damage. Back in the kitchen, I lean against the counter and listen to the stillness. Unlike at the stilt house there are no neighborhood sounds—no cars, no children playing, no dogs barking. For the first time in two years, I feel completely alone. Graduate school is over. Moira is on her way to Arizona, to begin a Ph.D. program. Andrew is gone. Mitch and Forrest are long gone. Even my parents, closer by an hour than they were when I lived in Augusta, feel further away because of how their shared struggles with illness have turned them inward. This vacant, pained house is like a caricature of the emptiness I feel inside.

I start outside to begin bringing my things in, but I have no sooner turned toward the door when I am brought up short by a new and particular horror: *There is a gap in the counter where the stove should be.* I whirl around. *There is an empty cavity where the refrigerator should be.*

A sea of nausea wells up in me. I sink to the floor, my back against the wall. I stare at the faded green linoleum curling up and away from the counter baseboard; a trail of mouse droppings runs the length of it like a long ellipsis. My mantra of self-pity kicks in: this is what I get (stolen appliances, punched-in walls, mice) for following my dreams (leaving Andrew, throwing Jay and Diane out of their house, wanting to live here). *This is the life I get for destroying someone else's.*

There is a fluttering on the other side of the kitchen door that pulls me from my reverie. Without getting up, I crack the door. Flapping against the mudroom window is a tiny brown bird, lured into the dim room by a shaft of light, but unable to find its way back out. I get up and go into the mudroom, careful to pull the kitchen door shut behind me, then raise my arms and walk toward the bird, steering it, with my body, outside. Once it is gone, I go to my car and start bringing in my boxes. Later that afternoon, I ask the man from the phone company to help me carry in my L-shaped sofas.

"Where's your stove and stuff?" he asks as we maneuver through the kitchen.

"The last tenants took everything," I say, but it makes me wonder: since he saw right off that the appliances were gone, how I did *not* see it? I, at first, decide it was inattention: I was focused on the chill, the smell, the quiet. But in thinking about it later, I will decide that I *did*, in fact, notice right off, and I will invoke my brain's famed duality to explain my delayed reaction: half my brain was gathering facts (*the appliances are gone! The house is barren!*) while the other half, inspired by this theme of barrenness, set off to navigate its own thought-trail of personal emptiness. In the end, in an emotional climax of clear-eyed understanding, they informed each other: *The house is empty; I am empty. This house and I are one.*

This is when another thought will appear to me, seemingly out of the blue: it wasn't a bird in my mudroom, but *the* bird, the very same one that, six years earlier, delivered my message about the supposed healing powers of addiction, and later the healing powers of recovery; the same bird that warned against Mitch, and that planted an early, cautious hope about Andrew. In its latest visitation it is smacking its wings against the confines of my new house, this time bearing a message not of hope or consequence, but of predictability. Whatever duality I profess, there is but one truth: the habitat of my emptiness is the expected—*and unsurprising*—outcome of my own perceived emptiness. It is a message of logic, of reason, of the brain and body's inevitable interdependence, that I will enact that which I feel, and that which I feel I will make visible around me. It is the oldest lesson of anorexia, and it is, in the Rollercoaster Road house, my earliest sign that the war inside is ending. That, in spite of how I still grope and measure and weigh, I am moving forward, into the rich and tenable realm of the undivided mind.

* * *

A week after the move, Moira drives up for a visit. It is the last time I will see her for a while.

"This place is not that easy to find," she says, wrapping her broad arms around me in the kitchen. It feels good to have her in my sights again, to feel her body-compressing hug that always makes me feel both broken and adored. "You can't see it at all from the road."

"I know," I say. "I love that about it. It's like a little hideout."

"Except you're not hiding out, right?" Moira says. "You have a great new job, you're *available*... aren't you *excited?*"

"I *am*," I say.

I don't say that, in light of what I now know about my new job, my decision not to go on for a doctorate feels misguided. My reasons, at the time I made the decision, were clear to me: after just two years of grad school, I was already feeling the tinges of burnout and wasn't sure I should devote another four years to school. And in spite of the fact that I was doing well in a Master's program, I wasn't sure I would do well in a doctoral one. So at twenty-four, still looking to my mother to draw the margins of my life, I ran my uncertainty by her, knowing her advice on matters of import was historically whimsical and frustratingly uneven. ("I thought Neil was wonderful, a real class act!" she says, years after she has rallied bitterly, along with my father, against our relationship. "You made this bed so you figure out how to get out," she said of my anorexia. "This has nothing to do with us.")

On the issue of a doctoral program, my mother is quick to weigh in.

"You haven't even travelled!" she says. Her message is clear: travel is the hallmark of intellectual sophistication without which I cannot hope to compete in a Psychology doctoral program. I don't argue. I *haven't* travelled. But rather than unmasking this pronouncement, revealing it as the capricious and fleeting and possibly innocently misguided assessment it is, I instead take it in as clear and objective confirmation that I am lacking in what it would take to complete a doctorate. Only now, standing in the Rollercoaster Road house kitchen with soon-to-be-Dr. Moira, who is asking whether my new life doesn't excite me, I feel a mounting anxiety, not unlike what I felt just before Andrew moved in with me: that this new life is a parking space I have blindly backed into.

Moira opens the cabinet door over the sink in search of a glass, and a shower of mouse droppings rains out onto the counter.

"Jesus!" She jumps back and slaps at the front of her chest, then stares at me with a disbelief. "What the *fuck*?!"

I stand in the dark cavity of my kitchen, my hand over my mouth. "The last tenants had a little problem with mice."

"A *little* problem?!" Moira slaps at her chest some more. Then she grabs my shoulder and looks behind me, into the cavity.

"Where is your refrigerator?"

"The last tenants took it when they moved out. Stove, too."

Moira's mouth drops open. "They took the *appliances*? Weren't they in your *contract*?"

I don't tell Moira there is no contract. I can't tell her, because the seemingly effortless and infinite equanimity with which she conducts her life just makes the rocky and ad hoc way I conduct my own stand out in hideous relief.

"Well your landlord owes you a stove and refrigerator. I've never heard of a rental unit without them."

"I don't want to make waves," I say. (Most likely I feared the landlord might do to me what he'd done to Jay and Diane.)

Moira laughs. "Oh, please! He's lucky to have anyone renting this dump. What's his number? *I'll* make waves."

Rather than tell Moira about having a family of four evicted so I could move in, I dig Mr. Blevins's number out of the kitchen drawer, dial it, and hand her the phone. Then I go into the living room to wait. That Moira will always take care of me has been obvious for some time. I can hear her voice, melodic but professional, as she grapples with Mr. Blevins over my rights.

"Okay," Moira says, walking into the living room. "He's pissed but you'll have a stove next week. You're on your own for a refrigerator." She smiles broadly. "You're going to have to learn to do these things yourself," she says. "I won't always be here for you."

Moira stays one night, sleeping on the L-shaped sofa. She is disgusted by the Rollercoaster Road house, it is obvious, but I barely hear her protests about crooked window sashes and cracked linoleum or the front door with the nail for a knob. I know all about these problems, and there doesn't seem to be any reason to make more of them than what they are: evidence that Moira and I are in different places, and that we embody and respond to the truths of our lives accordingly. In emptiness, I draw inward, starvation my icon. Moira, in her hunger, expands outward, as naturally and as unconsciously as her own body.

* * *

After orientation week, which includes filling out a mountain of paperwork pertaining to health insurance (for which I document, in excruciatingly personal detail, my anorexia history, not knowing that I am not required to do this), I am instructed to shadow a Sheltered Workshop supervisor at an adjacent county to the one where I will be working. I am depressed before I even arrive. Already I have spent a week bemoaning the fact that I am not a therapist addressing high-minded thoughts, but a behavior management specialist addressing low-level behaviors. While I have resigned myself to working the job for a year before I bolt, I can't seem to quell the emotions that well up in me when I think about how thoughtlessly I progressed into my erroneous job, and I arrive at the workshop where I am to shadow the supervisor at ten minutes until eight, prepared to be sickened.

The workshop is housed in a simple, one-story, brick building with narrow vertical windows and long wide wheelchair ramps leading to each door. It is surrounded by twenty-five wooded acres and a chain-link fence. Just inside the door, I detect the faint acrid smell of bleach mixed with baby powder. The director, Sally Winfield, meets me in the main area, welcomes me "on board" (as if my job were a giant ship), and leads me through the swinging doors to the workshop itself.

In spite of my plans to be disgusted, I am immediately mesmerized. The workshop is a lively and noisy and interesting place. There is a large, open area, which is where clusters of clients sort bolts into containers or package tiny tubes of sunscreen and toothpaste into slightly larger boxes on a large conveyor belt. There is even a table on which are arrayed a complex assortment of radio parts to be assembled, a task I myself could not do if called upon. Every so often, a voice bellows over the intercom, directing a staff member to pick up a certain telephone line. Around the perimeter of the room are several offices inside which staffers are barking into telephones, scratching in charts, and holding important-looking meetings. The whole place looks like a command center where crucial business is being conducted: plans for an imminent rocket launch maybe, or a war-room drama. I am reassured by the activity. In my mind, thinking only about how I was not going to be the therapist I always wanted to be, I'd envisioned the sheltered workshop as a dingy, sub-verbal entity, where staff members were indistinguishable from clients.

The director points to the back of a man standing in the middle of the room, holding a clipboard with a sheaf of papers threatening to explode from it. He is tall—nearly a foot taller than me—but there is something almost comical about him from behind. His slacks, lime green and polyester, are too tight and three inches too short. His rear end is round and cinched up high like a package. His shirttails hang out of the bottom of his tan sweater like twin flags. A cluster of clients is gathered around him, watching his face and listening intently.

"Fisher." Sally Winfield says, softly but importantly.

Fisher wheels around at the interruption. His collar is unbuttoned, and on the front of his sweater is a long stain, like the scratch in a car that's been keyed.

"Yes, Ma'am," he says loudly, but there is none of the Southern drawl I have come to expect. Instead, his is the baritone, stick-straight speech of a Northeasterner.

"This is the new behavior specialist, from Augusta," Sally says. "Let her shadow you today."

Staring at the comical sight of the too-tall man in the too-short pants and stained sweater, I am visited by the urge to laugh, as if he has dressed himself wretchedly as a great joke, to keep the tension in the room loose. But when Fisher looks at me, I am visited by something else entirely. There is, engraved in his strong face and echoed in his bracing blue eyes, a naïve wonder and a studied gravity that make me catch my breath. This is, quite possibly, the handsomest man I have ever seen. Fisher smiles, and his eyes soften under the curtain of fine brown hair that is cut in a bowl shape around his head (later he will confirm that he did use a bowl). For the rest of the day, in a foreshadowing of the two years to come, I will move about practically inside Fisher's footsteps, like an emerald green meadow in the embrace of a mountain.

Chapter 27

Ways to Live

THERE HAVE BEEN TIMES when I could feel myself stepping from one phase of my life into another. It is like standing at the edge of a creek or cliff and looking across the chasm into a whole new land. Suddenly, I see that the way I've been doing or thinking about things is outdated, maybe has been outdated for a very long time, but it took until that moment to notice that either the creek had dried or the land had drawn in on itself; either way, the space between where I am and where I'm going has narrowed enough to jump.

This happened at age twenty, when I walked into my first anorexia support group and realized I had already moved on from the worst of my illness. While my weight still hovered at ninety pounds, thirty pounds below what was reasonable for me, I knew, without question, that there had already been a fundamental shift in my thinking. Weight gain would not come immediately, but never again would extreme weight loss hold the blind promise of redemption.

It is this jump, from one phase of my life to another, I believe I am making again the day I get my first paycheck from the Northwest Georgia Mental Health Center. Check in hand, I stare across the abyss into the eyes of a very wealthy me.

I call home. My father answers.

"Guess how much I'm putting in savings this month?!" I shout into the phone.

"Twenty-five dollars?!" he shouts back.

"Nine *hundred* dollars!" This is two-thirds of my paycheck. I press my ear to the phone, listening for my father's audible shock and pride. *Nine hundred dollars!* he is thinking. *How responsible! How dedicated! How mature!* The hum of his electric typewriter falls off into silence. His chair creaks and I can almost see him leaning back from his desk, smiling.

"That's terrific, Sweetie," he says. "But you should have some fun with your money too. Go buy yourself something."

"I will!" I say.

But I won't. I won't because, of course, saving money is another tentacled arm of anorexia. Already I am making plans to save a thousand dollars next month, over a thousand the month after that. I don't think about *what,* exactly, I am saving for, or how I will know when the time is right to spend, or about the fact that I actually need some of the money I am stashing away from myself to survive on, to pay for rent and groceries and utilities. And I certainly do not consider how this savings bank of money echoes the savings bank of calories I used to maintain in my head on the pretense that I would reward myself with a slice of cheesy pizza or a rhomboid of silky, chocolate cake as soon as I'd built up a large enough reserve (i.e., lost another two or five or ten pounds). Instead, I think about how grown up I am. How like a real adult it is to delay gratification (read: not meet my needs; read: not follow my dreams) until such time as I have somehow determined I've earned the right.

The "somehow," of course, is what is at issue. How I will determine it is time to reward myself is a mystery even to me, and it is because it does not matter, is not the point. It is the *saving*—some might call it denial—the hoarding of surplus (calories, money)—that is the point, that is for me a safety net woven from the things I desperately want but cannot have.

"A half-sandwich is the hallmark of a whole woman," my mother's voice comes back to me.

"Don't you want it?" I asked her, of the discarded bread cap.

"Oh, yes," she said, and proceeded to eat her exposed sandwich as if the bun-top had ceased to exist.

Desire without gratification was my mother's mantra before it was mine. In one story, she tells me, her own mother indulges in creamy milkshakes while she, ten years-old and chubby, stands behind her, hoping for a spoonful. Because my grandmother was embarrassed by my mother's weight, she withheld the sweets my mother craved. Presumably, there was a promise behind it (you can have one when you lose weight) but, as often happens—be it habit or the mind's attempt to accommodate the new order of things—the longer you do not get what you believe you want, you begin either to crave or question it. For my mother and, later, me, the promise itself (starve, save) became the focus, the thing we were wedded to more than the reward (eat, spend), satisfying as it did some other craving: for control, most likely. *How much discipline we have! How not like others, or how like a real adult!* Soon, the withholding itself became the seductive thing that completed the cycle of desire.

* * *

I don't tell my father my plan to save thousands of dollars a month. In time, I will call and surprise him with how much I have saved. ("Guess!" I will say again, a few months from now. "A thousand dollars?" he will say. "*Ten thousand* dollars!" I will say, and again I will hear the hum of his typewriter fall away, my signal that I have superseded in importance, if for only a moment, his work.)

I race to the bank. Beside me in the passenger seat my paycheck lies open and smoothed flat, and every few seconds I look over at it admiringly, like it is a new baby. Maybe I will heed my father's suggestion and go to the grocery store after the bank and buy myself a *Glamour* magazine. In front of me on the narrow rural road is a wide, brown Plymouth that seems to have too much weight in the driver's side and keeps drifting toward the center line. Ordinarily, this kind of sloppy driving would just irritate me, but today it infuriates me, and I push harder and harder toward the car's bumper, trying to deliver a message of *hurry up*. The driver of the car doesn't get it, and I arrive at the bank two minutes past closing.

Fuming, I vow to deposit my paycheck the next morning before work. I fold it and stuff it into my pocketbook and drive another ten minutes, at breakneck speed for no reason, to the ShopRite. In the front window are signs announcing that chicken livers are twenty-four cents a pound, cigarettes sixty-four cents a pack, and that food stamps are accepted. Chicken livers are actually something I have learned to eat, however without a refrigerator or stove (which the landlord is to deliver sometime in the next two weeks), I can only buy non-perishables. Along with my carton of Marlboro Lights, I plunk down a six-pack of Diet Coke and the *Glamour* magazine on the conveyor belt and start to scrounge in my pocketbook for a twenty I've forgotten I gave to the water company earlier in the week.

"How's the house?" says a soft voice. I jerk my head out of my pocketbook. Standing in front of me on the other side of the conveyor belt, wearing the sky-blue, button-down smock of the ShopRite employee, is Diane.

A frisson of anxiety darts up my neck. "Oh! It's—good," I say. "Are you working here?" It's a ridiculous question. Diane looks older, like in the space of a few weeks, her cheeks have lined out and her eyes sunken into the creases. My face is hot and tingly. She bags my purchases.

"Your total's eighteen dollars, twenty-three cents," she says. "We got us a place not far from here. It's real clean and all."

I feel a pang of envy at the mention of clean. "That sounds great."

"It's small," Diane says. "The boys had to go live with my sister in Mobile till we can get us a bigger place."

The pang of envy turns to a sharp stab of guilt. I begin to sweat. I paw through my pocketbook but nothing looks familiar. At last I catch sight of my paycheck. Regretfully, I extend the oversized, tan, handsomely printed and carefully signed check (complete with MS, for Master of Science, after my name) to Diane.

"I thought I had a twenty but I can't find it."

Diane reaches for the check and a shadow slides across her face. "We don't have this kind of money here," she says, almost condescendingly. She slides the check back across the conveyer belt and points to a sign by the cash register on which is scrawled, *Thank-You for shoping* (sic) *at ShopRite, $500 limit on checks.* My paycheck is fourteen hundred dollars.

"This is all I have," I say. I am sweating profusely now and my face is fiery hot. I would leave, except I need the cigarettes. I do not own a credit card, and I am so caught off guard by everything that it does not occur to me to write a check. Diane glances at the line forming behind me, takes my paycheck and goes to the manager's station. Although I do not turn around to watch, I can feel their eyes on me. When Diane returns, she counts $1,381.77 into my shaking hand. We do not make eye contact again. I thank her and walk stiffly out of the store. Outside, the late afternoon sunlight is strange and the ground has become convoluted and uneven, and I must work hard to navigate the twenty feet or so between the door and my car without falling.

In the parking lot, I sit in the car and wait for my shaking to stop. There is so much I wish I could say to Diane. Most importantly, I'd like to tell her that I stew in a complicated regret made up of true sorrow for her troubles and true sorrow for my own, the result of the injuries she and Jay inflicted on the house. I would tell her that I had already made up my mind to live in the house before I knew it was occupied, that the landlord led me to believe that Diane and Jay were moving of their own accord, that by the time I understood what was happening, I was powerless to stop it. I would not tell Diane about my habit of choosing terrible houses the way other women choose terrible men, or that the Rollercoaster Road house, with its seedy prologue of eviction, surpasses even the dysfunction and ruin to which I have become accustomed. And I would not tell her, because I do not know yet that she, the focus of this latest house drama, is just a bit player, and that, in time, all the regret and sorrow and anger I feel will take its rightful place as nothing more than a distraction from the real issue, that of believing it is better to deny my needs than to satisfy them. Something tells me it would not comfort her to know this.

* * *

Cancer, meanwhile, has lifted its head from dreamy inconsequence to become, once again, a nightmare of great import. My mother gives me the news a few months after I'm settled into my new job, but I sense they've known about it longer.

"How bad is it?"

"It's cancer," she says into the phone, softly.

I know not to ask whether this means it is back for good this time, because no one knows. Not even the doctor, who told us early on that cancer is a fickle visitor, as likely to depart unexpectedly (which it did) as it is to kill. I also don't ask because, for three years now, the amount of time my father has been dealing with bladder cancer and its outposts of chemotherapy, surgery, and an excruciating bout with shingles, my mother and I have had an unspoken agreement to communicate only sketchily about the details. I suspect that she is protecting me from worry, although I tell myself that my father wouldn't dare die now, that he will most certainly survive until such time as we have put issues of discord and disappointment behind us, that he *owes* me at least that. I tell myself that when my father's time is up, I will be at an age (fifty at least) and a level of maturity (neither frightened by, nor inured to, the reality of his death), that it would be, while not welcome, not a shock either, not something that makes me rail against time and my own stubbornness for the way each cheated me out of a loving relationship with him. My father will be into his eighties by then, the age at which many lives come naturally and expectedly to an end, and he will leave behind, in me, a healed connection, replete with appreciation and forgiveness and respect and admiration. No longer will I cling to hurtful memories of my college years when, angered by my newfound sexuality, he accused me of promiscuity and drug use; nor will I carry the sting of his admonition that if my brother hit me, I must have done something to deserve it. He will have apologized for his insensitivity, and I will have apologized for hating him for all the things he did imperfectly, like not tucking me in after age eight because I told him not to, even though I really wanted him to; for how he drove me to school in chilly silence because we could not talk, and then, slumped over my books in homeroom, I immediately missed him. I will have apologized, above all, for not understanding that his missteps were human and unintentional, and most of all, regretted. Then and only then will he die.

"We're doing everything we can," my mother says.

* * *

Reassured once again by the magic of blind certainty, I tuck away the information about my father and continue about my life. I am quickly at ease with my job. I have discovered that administering IQ tests to earn a salary is no different from administering them to earn a grade in school, and while it isn't interesting, it also isn't hard. Images of Moira, whom I haven't heard from since she left the Rollercoaster Road house three weeks earlier, and of Andrew, working at the prison in Augusta, bubble up, but though both depress me, I can't push them away. I'm envious of Moira's seemingly fluid life, and sad for Andrew's seemingly stagnant one. And while I can't know the veracity of either, they keep my gaze comfortably averted from my own lackluster life. Mercifully, a new image soon bubbles up in their place: the memory of the sight of Fisher, tall and solid, his strong, straight shoulders and muscular voice commanding the attention of an entire workshop.

"Where do you live?" he asked me the day we met, meaning, did I live in Fort Oglethorpe, where the main office was, or did I live in Summerville, where my workshop was based. But I was so busy studying the generosity of his angular jaw, swimming in the swells of his ocean-blue eyes, that I answered in embarrassing specifics.

"In Chickamauga," I said. "The corner house on Rollercoaster Road."

Fisher nodded, and his umbrella of shiny brown hair shimmered under the fluorescent lights. "I know that place," he said. "Always wanted to see inside it."

At the time, my heart skipped with excitement, but although I'd said I'd be glad to show it to him, neither of us followed up. More and more now, during the long mornings testing clients and the long

247

afternoons crafting vague, lifeless notes in client charts about behavior goals (*M. seems to be more aware of positive and negative consequences of his behavior and the incidence of failure to act in appropriate manner appears to be decreasing, according to his Level One supervisor)* I relive that first meeting with Fisher, and am surprised to discover that it still thrills me. I consider calling Moira to ask how to proceed, but I quickly let this thought go. I'm fairly certain that Moira, en route to her doctorate, would now see man problems as the trivial time-suck of people without better things to do, and I do not want to open the conversation that will make me see it, too. And so, as I try to do with my thoughts of her and Andrew, I push thoughts of Fisher and his shimmery hair and eyes out of my mind.

But it doesn't work. Two weeks later, when a memo circulates to all behavior specialists and workshop supervisors stating that we are to attend a staff meeting at the main (read: Fisher's) Sheltered Workshop, I am elated, and I vow that, this time, if Fisher mentions my house, I will throw open the door and yank him in.

I am so excited about the meeting that I practically can't sleep the night before. I plow through my closet in search of a sexy top (which I do not own; all of my tops are long and loose) to pair with form-fitting slacks (which I also do not own). Finally I settle on my favorite pair of jeans, snug in the hips and ankles, a long black sweater, and tan boots, although long after I am in bed I continue to mentally rummage through my closet for something cuter and sexier. At midnight, irritated by my shallow desire, I finally fall asleep, and at six a.m., my eyes pop open and I am again instantly irritated by my own anticipation of the moment I will see Fisher again. I shower, feed Jesse and Keithan, eat a breakfast of six peanut butter crackers and Diet Coke, and dress. I brush my hair until it, like Fisher's, shimmers, and I paint narrow black lines under my eyes. I even dot a tiny amount of blush on my cheeks, something I do not do on an ordinary workday. I wave goodbye to Jesse and Keithan rather than hugging them, because I don't want to chance getting dirty, and drive the fifteen minutes to the training center, awash in a nervousness that further aggravates me. If Fisher doesn't ask me out, I don't know what I will do; if he does ask me out, I know I won't be able to concentrate until the moment of our date. Either outcome will prompt a call to Moira, I tell myself, doctorate or no doctorate.

The scene inside the workshop is much as it was the first time I was there. Fisher, this time wearing snug jeans, the same too-small tan sweater, and running shoes, stands at the center of the room, clipboard in hand, the din of chatter and busyness encircling him like water. His rear, no longer looking like a silly package waiting to be mailed, is round and firm and brilliantly displayed in faded Levi's of ample length.

For several minutes, I watch the clients watch him. That they respect Fisher is obvious. They flock around him but keep an admiring and appropriate distance. They do not reach out to touch his hair or sleeve, as my clients do with me at my training center, or appear in his path to make demands or declare their affection. Instead they part to make way for him when he walks across the room. They quiet when he speaks, smile when he smiles, laugh when he laughs, and not before. Likewise, the older female staff members—the woman who drives the van, the field services manager, the program director—seem to admire Fisher in a blatantly maternal way, one of them even informing me that Fisher needs a wife, and that until he finds one, she will continue to fix him supper and leave it outside his apartment door twice a week.

"Can't he cook?" I ask.

"Oh, honey," she says.

In the staff meeting, it strikes me that it is exactly this combination of Fisher's commanding presence and boyish vulnerability that is so appealing to clients and coworkers alike. He is at once father figure and adopted son, inspiring and irresistibly pamperable. Clients seem to stand straighter in his presence, women to preen and smile. Fisher is one of those rare people, it occurs to me, who move others to greatness, who is in possession of some kind of magical mirror whereby those in his presence, from the able-bodied to the handicapped, see themselves as they see him: as powerful and handsome, kindhearted, and lovable.

By the time Fisher gets to my house that evening, I have swept and tidied all the rooms and thrown away the Sunday paper from two weeks earlier. I have cleaned the bathroom and arranged a stack of books on the coffee table with *Zen and the Art of Motorcycle Maintenance* on top. I have also showered, changed into my other pair of favorite jeans, and tried—in vain, of course—to light the wood stove. I am vaguely aware of going to a lot of trouble for Fisher's visit ("I'd just like to see the inside of that house and then I'll be on my way," he'd said), but I tuck the information away from myself, into a receptacle labeled *What You Do When Company Comes*, rather than leaving it where it belongs, in the receptacle labeled *What You Do When You Might Be Falling In Love With Someone You've Only Just Met, and the Image of Your Ex- Boyfriend Is Barely a Month Old*.

At six o'clock, when Fisher arrives, Jesse and Keithan make a huge racket in the kitchen, barking and leaping onto each other's backs and snarling in mock rage. As soon as I open the door, they throw themselves against Fisher's legs, and without a word to me, he sinks to his knees in greeting. I am reminded of Forrest fawning over Keithan the first time he came to the quadruplex, and I am as overwhelmed by the gesture now as I was then.

"This is great!" Fisher says, unfolding himself from Keithan and Jesse and rising to his full height again. He is looking past me into the living room. He grabs my shoulders with both hands and squeezes, which unleashes a warm current of adrenaline in my groin. Then he strides across the kitchen floor past the cavernous dark holes where the stove and refrigerator should be, and plants himself in the center of the living room, legs slightly spread, hands on his hips, the sleeves of his sweater pushed up high and bunched over his biceps. In his tight jeans, and with his bulging upper arms, he looks like some kind of plain-clothes police officer, daring ordinariness to show its face. I feel cupped in his presence, and giddy with admiration.

"Wow," he says, nodding his head slowly as he takes in the dingy white walls, the low ceiling, the uneven window sashes. "This house has so much *character*." He raps his knuckles on the cold wood stove, walks over to the windows and looks out at the grass growing on the front porch, then up toward the mountain, where the far-away outline of Covenant College, the alma mater of his fundamentalist religious education, is visible in the fading light. Fisher exhales softly.

"There's a real presence here," he says. "I can feel it. It's Godly." He turns around to face me, his bright blue eyes shining out from behind the blunt-cut curtain of his hair. "You know that?"

Suddenly, I feel I have not appreciated the house enough. It does not occur to me yet to wonder why Fisher might find the Rollercoaster Road house, with its drab carpets and curling linoleum and missing appliances "Godly." And it certainly does not occur to me to consider that Fisher, unable to dress or cook for himself, might, like the house itself, have good bones but cavernous deficiencies. And although the word "Godly" gives me pause, I tell myself it is because of my disdain for spiritual language. I myself had no name for the ache of desire I felt upon seeing the house for the first time and smelling the seductive aroma of wood smoke and maple syrup. I couldn't explain to Moira, though I'd tried, the comfort I took from the protective arm of the undeveloped cul-de-sac encircling the shoulders of the property. And yet, I felt so strongly about it that, even though the house was inhabited by people who arguably needed it more than I did, I felt compelled to make it mine. If I had to come up with a word equivalent to Fisher's "Godly," then I would have to say I *craved* this house, similar to the way I had craved the cornfields behind my apartment in Tifton the first time I saw them, and forgot altogether about my plan, months in the making, to bring Keithan with me.

"Have you ever felt like you *had* to have something," I say, "like there was some kind of a seductive pull that you couldn't explain, but knew you were helpless to resist?" I am talking about the house but I am looking up at Fisher's angular face, onto which an afternoon shadow is beginning to creep, at the way his hair grazes the top of his sweater collar and then kicks out in ten different directions. A bead of sweat forms on his temple, then inches its way down, quickening over his cheek.

Fisher looks at me solemnly. "I think so, yes," he says, tugging upward at his sleeves. His forearms are wide and flat.

"Well, that's how I feel," I say, adding quickly, "I mean *felt*. That's how I felt about this house when I saw it. It had *that* kind of pull."

I show Fisher the rest of the house, which is still mostly empty. There's a small area between my bedroom and the living room that I call a dining room, though I don't have a table. In my room there is a mattress but no nightstand or dresser. I open the spare bedroom door so Fisher can see the punched-in wall, a sight which makes him groan. I tell him about Diane and Jay, the eviction and the gun, the stolen refrigerator and stove. He listens with an intensity I never saw in Mitch or Forrest, an intensity of which, it occurs to me, only men with a certain hue of blue eyes are capable.

We sit for a long time on the sofa as the light fades from the room, and talk. Fisher is thirty-six, and has been at the training center for ten years. He loves his clients, his parents, his brothers, God. He loves the van driver who brings him dinner two nights a week. He lives for the New York Jets.

"If I could do anything," he says, "I'd be a writer."

At eight, we share a pack of peanut butter crackers and a warm Diet Coke. He asks about my family, how many siblings I have, why I moved to the area. I tell him about my father, about the cancer. Fisher's face turns grave.

"No, no, he's going to be fine," I say quickly. "This is just a temporary thing." As if tumors were pimples, or cancer a bad cold.

Fisher nods uncertainly. I change the subject to his family. He has two brothers. He grew up in a fundamentalist Christian family. His parents were strict: no dancing, no music, no cursing, no dating.

"Clean living," I say. I don't think about the irony of a "clean" upbringing resulting in a stained and tattered man, although I should. I am too busy staring at his perfect face with its rugged features, the solemn blue eyes, the shiny hair. Likewise I don't think about how much my father would not like him, how, if my relationship with Gentile but religiously unaffiliated Andrew was "devastating" to him, a relationship with a dedicated Christian might just be ruinous.

At nine, Fisher gets up to leave and there is a moment of awkwardness as I wonder whether he will kiss me. Because I sense that we are not ready for the intensity of a kiss, I hope he will not try. Fisher looks down at me on the sofa.

"I like you," he says simply, and a flush of gratitude goes through me. That he has not gushed some emotion-laden, false-sounding accolade, like, "We're soul mates," or, "I could really see us having a future together," relieves me.

"I like you, too," I say, looking up at him.

He nods, looks around the living room one more time, then back down at me. "Maybe we can take a drive sometime."

"That would be great," I say.

"I'll call you at the training center. I don't have a phone in my apartment."

"You don't have a *phone*?" I say. "Geez, Fisher, together we could practically unfurnish a whole house."

He throws his head back and laughs.

After Fisher is gone, I walk through the house and try to see it through his eyes. I open all of the doors, staring especially long at the punched hole in the spare room that made him, like me, recoil in pain. *This house is just how I hoped it would be inside,* he had said after the tour, and I turn this simple yet somehow momentous statement over and over in my mind. Here is a man for whom my house is a source of pleasure, a man who sees beyond its obvious problems to the beauty at its heart. Even in my romantic reverie, at the heart of which is an entrancing dream about the loveliness of Fisher's sincere, attentive gaze and the way it attaches itself to me, the profundity of what he has said, and what I believe it means, is not lost on me. Fisher is a man who will see what is beautiful in me amid everything that I currently believe is unbeautiful. I lie down on the mattress in my bedroom, pull a blanket against the cold, and sleep. In the morning, I dress for work but think only of Fisher, square-jawed and silent and gazing at the mountain, the outline of Covenant College in his eyes and a strange and fundamental longing etching a crease down his cheek. After work, I come home and walk through the rooms of my house again, listening for the lingering echo of Fisher's voice. I actually think I hear it, ricocheting off the walls and floors, but then I realize it is the voice of my landlord talking to his son, as they struggle to carry my new stove into the kitchen.

Chapter 28

The M&M Cure

A MONTH INTO MY JOB, I become aware that M&M's are the panacea of the Sheltered Workshop. In every chart I review, many dating back ten years or more, the little brightly-colored candies have been the standing go-to for behavior changes big and small. When Debra, one of the instructors, needed a reluctant client to board the center's bus for home, she could usually get him on it with M&M's. When she needed to train another client to flush after using the toilet, she did it by pairing flushing with the receipt of M&M's. And when she needed to put an end to her client, Manuel's, intermittent clapping outbursts, she did it by offering M&M's in exchange for silence.

Many of the behavior modification plans ("b-mods," they were called), including Manuel's, were exquisitely detailed and clearly spelled out by Damien, the previous behavior specialist, who also provided behavior tracking forms to instructors for monitoring progress. If the instructor was vigilant about following the plan and recording the results—in Debra's case, this meant making notes several times throughout the day about how many times Manuel clapped—then gauging whether it was working was as easy as glancing at the forms. If there was no progress or progress was too slow, Damien could revise the b-mod plan and the whole enterprise would go forward again with the new revisions in place.

It is a beautiful system, behavior modification, and I was immediately drawn to the brilliance of it in graduate school. The supposed ease of getting what you wanted out of people simply by manipulating rewards and punishments fascinated me. It was like seeing behind the scenes of a magic trick. Once I understood how to do it—by rewarding closer and closer approximations to the ultimate, desired behavior until the behavior itself was achieved consistently—I trained Jesse to sit, stay, and heel in a week using dog biscuits. During the time when I was angry with my father, I trained my mother to call me for weekly chats and not him, by rewarding her with my newsy, happy voice, and punishing him with petulant silence. It seemed to me there was no behavior you couldn't mold, given enough time and the right incentives.

By the time Damien quit and I was hired, Manuel's no-clapping plan had been on the books for five years. According to Debra's formal request for a new plan, which I have just now received, Damien's plan never really worked, and although Manuel's clapping only got worse, Damien refused to make changes.

I flip through Manuel's chart, looking for the chink in the magic trick. It doesn't take me long to find it. Manuel is to receive five M&M's at the end of every ten-minute span he goes without clapping. This means that, over the course of a six-hour day, he could receive as many *a hundred eighty* M&M's. Most people, including the intellectually challenged, only really enjoy a finite amount of candy before they get sick of it and no longer want any more. This is why using a few M&M's to mold low-occurrence behaviors like boarding a bus or flushing a toilet is fine, but giving someone thirty per hour is pointless.

And Manuel's plan is not the only one with an M&M problem. M&M's are written into almost every b-mod plan in the center, and even when they are not effective—and the evidence is right there, in the behavior tracking forms—no one, as far as I can tell, has ever said *let's try crackers*, or *how about nuts* or for that matter, *what about something that is rewarding in an entirely different way, like one-on-one attention, or a special walk around the grounds?* Instead, even though the center is rife with sugar-sated, behaviorally challenged clients, M&M's are still handed out like medicine, and there are cases of them in the cabinets, along with flashcards and interlocking blocks with numbers on them, under the pretense of being a true and useful tool. *My center needs a b-mod plan to wean it off M&M's,* I think, and just as I start to consider how I would do this, Sherry, the center secretary, beeps the intercom on my phone and announces that Moira is on Line 1.

It has been two weeks since we talked. I am so happy to hear Moira's voice that I forget about M&M's. She tells me excitedly about registering for classes and meeting her professors, and how they already call the students *"Doctor* so-and-so." A pang of envy goes through me. I say I'm happy she's happy, and then I tell her about Fisher and his visit to the Rollercoaster Road house.

"He said it's *Godly?"* Moira says. I can hear the enormous smile lighting up her face.

"He said he's always known about the house but never seen inside. He said it's just how he'd hoped it would be."

"He hoped it would be a dump?"

"Moira!" I say. "It is *not* a *dump!* I have a great view of the mountains now that the leaves are almost gone."

"I've been there," Moira says. "You have exposed wiring. You have a *nail* for a doorknob. You have mice crapping on your plates. You have no *heat.* What do you plan to do when winter gets there? Freeze to death while appreciating the view?"

I squirm in my chair. I used to think Moira would be a good therapist because she could always shake me up but still make me feel loved. I tell myself it is because she is so far away now that her confrontations feel like accusations. In truth, they feel bad because I am depressed, and I am depressed for exactly the reasons Moira mentioned, and then some. The house is already uncomfortably cold. Mice are scratching inside the walls. On my desk is a stack of requests for b-mod plans, repetitive requests for repetitive behaviors that, as far as I can tell, will remain present as long as M&M's are the magic pill. I am uncomfortable at home and frustrated at work. I am beginning to see that my plan to escape Andrew might have been too hastily committed to, enacted at the expense of a more well-researched one.

"The wood stove works. I just haven't figured out how to keep it lit," I say. I tell her that I bought a kerosene heater at the flea market, but I don't tell her that it belched a thick greasy plume of smoke, blackening the ceiling in my living room and making me cough all night from the fumes. "Fisher said he'd show me how to build a fire in the wood stove that won't go out."

"So, *Godly*, huh? Is this guy a Jesus freak or something?"

I lower my voice. "I think he's just really *spiritual*," I say, hating the way it sounds before it's even out of my mouth. Still, that Fisher felt a connection to the house that seemed to sidestep an appreciation of architecture or decorating or even functionality was obvious, and while I will later call it what it really is, a shared material anorexia, for now, "spiritual" is the best word I can come up with.

Moira cackles. "*Shee*-it," she says.

I glance out my door to the main office where Sherry sits answering the phone, and for a moment my attention peels away from Moira. Sherry's obesity depresses me, unlike Moira's, which I practically hold up as a philosophical statement. While Moira and I have discussed at great length all the ways we've let our weight define us, Sherry, I presume, is blind to the underpinnings of her weight problems. Why this should concern me in this moment I can only conjecture later: a part of it is jealousy couched as irritation: doesn't she deny herself *anything?* But the other part is that, suspended in a job that screams self-sabotage and talking to soon-to-be Doctor Moira, Sherry is the physical embodiment of my own robotic march toward decay.

"You still there?" Moira says.

"You don't get it," I say. I tell Moira that Fisher has a real sense of what's important to his life. That he lives in a studio apartment and that the only thing he owns besides clothes is a pickup truck. That he doesn't even have a phone. I squash down the niggling anxiety that is pecking, like a new chick, at the shell of my own disbelief. (*I know why I have nothing; why does* he *have nothing?*)

"He says he doesn't believe stuff makes us happy," I say. (Actually, Fisher said that material possessions interfere with a person's relationship with God, but I am not about to repeat this.)

"Holy shit!" Moira shouts into the phone. *"You've found yourself in a man!"* Moira cackles with delight. I stare glumly down at my desk, on which Manuel's bulging chart lies open like a bloated pig.

"I gotta go," Moira says. "Keep me posted on the Jesus freak. Don't immaculately conceive anything!" She cackles some more and then punches her phone's off button with a fingernail that I know is cherry red and flawlessly manicured.

For several minutes after the line goes dead, I sit in the chilly silence of my office, an intense loneliness bubbling up inside me. When Sherry's phone rings again, I close my eyes and wish for it to be Fisher, although, based on what I now know about him, I suspect it could be several weeks, maybe even months, before I hear from him. *If* I hear from him. In the void created by the end of my phone call with Moira, and the new, unwelcome thought that Fisher's ascetic strivings might extend to relationships, I feel immobilized, crushed in the helix of a job I do not want, a barely habitable house, and growing feelings for a man whose quest for spareness may outspare even my own.

With enormous effort—my body feels like it weighs a thousand pounds—I get up from my chair and start out to the workshop to talk to Debra about Manuel. On the way, I catch a glimpse of myself in a darkened office window and am surprised to see that my reflection is not one of massive proportions, that, if anything, I look gangly, and even sort of gaunt. I remember being in the hospital five years earlier and inspecting, with great distress, a stubborn roll of flesh around my waist. I was sixty pounds underweight yet the visuals of fat were all I could see. Later that same day, walking past the nursing station window, I caught an unexpected glimpse of myself and was stunned by what I saw: the literal *scaffolding* of my body poking through my clothes; so undernourished was I that I could not believe I had enough life left in me to still be walking around. Starvation made a trickster of my mind, so that I saw myself as flabby when in fact I was emaciated. Caught off guard by my own reflection, however, with no time to "fix" what I saw, I saw the truth. At the moment I walk past my reflection in the darkened office window on my way to Debra's workshop, expecting heft but surprised by gauntness, I am reminded yet again of the message inherent in my chosen disease: emptiness is my modus operandi. I seek it out, I inhabit it, I covet it, I feel great pain around it. I then deny the emptiness, until such time as it makes itself undeniable. Endlessly repeating behavior is the province of any good behavior specialist, the cycle of which I am seemingly unable to break.

* * *

"Thank God you're here," Debra says. "Manuel's driving me batty." She folds her freckled arms across her chest and gives a quick, exasperated shake of her head. Her body is a rectangle. A shiny "D" hangs from a gold chain around her neck.

Debra's workshop, which is the size of a large classroom, smells of chlorine bleach. Twenty-five clients sit two to a table, trays of brightly colored pegs and pegboards in front of them. Amid the din of repetitive speech, formless laughter, and the radio playing country music, is the occasional sound of clapping. It is so noisy that I wonder how it is possible for her to find Manuel's clapping disruptive. But rather than question her complaint (which, I have been told, is what "sank" Damien), and although I already know what the problem is, I begin the line of assessment that precedes any good b-mod plan. *How long have you had this problem? How have you tried to fix it? How did that work?*

Debra says she's had the problem with Manuel "forever," that she gives M&M's in exchange for him not clapping, that it works for about half an hour.

"Manuel knows the clapping aggravates me," Debra says. She whirls around and points at him. "Don't you, Manuel! Don't you know it aggravates me!"

Manuel, a chubby, middle-aged man wearing a V-neck white undershirt and loose-fitting blue jeans, smiles broadly and claps rapidly twice in the air.

"Manuel, stop!" Debra barks.

"Manuel, stop!" echo several clients.

"Manuel, stop!" says Manuel, clapping the air twice, obviously delighted by the way his name ricochets about the room.

My head begins to throb. "What kinds of things does he like?" I ask Debra, "that we could use to reward him for not clapping?"

"Just M&M's," she says.

I explain the problem with sweets in general.

"Well, I don't know what else he likes," Debra says. "And I got too many other clients to worry about without having to keep Manuel happy."

My pen begins to tap a novel of Morse code on my thigh and a thick black cloud anchors itself behind my eyes. "Okay, then," I say. I tell Debra I'll make a home visit, talk to Manuel's mother, and try to come up with some ideas.

"But for now," I say, "just try *not* to hear the clapping. Knowing it bothers you makes it fun for Manuel. If you were to stop responding to it, my guess is he'd quit doing it. So we might not even need a plan."

"So when do I give him the M&M's?" Debra says.

Which is when the storm in my head explodes, and I go into my office and call my boss and make an appointment to talk to him at the first of the month.

* * *

Ted Bolin is a stout, balding man in his early forties, with kind brown eyes that constantly search the room as if looking for a way out. I thought this was inattention the first time we met, but eventually came to believe that it was self-protection. That, as the head of Developmental Services and the boss of more than three hundred people, he was constantly compelled to search a room for escape.

Ted smiles warmly and points to a chair when I walk in. "What's up?" he says.

Although I have planned for this day, and even discussed with Moira how to go about asking for a transfer, I am nervous. I am not, as I was just a few weeks earlier, desperately unhappy. Some of the shock and sorrow of having accepted a job where I couldn't do any counseling has worn off, and been replaced by a kind of grim but tolerable acceptance. Upon serious inspection, I have decided this is a form of maturity and not more self-denial. I have ceased fighting against what is, and am instead looking for ways to amend it.

I tell Ted about my findings at the training center, how M&M's are written into every behavior plan. The instructors know they don't work, and the previous behavior specialist knew they didn't work, but nobody did anything differently. I tell him that when I made the effort to talk to Manuel's mother and came back with a list of things Manuel liked that did not involve food (stickers, looking at picture books, putting stickers *in* picture books), Debra said she did not have time to fool with a new plan and she would just live with the clapping. I summarize by suggesting that my skills are being wasted at the training center, and that I could potentially do as much good in two days there as I am currently doing in five.

"I wonder," I say, "whether I could cut back to two days at the workshop, and work three days at the mental health center seeing real clients." I don't mean to say "real." Ted cringes and his eyes dart about the room.

"I mean normal," I say. "I mean of normal intelligence."

"Debra is probably just frustrated," he says. "I'm sure you'll bring her around. That's why we hired you, to help the instructors feel less frustrated and give them some tools they can use in their classrooms."

"I know," I say, "but—" I look at Ted across the expanse of his cluttered desk. His hands are folded in his lap, his face, apart from his darting eyes, a mask of calm. *But what?* If it is my job to give the instructors tools they can use, then *what* exactly am I asking for except for this *not* to be my job? For him to nod his head vigorously and agree with me that the workshop clients are a depressing collection of moaning, wetting, sugar-sated hand-clappers, and the instructors have all given up on them? For him to burst forth from his chair and exclaim that, indeed, my skills as a therapist *are* being wasted? That he is reassigning me immediately to the mental health center up the road, where I can rejoin my spiritual—yes, *spiritual*—side on the path to psychological superhero?

Ted Bolin is not going to say or do any of this. "You're doing an excellent job," he says. "You just have to celebrate the small successes. Getting them on the bus without a fight. Getting them through the day without a bathroom accident."

I stare down at my hands and fight the urge to disgorge a monumental amount of tears onto Ted's office floor.

"Your coworkers really like you."

My head jerks up and I look into Ted's admiring eyes. "They said that?" If my coworkers truly like me, then maybe this is a measure by which I can see myself as a helper. My spirits lift and the urge to cry scatters away like a thin cloud blown off the horizon by a strong wind.

"I've had no complaints about you," Ted says, smiling confidently, and I realize with sickening clarity that I am being "handled," that Ted Bolin is manipulating facts to make them sound like something they are not, so that I'll go away. That my coworkers haven't said they *don't* like me does not mean that they *do*, but it hardly matters. The extinction of my negative behavior is the goal here, the quashing of my ideological complaints, which Ted attempts to hurry along by punishing my tattletale-style reporting-from-the-trenches with barely palliative responses.

It does not occur to me that I might be wrong. That my presence at the Sheltered Workshop, regardless of whether behaviors change or not, is a hopeful one, a calming influence. It does not occur to me that the fact that my coworkers have not complained about me *does* mean that they like me, or that Ted Bolin really does have confidence in me, which really is why he hired me. Nor does it occur to me that he is actually considering my request for a transfer, or that, in time, he will come through for me.

* * *

When Fisher finally calls three weeks later, it is late one evening after work and I can hear the rush of traffic over the pay phone. Because I have stopped waiting for him to call, it takes me by surprise. I immediately wish I'd been able to prepare myself, although I don't know how I would have done this. It isn't like Fisher is asking difficult questions.

"How've you been?" he says. "How's the house?"

As soon as he asks this, I realize that *prepare* isn't the right word:

the right word is *anticipate*. Had I been able to anticipate Fisher's call, I tell myself, the drama around behavior plans and M&M's would not have swollen to such magnitude. What I do not tell myself is that, for the first time in a very long time, without a man in my life to distract me, I was focused on the problem at hand, as best I understood it (too many M&M's, too much downtime at the training center) and fairly quickly acted in my own best interests.

"The house is great!" I say. I don't want to complain about anything, because I don't want to sound negative. "My landlord brought me a stove finally. Oh, and I got a kerosene heater."

"I told you I'd show you how to use the wood stove," Fisher says. "If you want. You know, sometime."

Fisher's forwardness coupled with a sudden pulling back is intoxicating. Here is a man, I imagine, who, just as I am about to feel smothered, will retreat so far away from me I will feel instantly lonely. It is, I will come to realize, an enactment of feasting and then fasting, the tantalizing combination of too much of a highly desired thing followed by the agonizing, and yet somehow reassuring, surrender of it.

"That would be great if you could show me," I say.

Fisher tells me he'll be at the house Sunday morning, which is five days away, and I fight the urge to say, in my most childish voice, *not till SUNDAY?* Fisher-time, I am beginning to understand, runs on a clock all its own, its movements unhurried and, for the most part, indecipherable.

* * *

At the time I cannot explain how it is I know that I can have sex with Fisher without the baggage that dogged my sex life with Neil and Mitch and Andrew. What the attraction feels like, interestingly enough, is a gnawing hunger, a description that suggests, by its comfortable reference to appetite, something new at work in me, some loosening of a grip or striving toward a new, physical reality that will allow all parts of me to feel. What I will understand, years after the

Rollercoaster Road house era and under the microscope of therapy, is that Fisher and I fit together like puzzle pieces, and while this is always so, no matter whom we are with, it will never be as clear to me as when I look at my sex life with him. Born and raised under the iron fist of fundamentalist Christianity, Fisher had been taught to equate pleasure with sin. Along with drinking and smoking, and sex outside of marriage, it was inadmissible, in Fisher's household, to dance or listen to music. It was a childhood of prohibitions against most things gratifying, and by the time Fisher and I become a couple, it only makes sense that he covers his body in ill-fitting clothing, is unable to cook for himself, owns nothing but a small pick-up truck, and reads fervently from his Bible on the heels of intercourse, in an earnest attempt to repent. How like my own quest to empty my life out, I will see, but with a twist: instead of denying myself the pleasures that led to punishments, I denied those that led to rewards.

* * *

From the kitchen window I watch Fisher get out of his tiny truck. He is too tall for it and emerges comically from behind the wheel, the shape of the cab space repeated in the shape of his body. He stretches, removes his light blue ski cap, shakes out his hair, and pulls the cap over his head again. *He looks like a criminal in my driveway,* I think, and a little thrill darts through me. Although my first instinct is to race out and jump into his arms and let him carry me back into the house like a newlywed, I lean against the oven and wait while he stomps into the mudroom. I listen to Jesse moan excitedly and Keithan bark her shrill greeting, as if Fisher has been gone on a long voyage and has finally come back home to them, instead of the truth, which is that they have met him just once before.

When at last Fisher bursts through the kitchen door, I have to laugh. His head, hugged by the tight ski cap, looks large and misshapen, and tufts of brown hair peek out around the bottom edges. His eyes, blue like his cap, radiate like headlamps.

"You look great," Fisher says, then looks embarrassed and stares down at the floor. It is the same loop of forwardness coupled with reticence that I found so appealing on the phone. In person, it's even more attractive.

"I like your hat," I say.

"Oh," Fisher says. "I should take that off. Sorry."

"No you should keep it on," I say. "It's pretty cold in here."

"Right," Fisher says, heading into the living room where the wood stove has not sustained fire since I moved in two months earlier. I have shoved all manner of flammables into it, trying to get something to catch.

"I can light it fine," I say. "But it always burns out." I laugh an ironic little laugh. "Story of my life," I say, but Fisher just looks at me quizzically, and I remember with embarrassment that we aren't on this page yet, the page where I make jokes full of innuendo about my past sex life.

Fisher sits on the floor in front of the wood stove's metal door. The opening is the size of a man's head, and Fisher puts his in it.

"Never do this when it's lit!" Fisher calls out from inside the stove, his voice fluttering out through the grill on top.

"I'll try to remember!" I call back. His headless shoulders are rounded and broad. His generous hands grasp the edges of the stove.

Fisher pulls his head out of the stove. His cap and nose are dusted with soot. Then he reaches back into it with one arm—the way I once saw a vet reach into my horse's anus to remove an impaction—and pulls out everything I have stuffed into the stove over the last month that did not burn: singed two-by-four pieces of wood, a melted foam cup, one heavy, blackened log the size of tree trunk (which he has to angle just so to remove), a badly burned wash cloth, and—this is the worst—a mousetrap.

"Were you cooking mice?" Fisher asks, holding the trap gingerly in the air.

"Oh, God no!" I say, embarrassed by the ridiculous assortment of items Fisher has laid out on the floor like a display of things to be reviewed and priced. "I found that in the cabinet and just threw it in there one night."

Fisher points to each item one by one. "No. No. No. No. And no."

He looks up at me. His eyes are serious, the set of his mouth grave. "You can't put any of this in there."

"Not even wood? In a wood stove?"

"Yes but not like this. You put a little paper, some kindling, then a small log, then a slightly larger log. Like a fireplace. Then, once you have it going, you keep adding logs before the old one is too burned up to catch the next one." He points to the tree trunk. "This is too big."

He spies the kerosene heater in the corner. "You didn't get that for in here, did you?"

I nod. "I don't think it works right. It stinks."

"That's a *shop* heater," Fisher says, "for using in an open area with plenty of ventilation."

"That explains the near-death experience."

Fisher wags his head but can't contain his smile. He goes outside in search of fire building materials and comes back with an armload of kindling and small tree branches. I watch as he expertly layers papers, twigs, and branches inside the stove, holds a match to it, then gently shuts and latches the metal door. Without a word he takes my hand and leads me to the sofa, and we sit in silence as the warmth grows around us. Something loosens in my chest, and for the first time in a month, I don't care that I have the wrong job and a difficult house and that Moira is fifteen hundred miles away. The welcome feel of heat and the comforting smell of wood smoke are intoxicating, and I think *this is the house I fell in love with months ago!* I do not think *this is all about a man.* I do not think *I am drunk on Fisher.*

Fisher and I look at each other, and smile. Without speaking, he pushes me gently into the sofa and lowers himself on top of me, his warm, masculine body a thrilling weight. He puts his mouth on mine and we kiss a long, but oddly tongueless kiss as I explore, with jubilant hands, the broad expanse of his bare back beneath his shirt, all the way down to the rise of his round, solid rump. Fisher moans and I wriggle out of my jeans, and as he raises up to unzip his fly, I pull my sweater off over my head. Within seconds we are rocking hypnotically in the quiet awe of how good it feels to finally be fucking. I don't think about the fact that neither his hands nor his mouth seek out my breasts or any other part of me, and I do not know, of course, that they never will, that Fisher will prove unable or unwilling to explore my body in any more detail than he is exploring it this day. I do not think—for *years*—about how ironic and perfect and fitting it is that Fisher, knowing or not knowing—it doesn't matter—how much I want him to touch me, *denies me his touch*. And because I don't know any of this, minutes later, when his head arches back and a deep, guttural groan erupts from his throat and he at last lies motionless on top of me, I am deliriously happy, contented to my core, drowning in the delicious warmth of wood smoke, and the utter rightness of unfulfilling sex.

Chapter 29

Good Bones

F ISHER AND I FALL INTO A RHYTHM. On Tuesday and Thursday nights, he comes to the Rollercoaster Road house after work and we eat a simple dinner on the rickety table between the living room and my bedroom, where the light is poorest, calling it romantic. After dinner, we take the dogs for a walk, and then we sit in the living room by the wood stove, where I read *Glamour* Magazine or *Psychology Today,* and Fisher either scribbles notes for a short story or reads his Bible. Occasionally he will stop what he is doing to tell me something that interests him.

"Did you know Samuel's mother gave him up when he was little?"

"Really?" I will say, struggling to fit a face with the name. "Is he at the training center?"

Fisher will shake his head and laugh. "*Samuel,*" he will say. "*Hannah's* son." He will watch my face, waiting for recognition to cross it. When it doesn't, he taps his Bible with a forefinger. "He became a prophet? It's in *your* Bible."

Fisher feigns dismay at my ignorance. It never occurs to me that he really *is* dismayed, that for him, characters in the biblical world are flesh and blood ancestors to whom we owe gratitude for the groundwork of faith they laid. The fact that I don't know their names—much less appreciate the enormous sacrifices they made for us—*for you*, Fisher is fond of saying—eats at him, and so, over time, he does his best to sprinkle the information into our conversations ("You know, Job also was dissatisfied with his work," and "Selfishness just never pays off; just look what happened to Lot."). Because Fisher is good-looking and bright and just thinking about him makes my knees rattle with desire (i.e., because I am in love with him) I really am hooked at first. I even go so far as to buy my very own combined New and Old Testament Bible, the first adult Bible I have ever owned and that does not have generous illustrations of God's disciples in elaborate, colorful outfits. But I quickly tire of what I call the "stilted prose" and the monotonous recitation of lineages, and although I take notes, I can't keep the names or relationships straight. Soon my mind is wandering from the crinkly, onion-skin pages of my Bible to the smooth, sleek pages of my *Glamour* magazine. After two weeks, I shelve the Bible.

"It's just not that complicated," Fisher says. He explains that I don't have to memorize the family lines, or even necessarily follow them. "Just think of it as back-story and keep going," he says, and it almost works. But, of course, the real problem isn't that it's complicated, but that it's forbidden. Even though my Old/New Testament opens without Jesus, I am familiar enough with the plot to know that *Jesus* is where it is ultimately leading me. And that, unless I want to have another conversation with my father addressing the destruction that men of wrong religions wreak, then it is best not to pursue an education in it, no matter how attractive it seems through Fisher's eyes.

"Oh, please," Fisher says. "It's *your* spiritual life."

"I just know how sneaky Jesus can be," I say.

"*Sneaky!*" Fisher says, his eyes darkening and the crease in his face seeming to deepen.

"Okay, *devious*." In my experience, I say, Jesus, can seep into holes in your life you didn't even know were there. I tell him about going with a friend to a church youth group meeting, against my parents' wishes, when I was fifteen. Instead of the cliquish, exclusionary treatment I was accustomed to at school, ten teenagers I'd never met before welcomed me enthusiastically. There were no snide remarks about the hated ten pounds around my middle, no furtive glances at my tomboyish attire or my frizzy long hair. There was an immediate acceptance of me for me, a nonjudgmental approval that transcended my looks and my personality. The youth group leader, a young man in his early twenties, was unthreateningly attractive, with a round face and a sweet smile, wearing neatly pressed blue jeans—*in church*. The experience was disconcertingly thrilling, like a drug high you feel guilty about but can't wait to repeat. I was desperate to go back again the next week, but didn't dare ask my parents if I could. Later that same year, I had a chance meeting with a minister on the heels of an argument with my mother. He was kind and sympathetic and listened attentively to my story of anger and injustice; he *understood,* he said, and I felt the same heady rush of unconditional acceptance that I couldn't seem to locate inside my own family. It was a delicious high, as thrilling as a free-fall through space.

Fisher stares at me. "That's not just unconditional acceptance," Fisher says. "It's Christ's *love.*"

"It's a *trap,*" I say. "A love trap. It's like Christian fly paper. You don't see it till you're *in* it, and by then it's too late, you can't get loose."

Fisher shakes his head vigorously. "Christian love isn't a trap," he says. "It's a *net.* There's a difference."

But regardless of how Fisher explains it or how convincing he is or how handsome, I do not return to the Bible. Fisher doesn't fight me on it and, soon enough, we push past it, until we are three, four, five months into a happy, if mostly secular, twosome. As I'd predicted it would be, our sex life is startlingly unfraught with the baggage that weighed down my previous relationships. Rather than a steadily declining interest in sex, as there has been with every other man, I am not only happy to have it, but often the initiator. And I surprise myself by my own lack of inhibition. Without warning, I will undress and plant myself on top of Fisher. Or brazenly unzip his pants and pull him onto me. Years of agonizing about what my body looked like, worrying over my supposedly flabby middle, concerned about whether I even deserved to be looked at or to have sex—all of it seems to melt away under Fisher's spell. I don't complain when, after sex, he thumbs through the psalms, and for two years it does not occur to me to be stunned and humiliated when he tells me he doesn't touch me "down there" because it is "wet and gross." It will take that long and longer before I will begin to put it all together, that Fisher's withholding touch from me and reading the Bible after sex is his way of assuaging the guilt he felt about it. These were his bargaining chips with God: as threatened as I was by Jesus, Fisher was equally threatened, and his solution was to have a kind of hands-off sex that somehow bent but did not break the rules.

With Fisher in my life, my unhappiness at work recedes into the background. I no longer agonize over ill-conceived M&M cures, and, in fact, stop fighting them, which seems to bring a sigh of relief from the instructors at the Sheltered Workshop. While this feels, on some level, like I have boarded some great big boat of apathy, it is also surprisingly comfortable. Less on edge, less determined to fight for change at the center, I stop plowing through my old behavioral psychology textbooks looking for ideas; if it can't be fixed with M&M's, then it can't be fixed. It is a life of newfound simplicity, completely structured around Fisher-time: eight hours a day, five days a week, I test new clients, re-test old ones, and write progress notes, all the while sucking down cigarettes and counting the minutes to Tuesday and Thursday nights.

It is a life that finally feels vivid and complex and urgent. I would eventually see this emotional intensity for what it really was: romantic love, into whose clutches I always thought I was too rational, too independent, to fall. But because I am unclear about myself, and because what I need most in my life is to feel important, I hang my newfound contentedness on my arrival at some external platform of mattering. Events of the outside world—sad news of the Challenger explosion, for example, which I watch over and over on TV—join hands with the events of my personal world—my father going in for more tests, my sister's pregnancy—to form a kind of meta-adulthood, a place that is deeply uncertain but also vibrant, if only because it is counterpoint to the numb, cement-headed feeling of my early twenties.

And then, a giant step (as I see it) on the ladder of my achingly slow recovery: I get a refrigerator. I liken the occasion to the moment four years earlier when my period, lost for two years to anorexia, suddenly reinstated itself. I was working my internship at the State hospital, and was so excited to see blood that I ran out of the bathroom and called my parents.

Manufacturing enough estrogen to menstruate was, like weighing over a hundred pounds, like expanding my food choices from things I could measure in tablespoons to things like sandwiches and meat, an indication of recovery. I was aware that until such time as I gained enough body fat to do so, my mother would watch over my meals and my weigh-ins. There would come a time when I would appreciate recovery for more than the shaking of the parental monkey off my back, but at that moment, freedom from their oversight was paramount. My period also awakened something in me. As I pressed the phone to my ear, I stared lasciviously across the dayroom and into the counseling office of twenty-eight-year-old, silky-haired Steve. There was, emanating from the same place where bright new blood coursed, a sudden pulse of attraction.

The refrigerator is on Manuel's mother's front porch the day I visit her to talk about his clapping. It is hideous: rusty around the edges and plastered with red, yellow, and green stickers. It is on its way to the landfill.

"There's nothing wrong with it. I just got me a new 'un," Manuel's mother says.

The information—that Manuel's mother, eighty and subsisting on food stamps and Social Security in a ramshackle, two-room house, has purchased a new refrigerator *even though the old one still works*, while I am socking hundreds of dollars a month into savings and won't buy myself one because I believe it's an *extravagance*—washes over me. But instead of doing what I should do, which is to leave immediately and drive straight to an appliance store and buy a brand new refrigerator, I smile my sweetest smile.

"May I have it?" I ask.

The refrigerator changes everything, even before Fisher and I drive back to get it the following weekend. My last few days and nights without one feel impossibly long, my cracker breakfasts and peanut butter sandwich dinners like punishment, and by the time Saturday rolls around, I know I cannot live another day without this all-important appliance.

Just as getting my period re-awakened me sexually, getting a refrigerator re-awakens me to the reassurances of domesticity. I want to do a massive grocery shopping. I want to get all the things I've needed for the past several months in bulk, to shop like the head of a family of ten, or a prairie homesteader on her annual trip to town. I want not just to cook, but to *wield* things, things that take impossibly long, like real spaghetti sauce and complicated reductions and stews, and then to spoon them lovingly into airtight containers, and stack them neatly in my refrigerator. And although, in reality, I buy only a six-pack of Diet Coke, a head of lettuce, milk, and a jar of diet Catalina salad dressing, I see, as I stare into the refrigerator's gaping maw, a whole future of possibilities. Perhaps I will make friends, throw a party, take a trip, learn to sew or bake or fly. It doesn't matter *what*, only that there is the thought, and in the thought, promise.

* * *

Just before winter, my father has a heart attack. It is the first in a series of escalating health problems that will lead to his death less than a year later. Although the news alarms me—I am at work when my mother calls to tell me—I push it away firmly, with a lack of emotional involvement that I will later find heartbreakingly austere. *I didn't call him at the hospital because there was no phone in his room*, I write in my journal, and this is all I write on the subject, evidence that I do not allow my father's growing health troubles to break the crust of my own consciousness. The rest of the story—how long he stayed in the hospital, whether the heart attack was related to the cancer, which at the time his doctors do not know has multiplied and spread—is lost to the incurious. The reason for my indifference, I tell myself, is that I am busy—busy having sex, busy being in love, busy navigating my new platform of adulthood that demands I no longer bind myself to the wills and ways of family. But the real reason I don't follow up on my father's latest and most serious setback is that I am too afraid to think about it. After the initial conversation with my mother about the event, I will immediately forget what she has told me—and by forget I mean something more intentional than forgetting, as in *I will push* what she has told me deep, deep down into the loam of memory, where it will not be retrieved for twenty more years—which is that my father is getting his things in order.

* * *

I turn twenty-six. In the parking lot of Fisher's apartment building, Fisher cuts the engine of the truck. We've had dinner at his favorite place, a truck-stop restaurant with a hot bar where Fisher can load up on fried chicken and Salisbury steak for relatively little money, and I can get a limp but passable chef's salad. Fisher is in good spirits, full of food, and playful. He leans over and kisses me on the nose, talks to me in baby-talk, which makes us both laugh. Suddenly he sits upright and stares out the windshield.

"You all right?" I ask.

Fisher nods. "I have to tell you something," he says.

My stomach drops. The last several times a man had to tell me something it was that we would no longer be dating, either because I was too much trouble or he was already engaged. I hold my breath and stare at the side of his face for what seems like a very long time. Fisher looks grave. He turns to face me and takes a deep breath.

"I love you," he says. "I love you."

* * *

With Fisher's pronouncement, I stuff any and all thoughts about my family under the tectonic forces of work and sex and something new: possible marriage. Now on Tuesday and Thursday nights, we lie in my bed listening to the tinny hum of the electric heater my parents gave me for my birthday, our fingers tracing patterns on each other's bare backs.

"What does this say?" I murmur into the dark, my eyes closed, my fingers spelling out in large, loopy letters our future children's names.

"S," says Fisher, "a, l, e, m."

It is, for me, time suspended in a soft fog of denial, where not only is no one dying, new life, in theory at least, is flowering. Sometimes Fisher and I use protection, and sometimes we don't; there doesn't seem to be any real commitment to either preventing life or creating it, just this nether land of *maybe* with no plan, no thought beyond this moment, except for names we love. *Salem. Mason.* Two-syllable, gender-unspecific names whose letters lean artfully, drowsily, into one another. We are, above all, two people who love the shape of words, and words are what we are fornicating for, not children.

* * *

When at last I do go home to see my father, a month after his heart attack, I bring pictures. My parents have never seen the Rollercoaster Road house, but I have told them select things about it. How beautiful it is when the sun trickles down through the trees. How cozy it is with the wood stove going full blast and the dogs asleep in front of it. How Fisher says the house has *good bones.* I do not tell them a family of four was evicted so I could live there, or that, when they left, they stole the appliances. My parents have also never met Fisher, but I have told them select things about him, as well. How he taught me to build a lasting fire in the stove. How smart he is, how handsome, how much his clients love him. I do not mention religion, which is, of course, my father's first question.

"Is he Jewish?"

We are sitting at the butcher block kitchen table, rain is pelting the skylights, and my father's corgi is on the floor under his chair, his short legs jerking in sleep. My father's dark eyes are flat behind his gold-rimmed glasses and, although the doctors have said his heart is strong again, he appears to have lost weight. My mother stares at her lap. I know the right answer to this question, but I can't lie. Instead I fudge the truth.

276

"He's the most spiritual person I've ever met," I say. *Spiritual* is my counter-offer to *Jewish*, a word that is hard to find fault with. With it, I hope to inject a bubble of doubt in my father's mind, by suggesting that religious affiliation is an intellectual stance, while *spirituality* is the flesh and bones of true faith. Which is, of course, pointless.

"I don't understand why you can't find the qualities you seek in a man in a *Jewish* body," my father once said, which, at the time, conjured an image of men as chocolate candies, my task being to locate the outer Jewish shell, after which I could poke around until I found the desired filling.

I change the subject altogether by handing my father the stack of photographs across the table, which he shuttles through at lightning speed. Suddenly he stops at one of them.

"This is Fisher, I presume?" He turns the photograph around. It is a picture of Fisher posing in his underwear in the middle of my living room. I grab it from his hand.

"Whoops, I forgot that one was in there!" I say, attempting to laugh, to appear lighthearted, unembarrassed. But my father's mouth is pursed, his eyes have turned to stone, and he is staring into the space behind my head.

"There's nothing there to see anyway," he says.

It takes a minute for me to fully hear this. My brain folds his comment over and over, wrestling with the words, his intention, until I finally unwrap it: *my father is insulting Fisher by saying he has a small penis.*

A little spigot of shame gushes in my head, although what I am ashamed about isn't really clear. A few years later, a therapist will ask me why I brought the picture home in the first place. "Why was it important that your father see your boyfriend in his underwear?"

I will fumble for answers.

"Maybe I wanted my father to leave the world angry with me, so that we wouldn't have to miss each other."

"Maybe," says the therapist. "But what made him angry?"

"Sex," I say.

"Twenty-six year-old women have sex as a natural part of life," she points out.

Of course. My father himself had a two-year-old by age twenty-six, with my mother, who was twenty-two.

And so I go back to the conversation about Andrew, and my father's devastation, the disappointment—in himself, not me—the crux of his anger.

"Maybe," says the therapist. "What else do you know about your father?"

I recite facts: my father was a first-generation American. His father defected from the Czar's army in Russia when he was nineteen and escaped to the US. He was forty–six and his wife forty-two when my father, the last of three (living) children was born. At our house in Atlanta, when I was a child, my *Zaide* was a foreigner, someone I understood to be my father's father, but who was also alien, with his pillowy, bespectacled face and broad, hooked nose and bulky Russian accent. That my father had been brought up by this unapproachable stranger in a cloistered, Yiddish-speaking, observantly Jewish household within the broader, mostly Christian community of Chattanooga, Tennessee, would be incomprehensible to me when I got older, a confluence of the ancient and the modern, not unlike the memory of war in lovely places.

My father, as a result, was often uptight, perennially perplexed by the New World Order of the 1960s and 1970s, which included the loosening of not only of dress codes (*you're wearing blue jeans out to dinner?*) and marital conventions (*I married for life*, he told my mother during one of her threats to divorce him), but also sexual mores: the housewives of my father's time grew daughters who became, unlike their parents, outwardly sexual creatures. (*You're wearing your bra outside the house?* my father once asked me, when I appeared in the kitchen wearing a halter-top.) It was an unimaginable world my father found himself inhabiting, his wife and children pall bearers for the way things used to be. As for why I felt it necessary to inform him, via Fisher in his underwear, that the times were changing, I can only surmise that this grew from the part of me for whom self-punishment was still reward: knowing my father would be—rightly or wrongly—upset, I loaded the gun and aimed it at myself.

* * *

The grass in the dog yard is weedy and high, and although I now count myself as a fully functioning adult—the measure of adulthood being ownership of both a stove and a refrigerator—I do not own a lawnmower. One afternoon, poking around in the far end of the mudroom, I find, propped against a wall, along with a dirt-encrusted leather tool belt and an old tire, a machete. It looks like—and is, essentially—a giant knife, the kind of tool a well-muscled hiker or ranch hand would use to cut a path through dense woods. I take it out into the yard and swing it left, right, right, left, through the tall grass until I am exhausted, which turns out to be about five minutes. It is like attempting to sling a bowling ball through water, and at best, I manage to whack the tips off a few of the more tender weeds. I call Fisher in on the job, and even though he is skeptical, he does not say, as any rational person would, "A *machete?* To mow your *lawn?*" Here is a man who would have just as willingly taken a pair of scissors or a razor blade from me and attempted to trim a half-acre of land, blade by blade. But after a few powerful swipes with the dull machete, he, too, gives up.

By now, I have lived in the Rollercoaster Road house for six months, and I tell myself the unruly yard lends the house an English cottage look. The only problem is that the grass gives cover to field mice, who, like front-liners in a war zone, use the opportunity to scurry unseen from the dog yard to any of a number of cracks and crevices leading to the inside of the warm house. While I had convinced myself the mouse droppings I saw on move-in day simply pointed to carelessness on the part of Diane and Jay (they failed to keep the doors closed!), I can't deny that, even though I never leave my doors open, my mouse population has exploded, as evidenced by the astounding increase in droppings from one week to the next. By the time I swing a machete through the tall grass, I have already tried a few things to get rid of them. Once I pushed the dogs' faces into a basket where I heard a mouse scratching around. (The dogs looked up at me as if to say *we don't do mice.*) And once I put little piles of rat poison behind the refrigerator. The morning two mice staggered across my kitchen counter leaking blood from their tiny mouths and ears, I swore off killing. If cutting the grass doesn't stop the mice from coming inside, I tell Fisher, then we will just coexist peacefully, a decision so devoid of wisdom and so lacking in judgment that even now, twenty years later, it pains me to think about. How Fisher, for his part, agreed to these terms and did not insist on setting humane traps or calling an exterminator, or otherwise helping me to rid my house of the legions of mice defecating and fornicating in my kitchen drawers and beneath the eyes of the stove and on my broiler pan, I chalk up to the fact that he was, as Moira said, my mirror image, ignorant of the roots of his own abstemious lifestyle, and therefore every bit as willing to take a machete to a lawn as to give in and live peaceably with a growing nation of rodents.

Not long after I make my peace with the mice, two puppies appear at the Sheltered Workshop. Because I am from a suburban neighborhood, where dogs were either on leashes or retained behind manicured fenced yards, I declare that they are lost and that their owner must be searching feverishly for them. My coworkers smile indulgently and then explain that, in rural areas where people are poor, putting dogs out of cars on other people's lawns is how they "adopt" them out. Debra is taking the black and tan one. I lift the yellow and white hound puppy to my face. *I can't have another dog*, I say, but the part of me saying it goes unheard by the part of me instantly drunk on puppy breath and the warm feel of the bloatishly round belly in my arms. That evening I put the puppy down on my kitchen floor. Keithan and Jesse rush to sniff her and she urinates copiously, the pee running in rivulets following the slope of the floor. I have forgotten what it is like to have a puppy. Fisher names her Boomer, and my life curls instantly, happily, around the fundamentals of housebreaking, leash training, and watching her grow.

Around this time, an acquaintance from work named Karen drops by the house. I have spent weeks extolling its virtues —the view, the privacy, the lunatic road it sits on, and way the woods cradle the house—and Karen has found herself in the neighborhood and curious. Because I now think of the house as an English cottage, I have no notion at this point that the house looks like something that has been condemned. The knee-high grass in the yard requires parting with your hands to wade to the mudroom door. Just inside the mudroom, which is where Keithan, Jesse and Boomer stay when I am at work, there are piles of blankets laced with wet leaves and sticks they've dragged in to chew on. The linoleum in the kitchen, on a relentless quest to free itself of the subflooring, curls up like a wave at the edges, and the loose door knob on my bedroom door has finally jumped ship, leaving only a flat face and the ghost of a worn circle behind.

And there is the smell. What I also don't know, though other people do, is that the scent of wood smoke grows ugly with age, and permeates not just your curtains and your carpets and your furniture, but your clothes and your hair and your skin. That it overtakes you, insinuating itself into the very cells of your body, so that you unfurl the primitive whiff of fire every time you exhale or perspire. As I stand there in my living room in my unwashed jeans and Fisher's giant sweatshirt, entreating Karen to *sit, sit!* and pointing to a dingy sofa that is lopsided with the weight of books and newspapers, I do not know that I have become, in effect, a walking totem, the smoke-stench and disrepair of my house etched so artfully into me that I have become emblematic of it, my house and I a shared story of myriad discomforts, wrongheaded decisions, and the encroaching despair born of my father's illness. All of this, I will awaken to later, is why there was, on Karen's face, not appreciation for the cozy house with the great view of the mountains that I have been bragging about, but the horrified expression of a woman who has blundered onto the scene of a terrible crime. She is stunned by something, that much I can see, but not what it is, and so I do what I always do: I chalk it up to a fundamental difference in values, the fact that I am not materialistic, and that the rest of the world, hung up on big houses in expensive neighborhoods with stiff, formal furniture, cannot possibly appreciate my carefully honed lifestyle.

Within ten minutes of her arrival, Karen leaves (*backs out slowly* would not be an overstatement). I plop down on my lopsided sofa and the tower of books and magazines tumbles into my lap and onto the floor. While this particular mess annoys me in the moment, there is nothing underpinning the annoyance, no larger recognition of what

Karen saw that disturbed her here. This will not come for some time, and like the encapsulated hospital moment in which I suddenly and shockingly saw my emaciated self clearly, it will require the element of surprise, the rounding of a blind corner that, without the lubricant of expectation, will bring me face-to-face with the truth of my house and, in turn, myself.

* * *

It snows. The snow gathers on the roof and on the porch, shimmering like a frosting of jewels. The sun glows like a distant bulb behind heavy clouds. For three days, the amount of time the workshop is closed, I take the dogs for walks in the undeveloped subdivision, read, and watch television. As the third day winds down and I prepare (reluctantly) to return to work, I make a list entitled, "What I Really Want to Do," which, in direct opposition to my "Ways to Die" list, is more of a "Ways to Live" list. On it is everything I want to accomplish in my lifetime. It is a list I make and remake periodically, and that sometimes includes (solely as an interesting addendum) my favorite song of the moment. On this particular list there is: *help people, live in Europe for a year, start a farm for neglected and abused animals, learn to paint, get my PhD* (with a question mark), *stop worrying about weight,* and, ironically, *REO Speedwagon's "Can't Fight This Feeling."* It does not occur to me that my periodically updated list is like a recurring dream whose images are just that: visuals, and that their real meaning lies deep beneath the stone of sleep. It does not occur to me that my list is my salvo, my operatic call to the universe, letting it know that, what I really want, beyond the specifics of things (a farm) and activities (get PhD), is to feel the weight of *significance* bearing down on my life. And so when Ted Bolin calls on my first day back at work after the snowfall to tell me that, from now on, I will spend two of my five days at the outpatient mental health center seeing normal (he does not say *normal*) clients for therapy, an ocean of gratitude rolls over me, and I regard my newest list with something approaching awe, as if it, and not I, brought me to this important point.

* * *

And so, six hours a day, two days a week, I sit in what can only be called *rapture* of my mental health clients. Hour after hour I listen, spellbound, to their personal stories, their large and small problems, their (at times) seemingly directionless ramblings, all of which I believe is the meat and muscle of life lived, and therefore pertinent to the cure. My job as a therapist, as I see it, is to decipher the language, unravel the tears, and tessellate the over-long tales about surface events until, at last, we—the client and I—are chewing on the flesh of the matter. My approach, I tell myself, is demanding and intense: for the full therapy hour, I make unflinching eye contact and ask heart-scraping, difficult questions, which frequently cause my clients to cry. Once naked emotion is in the room—*the real vessel of pain*, I tell them—I sit in enigmatic silence until the moment is just right for me to venture an insight: *You are too focused on your husband*, I will say. Or, *it's not your boyfriend, or your mother.* Or, *it's not what happened to you but what you think about it, what you believe, what you're doing because of what you think and what you believe.*

One day after I have unfurled this choke of wisdom to a woman whose husband, a preacher, admitted he was having an affair, I look down to jot a chart note, and when I look back up, a bottle of cough medicine fished from her pocketbook rockets past me, so close that its breeze lifts a couplet of hairs on my forehead. The bottle crashes into the window behind me and shatters, and a thin violet oil slick slides down it. *You stirred something in her*, my fellow counselors tell me. *That's good.* It is the kind of peer affirmation I desperately need, and I tuck it deep down into my heart, but not so deep that I can't take it out and look at it every so often, like a beautiful marble I keep in my pocket, confirmation that I am on the right path.

It has been five years since I rode into Tifton, a ninety-five-pound superhero wannabe tucked safely inside my mother's car. If I am once again conducting insight therapy with too little of my own, I don't fully know it. I have glimpses of the fact that I am still tottering back and forth between full recovery and my (weakening) attempts to frustrate it. I still weigh myself daily, and at times still wear clothes that reveal how thin I am: form-fitting jeans and clingy sweaters that are slightly too small; I am still surprised when someone new remarks that I am too thin. Most of the time I don't eat with my coworkers because I have the idea that I still eat too little, although I am not sure exactly *how much* too little I eat. And I am in a relationship with a man whose discomfort with the female body and lifetime of abstinence from pleasure causes us to have a distant, hands-off kind of sex, and this almost comical, laissez faire lovemaking feels exactly right. This is what is healthy about me.

* * *

What is unhealthy about me, as I can only see it now, is that I have pushed the truth about my father's illness so far away that the truth's only recourse is to insinuate itself, like a rogue root system, into the very foundation of my life. This is, in part, evidenced by the slow, ongoing corruption of my house, which is sinking further and further into decrepitude. Here with me, like a fellow injured bird, is Fisher, perhaps the one man on the planet for whom my addled version of maturity and adulthood so syncs with his own. This rickety platform of interdependency we ride down a river of oblivious happiness, punctuated by interludes of sex and Bible reading, and capped off with repeated drives through the countryside to look at a property we dreamily refer to as "our house" but that isn't even for sale.

I push on. I push my therapy clients to get better, and some actually do. I staff cases with my coworkers, and get ideas for how to work with difficult clients. I housetrain Boomer. I make soups and save leftovers in the refrigerator. I ask Fisher to consider staying a third night with me. He agrees to think about it. And we decide it is time he met my parents.

By the time I take Fisher home, they have had several months to get used to the idea of our relationship; to the fact that he isn't Jewish, that he is eleven years older than I am, that one of my favorite things about him, even though it is inconvenient, is the fact that he lives without a telephone.

"That's how non-materialistic he is," I tell my parents.

"How, in this day and age, does a person not have a phone," my father said when I first told him.

I do not tell Fisher about my father seeing the picture of him in his underwear. Nor do I tell him my father is angry that he isn't Jewish, a fact that would surprise him, as Fisher is not angry with my father for not being a Christian.

"I love Jews," Fisher said to me early in our relationship, "You're the chosen ones."

Fisher, ignorant of his innumerable failings in the eyes of my father, but also, at thirty-seven, beyond the adolescent nervousness attendant to meeting a girl's parents, looks forward to the trip to Atlanta. Because he is not concerned about what my parents will think, but also because he does not know how to dress himself appropriately, he shows up for our trip home wearing blue jeans so tight I can see the outline of a nickel in his pocket. His shiny brown hair dusts the top of his shoulders. *No more bowl cuts*, I told him, and so he simply stopped cutting his hair at all, and while I think he looks cute, I can also see that he looks unkempt. I wear blue jeans also, and a sweater down to my knees that I think is fashionable but that will cause my mother to say I appear to have lost a great deal of weight. My hair, recently permed by a friend, hangs long and loose around my face, dry lifeless curls cascading down to my waist.

We sit in the stylish warmth of my parents' den, just the four of us. My mother asks Fisher about his job and his family as my father stares at the side of his head, smiling a thin, tight-lipped smile. Fisher answers my mother's questions and the three of us laugh and joke, but my father does not speak to Fisher all evening except to say hello when we arrive, and three hours later, goodbye. Although this makes me uncomfortable, and furious, it does not surprise me; I recall that my father barely spoke to Andrew, in spite of the lovely book cake.

At the dinner table, Fisher eats heartily, complimenting my mother's cooking and helping himself to seconds and thirds, which makes her happy. Afterwards, my mother and Fisher and I take my father's dog for a walk down the street, and at ten, we leave to drive the two hours home. The next morning, I call my mother to ask what they thought.

"He's sweet," my mother says. "He seems interested and involved in the world." She adds however that my father was not impressed. "He's not what Dad thought you'd come up with," she says.

"I didn't invent him," I say. She laughs and puts my father on the line.

"You don't like Fisher?" I ask.

"What is there to like about a man with no phone?"

From this point forward, my father will refer to Fisher as *the man with no phone*. Early on, it will irritate me for its shallowness, and I will find myself, paradoxically, wanting to feed him some other annoying, but more noteworthy, failing of Fisher's. *You think no phone is bad,* I imagine myself saying, *how about the fact that he reads the Bible after sex?* Or, for that matter, some failing of mine: *No phone? How about no stove? No refrigerator? No heat? No doorknobs?* Instead, I simply mull over his fixation with Fisher's telecommunications status—is it that no phone is impractical, or backwards, or irresponsible?—eventually arriving at the conclusion that no telephone is simply an emotional stand-in—like the photo of Fisher in his underwear—for something else eating at my father. Had he known about how I was living in the Rollercoaster Road house, first with no heat and no way to cook or eat properly, and later with the mouse infestation and the grass and the stink, I would say that what ate at my father was not that Fisher could not make a phone call, but that his own daughter lived a life of impractical and phenomenal discomfort, cut off from the world she was brought up to inhabit, not by technology or its absence, but by the astounding fact of choice. And, in the way that parents know the things we believe them not to know, there is perhaps the sense that my father did know, that when Fisher and I arrived in that elegant den, dressed like vagabonds and smelling of fire, I looked—we looked—like wild things: sex-whittled and feral-haired, two people for whom the world had become defined by lack and hunger and filth.

* * *

And then something so ordinary it might have gone unnoticed, except that it changes everything: A new employee, a young woman, comes to work at the mental health center. We walk in from the parking lot one morning and she mentions that she is looking for a place to live. An acquaintance told her about a small trailer for rent on an Arabian horse farm in Chickamauga. There are sixty acres. The landlords, an older married couple, are very nice.

"I'm jealous," I say absently, my mind on breakfast, on work, on the stone in my belly that is my father's ongoing vocal disapproval of Fisher. I have vaguely heard the word *horses*. "You should take it."

She's not interested, she says, but since I'm jealous she'll give me the number.

"Oh, I'm not looking to move," I say. "I love my house."

In the waiting room we part ways and I turn to go into my office when, like an apparition, the Rollercoaster Road house appears before me as if picked off its foundation and set down by a tornado. Except it is not the Rollercoaster Road house as I know it, but a gross replica. The mudroom is obscured by tall grass, its windows cracked and filthy. In the kitchen, the linoleum is pulling up from the floor in a long U-shaped wave along the baseboards, and the refrigerator is covered in filthy stickers. In the living room there is the dark stench of stale wood smoke, dense as fog. Only slowly does it dawn on me that this is the Rollercoaster Road house unembellished by the glaze of desire and denial. Only slowly do I understand that, stripped of expectation, and without the salve of forgiveness, there is only ungodliness there, *bad bones*, a decrepitude that I have, until this moment, managed to ignore by shoving it under the rapidly shifting plates of my life. Only now, seeing the house for perhaps the first time, do I have a vision of what I saw in the nursing station window all those years ago when I caught myself off guard, the hard shell of defiance and fear cracked open by the element of surprise. Then, as now, I was able, at last, to see the fragile framework, that which is always hidden until true healing has begun.

Chapter 30

The Father Question

THERE IS A TRUE/FALSE QUESTION on the Minnesota Multiphasic Personality Inventory that reads: *My father was a good man.*

It is one of five hundred sixty-seven questions on the MMPI, a test I took twice as a graduate student, and administered hundreds of times as a psychological examiner. Of all of the questions, only two have stayed with me. One is the father question. The other is: *I have never stolen from my workplace.*

The first time I came across the questions, I was taking the MMPI in order to learn how to give it. The father question, which comes early in the test, caught me off guard. I studied it for a long time, unsure of what my answer might say about me. How was it possible to give a simple yes or no when my real answer was so riddled with ambivalence? I re-read the question many times, as if repetition might reveal a loophole, a previously unseen option besides true or false. I considered leaving the question blank. I marked it true, then false, then true again, then false again. In my head, I argued that I needed room for expansion so that I could explain about the gray areas—where neither true nor false was true—that plagued my relationship with my father, gray areas that plague *every* relationship, I thought, even the easy ones.

"It's a sticky question," I argued in class. I pointed out that many people consider the parent-child relationship too sacred, or are simply too brainwashed by abuse or control, to answer honestly, that a father could potentially commit heinous acts of aggression and still be revered. And the opposite was true as well: one's father could have been, as my father was, deeply committed to the idea of family, fiercely protective and an excellent provider, yet, because he could not or would not relate to me the way I needed him to, still be maligned.

I also did not see how the father question, as written, could possibly take into account the fact that the parent-child relationship progresses through emotional stages.

"People hate their fathers when they're fifteen and adore them when they're thirty!" I said, "even though their father hasn't changed!"

Additionally, it was possible, I argued, for your feelings to change from year to year, or even month to month, resulting in a different answer, depending on when you asked.

In short, it was a question that begged qualifiers but allowed none.

The other question, *I have never stolen from my workplace*, also gave me pause because, at that very moment, there were a multitude of pens bearing the name Medical College of Georgia, which is where I worked, rolling around in my backpack. I supposed that, technically, this was stealing, although I told myself I would return them by semester's end.

On the test, I claimed that my father was a good man and that I had never stolen from my workplace.

* * *

Eventually, Professor Singleton would explain that, while my fellow graduate students and I were busy weighing our fathers' crimes and agonizing over our final pronouncements, the MMPI was not designed as a prosecutorial tool for fathers. It is, he said, a complex personality puzzle that focuses on the test-taker's *pattern* of responses.

"Never draw inferences about a person from one answer alone," he warned us.

As for the question about stealing from work, the expected answer is true (as in *True, I have never stolen from my workplace*) regardless of the truth. The MMPI assumes that every employed human in the world has, either purposefully or inadvertently, taken a pen, a paperclip, or a sticky-note pad from the workplace. Lying about it (saying you have never done this) is expected and is called, "faking good," and it refers to the desire of people with healthy egos to project an untarnished view of themselves.

* * *

Even after I fully understand the role of the father question in the MMPI, I will, for many years, review and revise my answer in my head. I believe there will come a moment when I will be clear about my feelings, able to answer the question definitively and without hesitation. But until such time, I vacillate, convicting or exonerating my father on a daily basis for crimes committed and gifts tendered.

"I'm moving to a trailer on a horse farm," I tell my parents one evening shortly after hearing about it.

"How will you ever reach Fisher to tell him?" my father asks, and I think *my father is not a good man*.

But a few weeks after I have moved, I call home to say hello and my father asks whether the dogs have settled in, if they have enough room and a nice strong fence, and my heart expands, and I think, *my father is a good man*.

* * *

Were I to put the father question to my sister and brother, they would not waver. *True*, they would say, pointing to his many good deeds: he was a member of the Peace Corps, he taught Sunday School, he started a publishing company and helped aspiring writers learn their trade. He bought my older brother a car, my older sister music lessons, and me a horse; later, he sent each of us to college and helped with graduate school. All of this he did without expectation of thanks, the hallmark of a good man. That they would not hesitate only feeds my ambivalence: how can my siblings answer without vacillation that which I cannot answer—not without spending hours, months, *years*—shuttling back and forth between extremes?

And then, after enough years of therapy, after I have made my way through my twenties and thirties and partway into my forties, I will stop oscillating between *my father is a good man/my father is not,* and will find instead a richness, a depth of understanding, about which I do not have to prevaricate, which is that my father was good *and* bad. I will see then that he, like many fathers—like many *parents*—was supportive *and* reproachful, attentive *and* dismissive, loving *and* self-involved, and I will come to a place where it is no longer the father question itself that interests me, but how thoroughly seduced I'd become by the either/or-ness of it, so that even as I was arguing, in graduate school, that the absence of a yes-*and*-no answer failed to take into account the gray areas of relationship, I was living my life at just such outer extremes, fearing food and so refusing to eat it, fearing self-indulgence and so amassing an outsized savings account I could never tap into, fearing comfort and so living without furniture, without appliances, without heat—every wrongheaded and self-defeating decision I made from age eighteen to twenty-six a testimony to my black-and-white view of things, to the way I clung to polar definitives, so terrified was I of the middle ground, of the uncertainties and the unknowables, which, I did not understand, are the hallmarks of everyday life.

* * *

A trailer is really nothing more than a network of two-by-fours holding up plywood walls and a roof, surrounded by an outer aluminum shell. The average single-wide is twelve feet wide by forty feet long, a perfect rectangle, and like mine, sits atop a pillar of concrete blocks hidden from view behind an aluminum "skirt." It is a precarious foundation and one I do not understand, except in those cases where a trailer is temporary, for example, someone is building a house but must live on-site until it's done. My trailer has been in its current resting place for fifteen years.

It is three miles from the Rollercoaster Road house. In order to get there, I must drive a network of roads that wind further and deeper into the southernmost outskirts of rural Chickamauga, past the short-lived House of God, a fundamentalist sect that met for a time in an old convenience store/butcher shop. The trailer sits on a dead-end road just over a tiny creek bridge and up a long, straight gravel driveway. It is nestled in a grove of evergreens. It is vanilla with red trim, with a rusty hitch the size of a motorcycle that juts out from underneath the kitchen window, testimony to its traveling past. There is a bedroom on one end and a kitchen on the other. In between there is a living room, a tiny bathroom, a spare bedroom, and a little cove carved out of the hallway for a washer and dryer. There is orange shag carpeting in every room except the kitchen and bath, where there is yellowing, but intact, linoleum. The walls are brown paneling, and the popcorn ceilings are low enough for me to brush with my fingertips. It is unattractive by any standard. But ten minutes into my first visit I am standing in the kitchen gaping at the stove and refrigerator like I've never seen appliances before, when a rumble like distant thunder erupts from the hallway.

"The furnace," says the landlady, as if she's read the uncomprehending furrow in my brow. "The thermostat is beside the spare bedroom." My chest warms with gratitude at the thought of no more wood smoke, no more three a.m. awakenings to stoke the fire, or worse, seven a.m. awakenings when the fire has gone out, trying to shower and get dressed in the cold.

Back outside, and for the amount of time it takes us to walk to the barn, I tell Sally Wright about the Rollercoaster Road house, how the landlord tricked me into going with him to evict the family living there, how the father had a gun, how they stole everything in the house when they left and put a hole in the bedroom wall.

"Oh, my," Sally says, an *oh, my* of compassion.

Five minutes later, I am staring up at an airy, two-story horse barn. Its shell, aluminum like my trailer, surrounds gargantuan rafters and sixteen roomy stalls, eight to a side, between which is a hallway large enough to canter a horse in a circle. The loft is packed solid with hay bales, a clean, sweet smell. Ten or twelve mares, some with babies skittering at their sides, wait for dinner in the hallway, and two more amble in from the back of the barn, which opens onto still more pasture. To the west, the Lookout Mountain plateau and its sloping nose rises like a sentry, while to the east, dense woods divide Sally and Ed Wright's horse farm from the cattle farm next door.

There are many reasons not to rent the ugly little trailer: its rickety foundation of concrete blocks and the rusty hitch jutting unceremoniously out the front, to name just two; the tall, orange carpet and the low-slung ceiling, ill-informed structural and decorating decisions that give the whole interior a dim-witted look. But once again I am smitten by heat: not a fickle wood stove this time, but a gas-powered furnace with a *thermostat*. I am enchanted by land that is flung in all directions and plummets into the woods on one side, the mountain on another. But most of all, I am in love with the fat mares and their skittish, whirling foals. And so, true to my penchant for careening from extreme to extreme, I disengage without worry or sentiment from the Rollercoaster Road house, and marry the idea of horses. It is a move that, though in many ways positive, further rockets me away from the roots of my suburban, Jewish childhood, about which my mother reminds me.

"Jews don't live on farms," she says when I tell her about the trailer.

"Jews really *don't* live on farms," Fisher says when I tell him about my mother's comment. "For a long time, they weren't even allowed to own land."

"I know," I say, although in truth this is the first I've heard of it. I stare at Fisher's face, firm and taut and broad as a blocked canvas. He teaches me more about my Jewish history than I ever learned in Sunday School; I would explain this to my father, except that I know his response: Jewish-*knowing* is not the same as Jewish-*being*.

* * *

And so it is without fanfare—with the very *opposite* of the drama with which I embarked on life in the Rollercoaster Road house—that I come to inhabit the trailer. Over the course of a few weeks, my love for the Rollercoaster Road house begins to fade, and, in its place, an early, deep affection for the trailer blossoms. I marvel at how it is that I could love a house the way I did the Rollercoaster Road house, bragging about its loveliness to friends, even going so far as to make myself over in its smoky image, only to have its doorknobs fall off, its linoleum leap up, its holes, like wounds, not heal. To this I will bring to bear that which I learned first at Bridgeway, and again in graduate school and in therapy: that it is possible, sometimes even predictable, to revere that which opposes you, to love without reservation, even in the face of conflict.

Within days, I establish a routine for the dogs: outside when I am at work, roaming the perimeter of their large fenced-in yard, and inside with me when I am home. Within a week, I establish a routine for myself: Mondays, Wednesdays and Fridays, I muck out the horse stalls in the evenings, from six-thirty until nine-thirty or ten and sometimes later, for which the Wrights (unnecessarily) pay me.

And within a month, Fisher and I are fighting.

It is mid-winter and the kind of dark that feels like summer is a childhood you'll never know again. Night spreads around the trailer like a liquid, coating the windows and snuffing out the light by early evening. Fisher and I and the three dogs are illuminated in the cheery yellow glow of a tiny ceramic Kmart lamp I've bought and placed on the bookcase. Were someone to peek in on us, I imagine we would look like an enviable covey. One evening, Fisher kisses the top of my head, lays the Bible on the coffee table, and says, "I need to borrow two hundred dollars." Then he puffs out his cheeks to show he is holding his breath.

Fisher needn't worry. I have, of course, thousands of dollars sitting in savings. While I still have trouble spending freely on myself, I am perfectly happy to spend on others. The dogs are whisked to the vet at the slightest suggestion of illness. I buy lavish Chanukah gifts for my family (a vacuum cleaner for my sister, an expensive digital bathroom scale for my mother). Likewise, I give Fisher whatever he needs.

"I'll write you a check," I say, getting up to get my checkbook.

He reminds me he does not have a bank account, that he'd rather have it in cash.

"Cash it is!" I say, and I tell him I will bring it to his training center the next day. He is deeply appreciative and assures me he will pay me back.

All of which would have been fine had it ended here. Instead, I start to formulate a plan for Fisher's future, a future brimming with the accoutrements of maturity as I know them: a bank account so that he doesn't have to drive all over downtown every month to pay his light and water bill. Clothes that aren't stained, and that are all generous in crotch and length. And a telephone, so that, on days when he is sick, he can call his boss from his own apartment, instead of having to drive to a pay phone. Or call *me*, for that matter, just to chat when we aren't together. Conveniences and little luxuries that will be made possible by the new job Fisher is going to get that will pay better than his current one.

"You should get certified to teach!" I say. My eyes shine with confidence and pride. "You would be a *great* teacher."

"I don't want to teach," Fisher says. "I like my job."

"But it doesn't pay you anything! You could be doing something so much more challenging!"

To understand Fisher's rage at this last statement is to understand Fisher's greatest wound. But I don't understand it immediately, or for many more months, because Fisher himself doesn't. And because he doesn't, he can't explain how his church and his parents and his religious school demanded that he seek an unreachable perfection, how his failure to do so felt to him like an affront to God, and how, because of that, he lives in the shadow of exquisite failure every day. Instead of being able to tell me any of this, Fisher rises up to his full height from the sofa and shakes his head from side to side like there is something poisonous stuck to it he needs to get off. His hands are fists; his eyes travel their sockets uncomprehendingly, no longer taking in the scene that is the cozy covey of us.

"If you wanted someone rich, you should've looked for someone rich," he says, through clenched teeth.

I sit there in the little circle of light, my mouth open to no words. The dogs, surprised by Fisher gathering his coat and ski cap—the preparations that are made for a walk—are jumping around the small living room, knocking the newspaper and the ashtray from the coffee table in their excitement, everything a misunderstanding, everything skidding off in a wrong direction. I stand up too but by then Fisher is already heading down the narrow hallway for the door, and just before he throws it open (it is hollow, so the force slams it against the outside of the trailer and back again), he says, "Obviously, I can't be who you think I should be," and he adds, loudly, as he is getting in his truck and revving the engine, "I-AM-ONLY-HUMAN!"

I run to the kitchen window and watch Fisher's truck lights disappear down the gravel driveway, over the creek bridge and up the road. *Surely he is coming back!* After several minutes the dogs groan and lie down again. I retrieve the ashtray from the floor and sink into the sofa, smoking cigarette after cigarette until my eyes burn, replaying the scene over and over in my head. I call my friend Dolores and tell her what happened. She knows Fisher well; she is one of the older women at the training center who used to take him meals.

"Don't worry honey, he really loves you, he'll call you tomorrow," she says.

The next day, as I am getting ready to test a new client for the training center, Sherry, the secretary, pokes her head in my office. "Fisher on Line 1," she says, wearing a broad, we-told-you-so smile, because I have been talking all morning about our fight and how Fisher misunderstood my comment and left angry and Dolores said he would call but it's already nine a.m. (then ten, then eleven). *Give him some time,* they said, and *no, you can't call him, it's his move,* as if our relationship were a chess match and there is a protocol, or worse, a strategy.

"Fisher?" I say softly into the phone. I am reassured by the simple act of saying his name to him.

"You obviously want something I can't be," Fisher says, words carefully chosen and practiced-sounding.

"That's not true," I say, my voice instantly pleading, sobs shimmying up my esophagus.

"I'm only human, you know," Fisher says, repeating the bizarre non sequitur from the previous evening, his response to my suggestion that he get a teaching certificate. "This thing is over."

I have been broken up with before, of course. By Neil in college, when I returned to school from the hospital; by Forrest, who didn't so much break up with me as indicate that I could continue to sleep with him although he was engaged; and by Mitch, who, as I sat in a pile of dead leaves laced with dog shit in the pool in the stilt house yard, announced that he was no longer having fun with me. But this breakup feels different. I don't need Fisher in some frightened, horny, college freshman way, like I needed Neil, nor do I crave the drama of men made more attractive by rage or moodiness, as I once craved Richie Deiner and Joe. Fisher is the one who walked into the Rollercoaster Road house and saw what I saw: not sloped floors and dingy carpet and sagging rafters, but the view of the woods from the windows and the promising smell of wood heat, a home with which, and in which, to fall in love. Likewise, he is the one who saw in me what I could *not* see, beauty and possibility and strength. This breakup feels like a death, because I have not yet learned to see myself as Fisher sees me. Without him, I barely exist.

I don't remember exactly what happens next. I know I cry, to my coworkers, to Sally and Ed Wright, to the dogs. I am sure that I cry in the barn, and that I think about the tragic and sad fact of shoveling my own tears along with the muck of the horse stalls and depositing them out back in the manure pile. I know that, at some point—a few days, a week later, maybe—my brother calls to invite me on a trip, and although I don't intend to tell him about my breakup with Fisher, I do, eventually wondering aloud whether the differences in our religion really were a part of the problem.

"That's why I don't date non-Jews," my brother says. There's a familiarity to dating someone of the same religion, he adds, like a book whose first hundred pages you can skip over, because you already know the set-up. Then he tells me about Cancun, Mexico, how much I will like it, how he has traveled with our sister but never with me, and that, as family, we should be closer. There are ruins to explore there, and snorkeling. He wants to go in February.

"If Dad is doing okay by then," he says.

"What do you mean, *by then?*" I ask, and he says, as if this is something I've already been told, that Dad is going to Sloan Kettering Cancer Center in New York for treatment. Perhaps I have been told, but, in truth, I can't remember, and much later, when I am trying to put things in perspective, there is no mention of Sloan Kettering in my journal. When I ask my mother about it years after my father's death, she says the treatment was canceled because my father's kidneys shut down.

I tell my brother I'll go to Cancun.

At the time, I don't know that Fisher and I will be back together by February, and that my brother's suggestion—that Jewish partners make for an easier road—will be filed away for future use. I also don't know that Fisher and I will have had several more fights, each more damaging, more perplexing than the first, and all of them ending with Fisher's proclamation that he is "only human." We are still, both of us, completely in the dark, blind to what Fisher is trying to say or why it keeps coming up. Between fights—stretches of time that expand to two weeks, at most—we continue to make strange, hands-free love. We still drive the countryside looking at fantasy houses, although when "our" fantasy house comes up for sale, we stare wide-eyed at one another and speed away, and never go see it again. If we have the sense that something is broken, something fundamental and necessary to our relationship, we don't talk about it. And looking back, I doubt that, had we even known what it was, we could have.

* * *

The mating of horses is hard to watch. It is part rape, part game, and the first time I witness it, I don't know what is about to happen, although I should. It is, after all, an Arabian horse farm I live on, a profitable *breeding* farm. One evening as I am mucking out, Ed Wright closes the enormous barn doors, removes a mare from her stall, and snub-ties her—her muzzle only inches from a post—in the hallway. From across the barn, a tall gray horse begins to holler and thrash about, kicking at his door, rearing up on his hind legs. The mare in the middle whinnies, shimmies side to side, tries to turn her head to get a look at the gray stallion raising a racket. Ed Wright attaches a lunge line to the stud's halter, then opens his door.

"Be nice," he admonishes.

What happens next happens in a storm of dust and a tangle of legs. The stud rushes the mare, paws at her flank, rears up. The mare squeals loudly, kicks out, keeps trying to turn her head, pull away from the post. The stud bites her neck. The mare waggles her rear end and dances from side to side, her legs opening up. The stud rears, lands hard across her back, and then—front legs pawing at her withers—snakes the length of himself—*two full feet it looks like from where I am standing, unable to look away*—into her vagina. After a few forceful grunts, the stud's body goes limp, and he slides, jelly-like, from the mare's back.

Ed Wright returns the stud to his stall, opens a folder, and jots down the date and time.

"Give us a little boy," he says affectionately to the mare, untying her and opening the barn doors. She snorts as if in agreement and trots out to join the rest of the mares in the pasture. From beginning to end, the mating takes place in under five minutes, though, I note, with more foreplay than I have had in almost two years. The thought surprises me, because I didn't know I ever thought about it.

Perhaps predictably, my next fight with Fisher draws fire from what I have witnessed in the barn. I invite him to a Jewish dinner with new friends, an invitation, he says, I should be "strong enough" to resist extending. We have a tacit agreement not to push our respective religious functions on one another, he reminds me, and this is me pushing.

"I am not pushing," I argue back, saying it's not pushing my religion on him to want his company at a dinner party, to which says he doesn't want to have to buy new clothes.

"Well, it wouldn't hurt you to have something nice to wear," I say, "You are a grown-up now." I know full well that this comment will ratchet up the fight, and, sure enough, Fisher leaps to *stop pushing me to be something I'm not* and *I'm only human!* To which I shout, "If you were *human* you would *touch* me when we have sex! Even horses know how to do *that!*"

It is as ugly and mean a thing as I have ever said, and it catches Fisher completely off guard. His whole chest deflates and his face caves in on itself, and I am instantly sorry I have said this since I have never mentioned anything about the strange way we have sex. But the fact is, I have only just gotten here myself, no longer instantly turned on by a look from Fisher, the shine of his hair, the set of his jaw. I need more than the dry bones of intercourse, and yet I know I cannot tell Fisher this in any sensible way that will not cause a fight, and so I say it when we are already at odds, already clawing away at what is left of our time together. As awful as it is to see Fisher hurt, and to know that I am the one who hurt him, I am hopeful that, in the wake of our pain, there will be something loving and soft and nurturing, something stronger and more real than what we had before.

It is magical thinking. It is not understanding that what I am fighting for—a better dressed, more attentive and mature partner capable of meeting my needs—is, in short, *a good man.* This is my mother's plaint. It is not understanding that what I am really demanding of Fisher are the intangibles—attention, comfort, patience, forgiveness—that I cannot give myself. And at its very core, it is not seeing that my desire for those things is a sign of my stepping forward into the world, where it is finally becoming apparent that I am, like Fisher, *only human.* For me, this means I have needs that are perfectly acceptable, and even *advantageous,* to meet; that my ego is finally beginning to claim its rightful spot somewhere near the center of my life. When this happens, I will recall the MMPI question *I have never stolen from my workplace,* whose correct answer is to lie in order to appear healthy—a sign that the ego *cares* what it looks like. In the small, arid spaces between fights with Fisher, I am surprised to find something new: *it no longer quells my anxiety to live like a pauper. It is no longer important to present to the world a face so obviously at odds with itself, because I no longer believe oddity makes me authentic.*

For now, there is no taking back what I have said to Fisher about not touching me. There is no uncrumpling his face, no inflating his chest. It is just another clash in what has become a long line of fights;

we are like miners chipping away at a quarry of need and frustration. Fisher will leave, come back, leave, come back again. Each time we will reunite amidst rounds of apologies and kissing and careful conversation. There will be more nights secure in the cozy lamplight of my living room at the trailer, but it will feel for me, and maybe for Fisher as well, as if something we cherished was lost in the move.

Chapter 31

The Death of Charles Black

THERE IS A NOTE ON OUR HOTEL DOOR when my brother and I return from breakfast.

Mrs. Dora Shavin called. It is important to call home.

The note confuses me. Dora Shavin is my grandmother, and she has been dead for twenty-six years. My brother is also staring at the note.

I say, "Dora Shavin?"

He says, "This isn't good."

I follow Mark back down the stairs to the hotel lobby to the pay phones. From each landing, I can see the Caribbean Sea glittering in the hot February sun. The wind smells like salt. It is not yet nine a.m., and the beach is already alive with sunbathers and the high whine of birds.

It is easier to reverse the long distance charges from Cancun to Atlanta than to use a credit card or feed an endless stream of quarters into the phone. Mark says, *collect call for Mrs. Norman Shavin,* which is when I understand the note: to the hotel *recepcionista,* Norman sounded like Dora.

I wait at my brother's side for the call to go through, impatient to talk to my mother. I am so homesick I am nauseous. I get this way when I feel especially vulnerable, which I have felt for almost our entire two days in Cancun. My brother and I have snorkeled, climbed the pyramid ruins at Cozumel, walked the beach, and eaten all our meals together, acting to the outside world like perfectly agreeable siblings. But the truth is, soon after our arrival in Mexico, we started to fight. Not fight like old times—at thirty-one and twenty-six, we are finally too mature to actually hit each other. We are more like bitter, longstanding rivals, compulsively judgmental, at times mean-spirited, and unable to hold our tongues. My brother's critiques are unwanted and invasive; my refutes feel to him like stonewalling.

"You shouldn't smoke," Mark says. "It's a terrible habit. Dad has cancer, you know."

"Yes, I know dad has cancer," I say, lighting up. "But I don't think I gave it to him."

And, "You're always unhappy," he says. "You never let up, or let anyone else have any fun."

"You think you're so perfect," I say. "You're so white bread."

He calls me pessimistic and controlling; I call him moralistic and uppity. At our lowest point, which was over tacos on our second night, we argued over who was worse company, each of us making our case for the other with shitty smiles and deep, disparaging sighs.

In fact we are both terrible company. I am anxious and depressed, and lonely for Fisher. We fought just before I left— barely recovered from the mean things I'd said about our sex life, he was newly angry that I was taking a trip without him, even though he admitted he wouldn't spend money on such a trip—and because he was angry, he refused to watch the dogs. I told him that just because he felt it necessary to constrict his life, I did not feel it necessary to constrict mine, and that I would continue to do the things I wanted to do, with or without him. Now, with the perspective that comes with an ocean between us, I can see how Fisher felt hurt and left behind, and I am sorry I wasn't more understanding. It is true that Fisher is a fiscal anorexic, but it is also true that he works a job that pays too little because he believes in helping others. True also that with the tiny vacation time he earns, he flies home to St. Louis to see his aging parents. Why I had to go a thousand miles away to see this, I don't know.

I am also anxious because I am eating unfamiliar, rich foods, including lobster with real butter and big, fat spicy tacos. There are no scales at the hotel, and so I am gauging my weight by the perceived roundness or flatness of my mid-section. Exacerbating my microscopic self-focus is the fact that half the things Mark and I are doing require my attendance in a bathing suit.

As for my brother, deeply private and not prone to sharing, he did confess when he invited me on this trip that he was lonely and unhappy at work. As far as I knew, he hadn't dated seriously for several years, and many of his friends already had families of their own. My brother has real dreams of a family, unlike me, for whom the idea of marriage and children is mostly abstract.

And there is the specter of our father hanging over us. When we left Atlanta, he was in the hospital, hooked to a machine that was sucking toxins from his kidneys, which had become unable to detoxify themselves. *He'll go home Thursday*, the doctor told us on Monday, *don't cancel your trip plans.* I stared at my father with his audience of machines hissing and sucking all around him, a tube snaking from his nose to a clear plastic container beside his bed, an earthy brown liquid burbling out. His face was sunken, his teeth seemingly enlarged. He didn't look like a man going home Thursday.

"This is just a setback, a complication," my father said, as if complications and setbacks weren't the advance guards of death. "Take your trip and I'll see you when you get back."

But for the two days we are in Cancun before the note appears on our door, my brother and I don't talk about our father. Instead, we rip and tear at each other's character, a habit so true-to-form from our childhood, when we couldn't know what the issues were, much less talk about them, that I feel now almost exactly as I did then. We are like a couple of hapless outlaws in a trite western drama, too mad to admit we're stubborn and too stubborn to admit we're frightened, and so we pull out our guns and shoot.

Mark is being a butthole, I will tell my mother when Mark finishes talking to her. *Mark is a self-centered know-it-all and he thinks he's perfect.*

Mark hands me the phone but before I can trot out my complaints, my mother says, "Okay, he died."

It is a strange, terrible sentence, an epilogue that seems to need a longer story to anchor it.

"He *died?*" I say, in a voice that is squeaky and incredulous. My mother says something reassuring —*it's okay, we'll be okay*—but because she is so far away, and with the suddenly cumbersome arc of the phone receiver between us, her words sound forced and empty. And although it should be anything but, the news is a complete shock. I am fairly sure I hung up the phone, looked at my brother's face, and said something, though all I remember is taking off running—running, like a child—back to our hotel room.

Mark and I pack and drive to the airport—in silence? talking nonstop? crying?—and begin what will be the herculean process of convincing the Mexican airline industry to allow us to break the terms of our tickets so we can get home in time for the funeral. They do not want us to leave, because as long as we are in their country, we are spending money. We are forced to say, over and over, *but our father has died*, words that feel at first like trying to chew up a washing machine, but that, by the time we get new tickets in place, which, in my memory, is six hours later, I feel like we've lived there for months. For the next four hours, Mark and I hang in the air, suspended between lives: the old one, in which we had a father, and the new one, for which he is anxiously penning the eulogy he will read the next day.

Someone picks us up at the airport and drives us to our mother's house. Condolences I'm sure, hugs, arched brows. My brother is stoic in the car; the next morning, I hear him weeping in the kitchen. At the funeral, he delivers his eulogy. *My father was a young man who died of an old disease,* is how it starts, but, like so much else, the rest of what he says falls off the face of my memory. I don't remember if the service was in a synagogue or a funeral home, who conducted it, where we sat, who was in attendance, or what was going through my mind. I do remember that my sister, Julie, spoke either before or after my brother, a sprawling, grief-mottled motif of indiscriminate memories and pain and regret. *A collection of neurons firing at random,* my brother will call it later, though some of it was poetry of the sort only Julie was capable, while other parts seemed an ill-conceived grab for compassion, as when she painted a picture of our "oft-maligned father" spending long mornings in the bathroom, struggling to have a bowel movement. It was perhaps here that my mother whispered fiercely into my ear, "I expect Dad to sit up in his coffin and say, *Oh, Julie shut up!*"

But for the most part, occupying the space in my brain where my father's funeral in the winter of 1988 should be, there is, instead, the funeral of my best friend, Bobbi's, father in the summer of 1973. This funeral, of thirty-three year-old Dr. Hathaway, whom I met only twice in my life, I can see like it was yesterday, almost down to what I wore. I can see the sanctuary where I sat with my mother and watched twelve-year-old Bobbi file in after her mother and sisters, her clothes hanging on her frame at an angle, the fault of a birth defect that made one hip higher than the other. I can see that she is arguing heatedly with her mother and that her mother is not answering her, and I can see them sit down and watch the funeral service with stunned, mask-like expressions.

I know that my father's casket was in the room at his funeral, but what I recall is staring at the mounded form of Dr. Hathaway's casket at the front of his funeral, not knowing it is a casket and thinking instead that I am looking at his rounded girth. I stare at Dr. Hathaway's draped form with great intensity, willing it to rise and fall with breath; when it does, I will jump up and announce, "*HE IS ALIVE!*" and everyone will be grateful to me for being so observant, and we will all go home. Instead, as I am waiting for him to take his magical breath, a man on the front row faints in his pew, and a collective gasp slices through the room as people rush to revive him. At home, that warm afternoon, an afternoon Bobbi and I would otherwise be galloping our horses to the Chattahoochee River, I sit alone on the floor of my room and move my model horses around, searching for a story to give purpose to their movements.

I don't fully realize that the memories of my father's funeral are supplanted by memories of Dr. Hathaway's funeral until many years later. There are many possible reasons for this displacement, the most obvious being that the death of Bobbi's father, because I was only twelve, changed my life dramatically, whereas the death of my own father, because I was twenty-six, did not. At twelve, there were

307

immediate, tangible losses: Bobbi sold her pony and moved away from my school and my neighborhood, leaving me with no other close friends. And there were intangible losses: gone was my twelve year-old's sense of safety, my faith in an unshakeable world, and my belief—albeit unrecognized—that a selective immortality spared those responsible for keeping my life on track. Fourteen years later, my father's death does not take anyone away from me except my father himself, to whom I am not close; it doesn't impact my friendships or my home life, or engender in me a child's terror of death and change. In fact, for a very long time, I tell myself that *nothing* life-altering happened as a result of my father's death, and I seem to believe this until that moment I turn my focus to his funeral, and realize my memory of it *simply isn't there*. It is this excised bank of memories that tips me off to the truth, which is that, although my father and I did not have a deep relationship, the effect of his death was profound.

* * *

Fisher does not attend my father's funeral. I don't blame him for his absence; I suspect that my mother and siblings—and maybe even I—discouraged his presence. And even though I remain at home for an entire week, sitting shiva after the funeral as friends and family pay their respects, he doesn't join me then, either. We do talk on the telephone once a day, although, the more I try to articulate my feelings about my father's death, the further away Fisher seems to go, until I feel as if I am talking to an empty room.

It is a somber week in my mother's house. The long days, during which I alternate between lethargic and bewildered, are punctuated by the arrival of many of my parents' friends and my father's coworkers, most of whom I do not know and whose presence in the house feels forced and strange. Several of my brother's friends stop by as well, a few of whom I had crushes on when I was younger, but their presence, too, feels strange, as if I am talking to them through a smeary window. There are a few cousins and an aunt. Conversation swirls around: which relatives are ill, died early, or died tragically, and among the names mentioned there is my paternal grandmother, Dora, the name the hotel receptionist inserted in place of "Norman." It is upon hearing her name that the full weirdness of the name glitch hits me: *Mrs. Dora Shavin says it is important to call home;* being *called home,* as Fisher has explained to me before, meaning, *to die.*

"It's like my grandmother was telling us to call her, because she had called Dad home," I tell Fisher the next morning on the phone.

"Wow, Babe, that's intense," Fisher says, but his words don't reach any emotional place.

And while I know that my own friends from high school must have stopped by—Kay and Lori and Deanna and the twins, and my neighbor friend, Denise—the only person I can recall with any clarity is Bobbi (who goes by Barbara now for work), and whom I haven't seen or talked to in over ten years. Her light-brown hair is shoulder-length and brushed to a luster, her clothes professional, her odd gait less pronounced.

"Isn't this ironic?" I say to her.

She looks perplexed. "In what way?"

"I was there when your dad died, and now you're here for my dad's death."

Bobbi nods but there doesn't seem to be anything behind it, no recognition of irony. At some point I would realize it really wasn't ironic, that visiting people when their loved ones die is one of the most common social niceties on the planet, and is, therefore, about as *un*ironic as things get.

Bobbi and I have little to say to one another except in the form of bare-bones catching up—*what do you do, what do you do, are you married? no, are you? no*—and then she drives away. I suppose I thought something might be rectified by this reunion, that the tragic loss of her father fourteen years earlier, which resulted in our loss of each other, would be somehow softened. Instead, her perfunctory appearance leaves me less comforted than before she arrived.

* * *

Every afternoon the week of sitting shiva, I make the walk down the driveway to get the mail. News of my father's death has not reached everywhere, of course, and won't for many months, so letters and bills and magazines addressed to him continue to pour in. I believe I am somehow sparing my mother the odd shock that comes with fielding my dead father's mail, ignoring the fact that all I am doing is compulsively reading his name on every envelope, then laying them all on her desk for her to go through later. But it is in performing this seemingly useless ritual that I am reminded of something I have always known, but that now strikes me as poignant: my father had an *alias*.

I was ten the first time I noticed catalogues in our mailbox addressed to a Mr. Charles Black. I told my mother about the mix-up.

"No, that's Dad," she said. "He uses that name for correspondence sometimes."

"Is it because he's famous?" I asked. My father wrote columns for the newspaper that earned him a bit of celebrity in Atlanta, and adults, on hearing my last name, often asked if I was his daughter.

"I'm not really sure why he does it," she said.

Discovering Charles Black was exciting. It was like finding a sixth person in our family where, all along, there had been only five. Mr. Black was mysterious and secretive; he got mail at our address but was, himself, invisible, and no one outside the family, not even the people mailing him things, knew the truth about him. Whenever I saw his name on a package or an envelope, I smiled and thought, *Your secret's safe with me, Mr. Black!*

The discovery that my father had an alias thrilled me as a child, but as a grown woman sleepwalking to the mailbox on the heels of his death, it feels emblematic. Who exactly I am grieving for is uncertain, and perhaps, I think, it's not even for my father. Perhaps I am grieving for Bobbi, whose brief visit reminds me of how much we lost when her father died. Perhaps I am grieving my brother, because there won't be another Cancun trip, or, for that matter, any further attempts to iron out what is wrong between us. Perhaps I am grieving for my mother, fifty-eight and suddenly alone, defined now by widowhood rather than marriage or parenthood. How odd, I think, that, in death, the spotlight of grief is turned away from my father and trained instead on everyone around him. And this, I decide, is the legacy of Charles Black. Not that my father had an alias in life, an anonymous identity to anonymous sources, but that, in grappling with my loss of him, what I find is not him, but everyone else.

* * *

And then the week is over. I climb into my car, which has sat dormant for ten days in my mother's driveway, and, fighting back the fountain of emotion that bubbles up as my mother waves from the dining room window, I leave. In the span of days from Cancun's end to now, my mother and brother and sister and I seem to have woken into a foreign land whose laws and customs we must now decipher. We tell each other we love each other, strange words in our mouths. For several months, my mother will call me three or four times a week, instead of once a week. I appreciate these calls; without them, she and I both know I will feel like I've slipped through some scrim of lake ice and disappeared. My brother will insist on moving into my mother's house.

"It's just for a while, until you feel comfortable being alone," he tells her. He stays nearly a year.

And my sister, whose cluttered eulogy mirrored a chaotic mind, announces that she has chronic fatigue syndrome. Soon, her visits home are accompanied by four-foot long bullets of oxygen, which must be delivered by courier service; it is what keeps her alive, she asserts. Five years later, she will move with her husband and daughter to Colorado, to a house that has been conceived for just such an illness.

It is not long after my father's funeral—a few weeks maybe—that my relationship with Fisher heaves its final sigh. For days, I have been claiming the tired, but, I insist, *transient* excuses of stress and grief and unhappiness at work as reasons for my constant malaise and lack of interest in sex. These are not lies, but neither are they transient: my father's death has lowered what I think of as a "dome of realism" around me that I can't ignore. It beseeches me to make something meaningful of my life (though a truer statement might be that it hounds me to quit my job at the mental health center, which has begun to feel tedious and hollow). At the same time, it warns me against making decisions I might regret. Marriage and children are two such decisions, and the next time Fisher begins a sentence with *when we get married*, I stare out the car window and say nothing. This is how the dome of realism comes to encompass Fisher's life as well, and how he knows, without my speaking the words, that the time for blind but hopeful speculation has passed.

Chapter 32

The Perfect Jew

I CLEAN THE BARN most of the nights the winter of my father's death and that following spring. Long after I no longer like my job as a therapist or love Fisher, I still adore the smell of horses and manure and oats. Four days a week, I live for the utter simplicity of pushing a heavy wheelbarrow down the rows of stalls, raking and shoveling until each one sparkles with dry wood shavings and fresh hay dropped down from the loft. Without Fisher, without my father, with a family rearranged, change feels inevitable.

"You can still get your PhD," Moira says. "It's not too late."

But it is too late. I am not the same girl I was five years earlier, hurtling down the highway with her mother toward her first mental health job, enamored of her own untested powers as a psychological superhero. The years, and my father's illness and death, have made me something different.

"I don't know what I want," I tell Moira.

"Are you still working with the horses?"

"Yes," I say. "I like it better than working with people."

Moira laughs. But the fact is, unlike with people, it is possible to make horses happy. All it takes is a clean bed of shavings and a little hay. And even though their stalls are sullied again by morning and the hay is gone, there exists, I believe, an equine faith in certainty, that all that is needed will soon be delivered.

* * *

When I was nine, my friend, Lolly's, brother was killed in a car wreck. The family was returning from vacation when a tractor-trailer hit them head-on. Tim died at the scene. In the newspaper account of the accident, there were pictures of the crumpled car, the jackknifed tractor-trailer, and the ambulance. In my memory, there were also pictures of Tim lying on a stretcher with a blood-soaked sheet pulled over his head. But this last may be my imagination. I probably just overheard Lolly telling the story of the accident to our teacher, Mrs. Paul, the two of them huddled like lovebirds at the front of the classroom, while the rest of us pretended to work on our book reports, secretly listening, our minds filling in the visuals of what we heard.

Before the accident, Lolly was just another girl in my fifth-grade class, but after the accident, she was practically famous. Teachers were constantly wrapping an arm around her, calling on her first when her hand went up, excusing her from homework. Even some of the other kids treated her differently, inviting her to parties when they hadn't before, picking her for kickball although she was terrible. For those of us still dragging unfashionably complete families behind us, Lolly's sudden rise to fame dangled like a carrot we could not reach. There were two other routes to instant popularity that I knew of: parental divorce, resulting in a move to an apartment with your mother, and a broken leg. Like death, these were hard-to-control events. When I was fourteen, it seemed I might be in line for divorce fame, until my mother changed her mind, making me just another kid with an intact family and strong, straight bones, neither of which, as far as I was concerned, did me any good.

By the time my father dies, I have lost the need for the kind of attention that suffering affords. Still, I am surprised by how little attention I get. A few friends hug me. At the mental health center, someone pushes an envelope with twenty-eight dollars in it into my hand, for donation to my father's favorite cause. Otherwise, my life resumes the pattern and the tenor it had before my father's death. I continue to see my therapy clients and to feel frustrated by their lack of progress. I continue to test and to write mostly ineffective b-mod plans at the training center. I continue to clean the barn several nights a week, my rake-shovel-dump, rake-shovel-dump routine a comforting meditation. My father's death is already woven so seamlessly into the fabric of my life that, except for the fact that I can't call him, it's almost like it didn't happen. How is it possible, I wonder, to lose a parent and then resume doing all the things you hate and love with no more thought, no more urgency, than you had before?

* * *

Summer comes to the trailer, and with it, a call from a man I've never met but whose name I recognize from the Jewish community. *Did I want to go out?*

"Out?" I say. "Like a date?"

The question takes me by surprise, although the voice on the phone sounds hopeful and kind. Still, there is something inside me pulling away.

"My father just died," I say, taking liberties with the word *just*.

"I know," says David. "A friend of my mother's came to your shiva."

This is reassuring, although I don't know why until I've hung up. It is the Jewish meeting ground that my brother mentioned a while back, the place that you start from when you date a fellow Jew, where you're already on familiar ground, are known right off the bat "for who you really are." At the time Mark said it, I'd scoffed.

"A little time to get back on my feet," is what I tell David I need, and he says that he will call me again in a few months.

"Oh," he says, "and I'm sorry about your dad."

Simple words that nevertheless go a long way. For a minute, I consider changing my mind, telling him I *will* go out now. As in, *right now*. But I don't. The dome of realism stops me, the part of losing a parent that has made me feel at once rudderless and at the same time more careful about what and whom to let into my life.

A month passes, then two. One day, upon returning from a full schedule of home visits for the training center, Sherry, the secretary, proudly hands me the sweater I'd worn that morning. It is my favorite piece of clothing, washed so many times that it had become little more than a fuzzy landscape of tiny fabric pills.

"It took all day but I got 'em off!" she says.

My sweater looks like it did when I bought it: deep, shimmery black and completely pill-free. I stare first at the sweater, which I adore, and then at Sherry, about whom I feel a creeping disdain.

"She spent her entire workday picking pills off my sweater," I tell Moira that night on the phone. "One by one. Hundreds of them. Maybe *thousands.*" For reasons unknown, I am staring at a picture of Fisher as we talk, following the deep crease in his face with my eyes, remembering how it once suggested something practically mystical about him.

"So?" she says.

"*So,* Moira? How much more pointlessly can you spend your workday?"

Moira cackles. "How about retesting IQ's that never change just to fulfill a state requirement? How about feeding M&M's to people and calling it a plan?"

"That's my *job,*" I say. "I didn't invent the re-testing of retarded people. *Or* M&M's."

I recall my father's comment to my mother that Fisher wasn't what he thought I'd come up with, and how I'd said, "I didn't invent him." Of course my father wasn't suggesting that I'd failed in the creation of Fisher, merely that I'd stumbled in the choice of him. Which is Moira's point: obviously the useless re-testing of IQs and the decades-long doling out of M&M's isn't original with me, but it has been my choice to keep doing it.

The aftermath of my father's death also finds me disillusioned with the mental health caseload I was so happy to be assigned just a year earlier. It is practically a basic tenet of counseling that most clients—even miserable ones desperate for relief—fight treatment. Enamored of the early promise of therapy—*someone who will listen! Someone who will support and take my side! Someone who will put an end to my anguish!*—clients are quickly deflated by the news (delivered, either directly or indirectly, by their therapist, i.e., me) that their pain is largely self-inflicted, and, as such, it is their own *selves* with which they must grapple, more so than their husbands or their mothers or their pasts. Therapy has now become something bigger and harder and muddier than it was in the beginning; now there is disillusionment with the process, which soon becomes disappointment in the therapist, which, for me, leads wrongly but inevitably to disappointment in the client. Somewhere along the continuum of elation to disappointment (another tenet of counseling: the green therapist will travel the continuum alongside the client, desperate, but unable, to alter the outcome), I would stumble across my memory of Mr. Jenkins's big bass/little bass lecture. It was what he used to illustrate his point that I needed to leave Bridgeway and go back to graduate school (the throwing back of the little bass so it can grow) if I wanted to be a good therapist. In this new strange land, however, where the structure of my family has been irreversibly altered and I have slammed up against the hard (though malleable) armature of my own future, the big bass/little bass analogy means something altogether different to me, namely that it is necessary to periodically toss our small convictions back into the pond we fished them out of, so that we can, at a later time, dip in and retrieve our larger convictions, those truly worthy of our fervor. In other words, although I once believed with every fiber of my being that I was born to be a psychological superhero, I am starting to believe that this is no longer where my passion, my direction, lies, and that there may be something altogether simpler, and at the same time, more profound, that is calling out to me.

But frustration with my mental health clients is not my only problem. Karen, the coworker who came to the Rollercoaster Road house and couldn't flee the mayhem she found there fast enough, announces to me that my larger problem is that I am passive-aggressive, and that, at the moment I felt my influence as a therapist did not matter, I stopped being available for staff meetings, treatment planning, crisis evaluations, or even just filling in at lunch when others wanted to go out. Instead—and she is right about this—I scheduled my own personal therapy sessions to coincide with the most detested hour of my workday, which was immediately after lunch, which granted me two full hours of blissful freedom (if you count as bliss the wailing and fuming I was doing in my therapy sessions, which, oddly, I did). I have, in other words, forsaken everything but my own bald cause.

At some point, I realize I am like a horse in high winds—eyes closed, head down, tail tucked, waiting for the danger to pass. Only the danger isn't an impending storm, but what it has left in its wake: the recognition, years in the making, that my emptiness, which for years fueled my depression and later my eating disorder, has not been miraculously quelled by helping. Being a therapist has not—and I realize now, cannot—imbue my life with the layers of meaning for which I am desperate. Fisher has been right all along: what I need is something bigger and more complex and more profound and more obscure than anything a simple job title can offer. What I need is a spiritual awakening. And so, when David the Jew calls again and says, *Remember me, I called you a few months ago,* I leap in with, "How about Friday?"

We agree to meet for lunch at an Applebee's restaurant.

"How will I know who you are?" I ask. He says he looks like a Jew.

I find him immediately. He sticks out in the crowd of mostly overweight, average-height men with the bland, flat face and side-parted hair that a friend from Hebrew School used to call "the curse of the Gentile." Like me, he is slightly too tall and too thin; also like me he is olive complected with thick, curly black hair and dark eyes. His nose is slightly downturned. Everything about him, from his pressed suit and polished loafers to the cloud of cologne that surrounds him stands in stark contrast to Fisher, with his chronically splattered shirts, wool ski caps, and butt-hugging Levi's. I feel a pang of guilt about this—I don't mean to compare Fisher harshly to David—and when I relive our lunch date later that night alone in my trailer, I will even the score. David is impressive, yes, but he emanates no alluring, earthy aura. His face, while handsome, lacks the deeply etched crease I so loved in Fisher's, evidence (I believed) of profound thought, which left its mark on especially reflective men.

We spend lunch covering the facts. David is the oldest and only boy in a family of three children. He went to private school and works with his father, a developer.

"Is that interesting?" I ask.

David looks up from his Cobb salad and puts down his fork. "We're destroying marshlands to build apartment complexes." He pauses. "The money's good," he smiles with his mouth closed and laughs through his nose. "But it's hard to feel good about what I do." There is something shy about his manner, like he is not completely at ease with the sound of his own voice.

"What about you?" he asks, without picking up his fork again. "What's a nice Jewish girl like you doing living on a farm?" He smiles again, mouth open this time.

"Not just a farm, a trailer," I say.

"A *trailer*," he repeats, a look of serious alarm on his face. "Jews don't live in trailers!"

"That's exactly what my mom said about farms!" We both laugh. He seems relieved that my mother shares his principles, and is probably thinking that it will only be a matter of time until her corrective influence sets me right, instead of the truth, which is that her influence has already come to bear, and I live where I live as a result.

For the rest of lunch, I study David's scrubbed face, white cotton shirt, carefully knotted blue tie. He is not the kind of man whose head would go swimming in a wood stove for me, of that I am certain. But he is bright and attentive and attractive, and when lunch ends, I am sorry to be leaving. It will take me a few more dates to put my finger on what, exactly, it is about David that does attract me, since he is so different from Fisher, but eventually I will realize that it is exactly that: all the ways he is not Fisher. The professional appearance. The fact that he lives in a spacious high-rise with hardwood floors and kitchen utensils, and not an airless, one-room apartment with a rented bed. The fact that he can, and does, call me at night on the phone, just to chat. In short, it is all the ways that David's manner and style do not resonate with the chronic self-denial and anorexic emptying-out that has for so long defined me, that attracts me.

And then there is the fact that he is Jewish. While I know this figures in from the very beginning, I don't realize exactly how much until I look back on our relationship with the perspective of several decades. Only then will I see how truly perfect David was for me in that moment: he had good social standing and a professional, well-paying job, yes, but most importantly, he was the Trojan horse under whose cover I would surreptitiously reclaim my place at the Jewish table. My relationship with him, which I fully believed would lead to marriage, was a gift to my deceased father, a donation you might say, to his favorite cause: preservation of my Jewish identity.

* * *

I get a new job at an outpatient mental health clinic in Chattanooga called New Life Center. Instead of therapy or b-mod plans, I take detailed mental health histories of new clients, render a diagnosis, staff the cases with the six other clinicians, and assign the clients a counselor. The whole thing from start to finish takes about two hours per client, and requires that I only see them one time. It does not matter if I like them, if they are bright or interesting, or whether they seem capable of change. I am relieved of the discouragement and frustration of my old job, in which expectations of me were higher but impossible to fulfill.

The glow of newness spreads relief to other areas of my life. Those issues that have for so long been baffling or problematic—job, home, eating, relationship—are beginning to sort themselves out and to fit together in a coherent way. Also, I have a new friend in a fellow clinician, forty-two-year-old Kim, whose signature stilettos and flowing skirts and ultra-long cigarettes make me feel mature and interesting in her presence. Two months after I start dating David, I tell her I think I've met the man I will marry.

"I did that once," Kim says, her voice deeply Southern. She pulls her long dark hair over to one side and combs her fingers through it. "Don't rush it. Just fuck for a while."

Which is exactly what we do. But I will never be as attracted to

David as I was to Fisher. Interestingly, with the addition of foreplay and intimacy to my sex life, there is something missing. The urgent, touchless sex Fisher and I had satisfied certain needs and frustrated other important needs, a dynamic that played directly into the hands of our shared issues with intimacy. In bed, we were like two hurtling trucks slamming into each other head-on at a blind intersection. David and I, less well-matched where sexual malfunctioning is concerned, arrive cautiously at the same intersection, then politely wave each other through.

Still, he's Jewish, good looking, and my mother likes him.

"I just feel like I'm finally inhabiting my life," I tell Kim.

She puts down her pen. "What does that mean?" We are sitting in her office, client charts and coffee cups between us. Outside her window, a man in a tan uniform is riding an enormous lawnmower around and around in circles. Every time he makes a pass by her window, he waves at us.

"Everything seems like it's falling into place. I don't feel like I'm recovering from something, or waiting for something."

She considers this, then nods. "Don't be fooled by a lull in the madness," she says.

Still, it is a blissful stretch of life that extends all the way from July to just before my twenty-seventh birthday, in November. At times my father's death seems blurry and far-fetched, as if it couldn't possibly have happened within the same year; at other times I can see, clear as a winter sky, the torn place in February out of which he slipped. Looking back at who I was before he died, I hardly recognize myself, and this, I decide, is one of the legacies of his death: the void of meaning in my work and love life that I became aware of after his death, which I would be compelled to fill, would in turn fill me.

Chapter 33

Sick to Death

A RASH OF ILLNESS runs through the horse barn. One of the mares dies. Two days later, her newborn filly dies. A week after that, the vet is back again, trying to save another mare. I stand at the second mare's stall door, utterly helpless and sick-feeling. It occurs to me to pray, but the only prayer I know is the Hebrew blessing over the wine. I whisper it under my breath. *Barukh ata Adonai Eloheinu Melekh ha-olam, bo're p'ri ha-gafen. Blessed art Thou, Lord our God, King of the Universe, creator of the fruit of the vine.* The mare recovers, though I attribute her recovery to whatever was in the outsized hypodermic needle the vet was pushing into her neck at the moment I was thanking God for wine. The whole sick-horse experience reminds me of moving my horse, Sheba, to a new barn with two other horses after Bobbi moved away. One of the horses colicked; the other broke his ankle and had to be put down.

"Bad things always happen in threes," a friend portended.

Every afternoon after school, I raced to the barn to make sure Sheba was still alive. When nothing else bad happened, and after my fear had subsided, I was able to see the naysayer for the bully she was. But the superstition of threes didn't originate with her, and I heard it again at different times in my life. Regardless of whether or not you were superstitious, there would always be examples from history or present life to give the theory legs.

Even so, when my mother calls six months after my father died to tell me her best friend's husband has died, I do not hold my breath for weeks and wait for the third bad thing to happen. Nor do I think *my mother is the third bad thing* when she calls three months after that to say she isn't feeling well.

"Not feeling well how?" I ask. I am hunched over my desk, writing up a client history. I don't notice right off that her voice sounds small and far away.

She says she hasn't eaten or eliminated in five days. I bolt upright in my chair. This, I realize, is the second time she has called this week. Three days ago, it had only been two days since she'd eaten or eliminated; I'd joked that that was what an anorexic called *just getting started*. She had laughed, and I hadn't thought about her again. Now I am terrified.

I hang up and call my brother. He says he will take her to the doctor. That evening, he calls me at home. That Mark will always be the one I share parent crises with seems inevitable.

"Cancer of the colon," he says.

* * *

There is a Henny Youngman joke that goes like this: *A Jewish woman has two chickens. One gets sick, so the woman makes chicken soup out of the other one, to help the sick one get well.* This is actually what I think about when my brother calls to tell me about my mother. I was woefully absent during my father's illness. This is my chance to get it right, to be present, to take proper care, and not nurse an outsized denial. It comes, of course, at the expense of both parents.

My mother has the first of two surgeries in November, 1988. Doctors remove the cancerous section of her colon (about six inches), and, for good measure, her uterus and ovaries too, veritable cancer sponges of the female interior. My mother is left with a two inch stump of colon, called a stoma, poking out through her abdomen, around which is something like a Ziploc bag, and through which she will eliminate. Although it requires intimate contact with her own feces and sometimes a noxious, fiery odor bleeds from it, she never complains about the bag.

"The doctor says people even have sex with them on," she tells me. She arches her eyebrows in a *why in the world would you do that?* look and shakes her head, but this is the most negative she will be about it.

When the re-sectioned colon is working smoothly again, which takes about a month, my mother will have a second surgery to open her abdomen and rejoin the stoma to the rest of her colon. Once that seam has healed, and she is eliminating normally again, all that will be required of her is annual colonoscopies. Her prognosis is good, and five years out, if there is no reoccurrence, she will be considered cured.

And so it is for one unbelievable month, inside the same year that saw my father's death from bladder cancer, that I travel back and forth to Atlanta every weekend to the very same hospital floor he was on to keep my mother company during the long days waiting for her colon to mend. We watch television, play cards, and sometimes draw. Occasionally, I sit beside her in the tall bed, careful not to displace her with my movements. Her torso and legs are thin and barely make a knoll underneath the sheets; my hundred-and-fifteen-pound body, by contrast, is a fortress of energy and strength.

In the evenings, I make the twenty-minute drive back to my mother's house, eat a salad, arrange myself in my father's recliner with his dog, Chelsea, and call David. But he can't keep me company all night, and so, after fifteen minutes or so, we say goodbye. No sooner do I hang up than the solitude of my mother's house, hemmed in by the ravine and dense woods I remember so well, settles around me, creaks and groans of the forty year-old structure punctuating the silence.

My fear of this house is almost twenty years old. I always believed it dated back to the robbery when I was ten and arrived home from school to discover that the house, as I knew it, no longer existed. The robbers, the police said, had been watching us from the woods. I imagined them inside our house, eyeing my sister's wall of books, my brother's bubbling aquarium, my plastic horses grazing and galloping across every surface in my room. Was there some kind of residue left behind by their wicked gaze, I wondered, some knowledge they magically took away of us that day?

Years later, curled into my father's soft recliner, my mother dreaming dreams of wholeness in her hospital bed across town, I wrestle with my decades-old fear of this house. Behind me, the sliding glass doors are locked and barred, their shutters pulled and latched against the night. Now and then, Chelsea's ears prick at the sound of a faraway car, and my pulse picks up in response. I once heard someone say that we can know fear intimately but never completely, and I think about this as I parse a terror I can only partially grasp. I am not afraid of my own houses. I am not afraid of bad neighborhoods, structural defects, people supposedly hiding in cornfields, a roof collapsing. If I am historically untroubled by the empty and ill-tended homes I inhabited in the past, then it is because on some level I have always known that, like my clients, what is mine to grapple with is not something external. What threatens has never been an outside intruder with only cursory knowledge of me. What threatens is the intruder inside (i.e., me) who has been watching as if from afar, to see what can be sacrificed.

* * *

My mother leaves the hospital cancer-free. I bring David home to meet her. We stand arm-in-arm in her foyer while she takes pictures. David and I smile huge, toothy smiles. Our hips are cocked in, touching. We are both wearing new jeans and crisp, button down shirts; we look like an ad for a Jewish dating service. *Aren't we tall and dark-haired and well-dressed and so very happy to have found each other!* In the pictures, the tiny star around my neck glitters. I have just started wearing this.

"I can die now," my mother says on the phone to me later.

I tell her that, if she dies, I am breaking up with David and marrying Fisher.

Chapter 34

The Way Home

I HAVE A RECURRING DREAM about a house. In the dream, I discover the door to a room I have never seen before, even though I have lived there forever. I know that inside this room are things I cherish but have forgotten about. Just as I push open the door, I wake up.

* * *

The thieves who robbed us in 1971 leave behind one thing in particular that I take with me into adulthood. It is a tiny paperback book called *Take Care of Your Backyard Pony*, a how-to manual crammed full of photographs of a little girl named Mary Jane and her pony, Lucky. My parents gave it to me when I was seven or eight. I loved this book. Although, since I wanted my own backyard pony more than I wanted anything else in the world, and they had no plans to get me one, the gift seems almost cruel in retrospect.

The photographs, none of which were in color, were terrible. They were blurry, shot from bad angles, and had poor contrast, more tan and white than black and white. Also, it appeared to be very cold in Mary

Jane's backyard: in each frame, she was bundled into a long winter coat, scarf, furry hat, gloves, and boots. The trees in the background were barren, the ground beneath the pony's feet grassless. In no picture did a single shaft of light peek through trees, suggesting a patch of clear sky. Even Lucky himself looked weatherworn and cold, with ice clots clinging to his whiskers.

None of this bothered me. I thumbed through the small paperback book reading and rereading every word hundreds of times, including the instructive captions underneath each photograph: *Mary Jane walks Lucky from the barn, always leading from the left-hand side. Mary Jane is careful to hold Lucky's reins while dismounting.*

I am preparing for the day that I will have only to come in from school, grab my freakishly complete set of winter wear, and step out the patio door where my own backyard pony awaits. Never again will I have to count the long hours until Friday afternoon riding lessons, only for it to rain, or to spend the entire hour ambling around a ring in single file behind twenty other girls on horseback, the instructor barking from the middle, "Shoulders back! Wrists supple! Heels down! Toes in!" With my own pony, in my own backyard, I will ride however and whenever I want.

Instead of a live horse, I get horse-themed merchandise: plastic model horses of every conceivable breed and color, doing everything from bucking to sleeping. A subscription to *Horse Digest*, which offers grooming, feeding, and riding tips, and comes with a fold-out feature called "Stablemate of the Month," a two-page spread starring a different spectacular horse each month, which I tack to my wall and stare at longingly. One year, I get an oversized hardback book chock-full of color pictures, called *The Treasury of Horses*, which I cherish and study (I know all the parts of the horse, including the "sheath"). I get novels about horses (*King of the Wind*, *The Black Stallion*, *Black Beauty*, *Misty of Chincoteague*, and my favorite, *The Horse That Swam Away*). I get a colorful fabric map detailing the various breeds' countries of origin, horse jewelry, sweaters with horses on them, a riding crop, a hard hat, and a set of English riding stirrups (sold separately from the saddle, which I do not get). None of it makes up for not getting the real thing.

One night, when I am about ten years old, I have a vivid dream in which my parents surprise me with a horse for my birthday. In the dream, I tear open an ordinary, gift-wrapped box, expecting a new model horse. Instead, I find a horse's halter. Astonished by what this means—outside, there is a real horse whose head fits this halter—I race out to our corgi's pen, where there stands a magnificent, chestnut-colored mare. My heart feels like it will explode. I erupt into great, gut-wrenching sobs of joy. I can hardly believe she is real, and if it weren't for the fact that I can smell her and hear her nickering to me, I would think the whole thing was a dream. I reach out to touch her face, and just as I am about to slip the halter over her head, I wake up.

For several minutes, I lie motionless in my bed, trying desperately to re-enter the dream, grasping at what's left of its still-vivid threads. But the noises of the house intrude: a toilet flushing, my parents' door opening onto the hallway, the *shush-shush* of my mother's slippers on the carpet as she makes her way to the kitchen. Despair washes over me. *I will never know this kind of joy*, it says, and I stare quietly at the ceiling as a resolution I know nothing about takes root. It begins as a resolution about a horse, but by the time I am in my late-twenties, it is a resolution about listening to my heart.

* * *

Predictably, David and I can't continue our relationship without problems. He is unhappy in his work and, although I encourage him to talk to me about it, he does not easily open up.

"I feel like we never talk anymore," I say one night on the phone.

He apologizes. His job is demanding. He is often tired at night, and just doesn't always feel like calling to chat, especially as we have already talked before work.

"Then don't call if you don't feel like talking," I say, although I don't mean it. David's calls are the highlight of my day.

Then he says he also feels pressured to ask me out every weekend.

"I might actually *want* to," he says. "But I don't like feeling that it's expected."

My heartbeat ramps up but I fight down the anxiety.

"Okay," I say, with an astounding degree of calm. "So just call when you want to, and only ask me out if you really want to see me."

David exhales into the phone. "Thanks," he says. "That feels better already."

It feels awful to me, but I tell myself this is how mature people hammer out a successful relationship.

"You have to work at it, make compromises, not expect things just to fall into place, right?" I say to Kim.

"*Twice* a *day*?" Kim says. "He's calling you *twice* a *day*?"

"Just once a day now, and then only if he wants to."

Kim shakes her head. "I can't think of anyone I'd want to talk to twice a *day*."

"You talk to me *ten* times a day. Every time I walk into your office, we have a conversation."

"I'm not screwing you."

"Screwing me makes me less interesting?"

"No," Kim says, "It just makes other things more interesting." She pauses. "Anyway, he wants out. That's what all of this is about."

According to Kim, David and I are not hammering out a successful union, but instead entering the Protracted Break-up Phase, where one person wants out but doesn't want to be the bad guy, so things drag on until it gets so horrible that it hurts less to get out than stay in.

"Almost all relationships go down this road to die," she says.

We don't break up right away. We continue to see each other exclusively, but because one or the other of us is always unhappy, about work or family or the demands we feel from each other, we are chronically on edge. Most of our dates end badly. Still, our relationship limps along like an injured dog, showing up for family functions, including a spring trip to Hilton Head that my mother promised us after my father died. David and I kick off the Hilton Head trip by making polite conversation all the way down in the car, then racing into the rental house to have sex before anyone else gets there, then having ugly disagreements the rest of the week about how to spend our time: a microcosm, practically to scale, of our now six-month-long relationship. At Passover at his parents' house that fall, we barely speak, mouthing the words of Exodus from the Haggadah like they were written for us.

I decide to start riding again. While my childhood goal was a horse of my own that I could ride whenever I wanted to, my adult self has been perfectly happy just to be around horses, cleaning stalls, rubbing faces, inhaling the scent of hay and wood shavings. A return to riding will be curative, I decide, and I saddle my favorite mare, a sweet-natured bay named Tinyah, and put her through her paces in the ring: walk, trot, canter, figure eights with lead changes, halt, back up, reverse. I'm as good a rider as I ever was.

One evening, after a particularly dull day at work, I saddle Tinyah and proceed into the exercise ring. My mind is far away, my thoughts on loneliness. I have not heard from David for two days.

I do not recall if something spooked Tinyah—a noise, the sight of something, some inadvertent way I poked a heel into her side—or if she tripped, but no sooner are we in the ring than she lurches forward and I fall off. Sally rushes into the ring, but by the time she gets to us, Tinyah and I have both scrambled up and are walking it off. My face is hot with embarrassment. It's bad enough to go careening down the side of a horse, wondering, in the seconds between losing your balance and hitting whatever you're going to hit, if it's going to hurt. But it's even worse when other people are watching, witness to your clumsiness and misfortune.

This is what I am thinking about the night I fall off Tinyah, lying in bed and feeling my hip beginning to throb where I hit the ground. In the account I am rehearsing for the next time David calls, I look heroic, even sexy, as I sail through the air. I stare at the ceiling, wishing for the phone to ring. Sometime around midnight, unable to sleep, it occurs to me that David probably would not be that interested in the details of my fall, or the fact that I was terrifically embarrassed, which is when it hits me: it isn't just the pain that makes breaking up so awful, it's how you believe you look in the eyes of the world as a result of your clumsiness or misfortune in love. It is time, I realize, to tell my mother, my brother, and my sister, all of whom like David, that we are finished. And then, since, by definition, a break-up means the person you broke up with is no longer there to comfort you in your time of sorrow, I will be all alone with my grief.

"Oh, please," Kim says the next morning. "Get a grip."

* * *

I have the first of a series of father sightings that will continue well into my forties. I am on my way to work and he is in the next lane at the wheel of a red car. My heart does a gigantic *TA-DA!* in my chest, and I actually think to myself, *He faked his death!* Instead of wondering where this ridiculous idea comes from, I follow it up with *He just wanted to get away from us!* It does not immediately occur to me that if he had really faked his death to get away from us, he probably would not have gone on to live his life in the same small town where I live.

After this initial sighting, I will see my father every few months: once he is at a hardware store where I am picking out paint. Once he is at the mall, strolling down the center aisle. Once he is in an Italian restaurant sitting with a woman I have never seen before. Sometimes it is my father from head to toe: hair fuzzy and thinned from chemo, long-sleeved shirt buttoned over a slightly rounded belly, khakis and hard shoes; other times it is just my father's moonish face, superimposed on someone else's.

"There's my dad," I will say, without drama, to myself and, eventually, to my husband, who will turn to look but, because he never met my father, can't say whether it's really him.

And although I give the thought no real credence, I think it every time: my father faked his death to get away from us.

"Why do you think your father wanted to run away?" a therapist asks me one day when I am in my late twenties.

"We weren't sympathetic," I say. "Before he got cancer, we considered everything he did, his workaholism, his headaches, his backaches, everything, a grab for attention. We were mean."

"You were angry."

"We were frustrated," I say.

"You were frightened."

"He said he sat in the corner chair at the dinner table because that's where we put him, in a corner."

"Who is *we?*"

"The whole family," I say. "My father felt like we were all against him."

"Are you *all* having sightings?"

I stare at her.

"Stop feeling guilty," she says. "Your father was perfectly capable of standing up for himself."

"Then why didn't he?"

"You tell me. Why don't most people step up and fix whatever's wrong in their lives? Why do most people blame their problems on something outside themselves?"

I know what she is thinking: that I'm angry with my father for not facing up to his problems because this is exactly what I'm doing.

"Think of your father-sightings as dream images," she says. "In that way, he's really you. You wanting to get away from something in your life."

"Everyone wants to get away from something," I say. "You could put that in a fortune cookie and a billion people would think it was written just for them."

She tells me she's not interested in everyone else, she's interested in me. But I have a hard time getting past this idea that, what I want is so universal, that virtually everyone in the world would raise their hand if you asked who wanted to get away from something in their life.

"I can't make you original," she says. "I can only help you with your feelings."

* * *

I throw myself into work. I study for licensure as a psychological examiner, which will allow me to open a private practice and test for the police force, the courts, nursing homes, the school system, hospitals, and drug treatment centers. At the same time, my living room fills up with pottery greenware and hundreds of tiny bottles of glazes. In my spare time, when I'm not riding Tinyah, I am embellishing pots with tiny, detailed paintings, designs of women and dogs and household interiors. I give them as gifts, and a few shops even express interest in carrying them. I know someone who makes his living as a potter, and there is a part of me that is beginning to flirt seriously with the idea. But instead of listening to my heart, I focus on passing the four-hour licensure exam. When my handsome certificate arrives in the mail, I get a raise and open a testing practice on the side. The extra money is good and my assignments are varied, and every morning, driving by what looks like a vacant art studio, I push away powerful feelings of sadness.

I am in a testing session when the first panic attack hits. My client is repeating a series of digits backwards when I suddenly have the sensation that I am being watched from inside my own head. My client's voice begins to echo. Within seconds—like a house in a gas fire—I am consumed by a terror so powerful that I leap from my chair and run to the bathroom. I do not think, as people unfamiliar with panic attacks often do, that I am having a heart attack. I do not think I am losing my mind. I lie down under the sink and press my cheek to the cold tile floor as my heart slugs away at the chamber of my chest. *I'm having a panic attack*, I whisper over and over into the tile, trying to keep myself from disappearing, like a dying person clinging to consciousness.

* * *

Were this one panic attack the end of it, I am fairly certain that I would look back on my life with sad relief, that I would tell my anxious clients their panic attacks are not their fault, as mine wasn't my fault. I would lay down my dreams of becoming anything other than what I was at the moment the panic attack hit, and proceed down the narrow corridor of my life, always looking over my shoulder for the thief who stole my future to return.

For this reason, I am grateful for the ensuing months of panic attacks and free-floating terror and despair. I am grateful for the number of times I had to pull off the road because I was too terrified to drive, or beg off work because I was too terrified to test. I am grateful that the attacks did not abdicate to the power of my clinically trained mind, did not acquiesce to progressive relaxation, biofeedback, therapy, hypnosis, or behavioral management. I am grateful that medication made me feel slippery and hung over. I am grateful that, at some point, a drug rep for Xanax gave me a mug which, when filled with coffee, magically revealed the slogan, "Panic attacks come from out of the blue." It is the futility of these words that wrests me at last from my frightened slumber.

Panic attacks don't come from out of the blue. They come from the colorful and knowable world of the psyche. What is wrong with me is nothing new and nothing mysterious, and is, in fact, something quite old and familiar. I am, as I did for so many years, ignoring the wise but wordless voice that knows exactly what it is I want and need for myself. I am happy to have gotten my license; I am making more money, and I have more freedom. But the passion that set me down on the highway to becoming a psychological superhero is long gone. Ministering to the ills of others did not cure me; psychological testing would not make my life meaningful. Such was the realm not of employment, I would come to realize, but of a mind and body at one with itself.

And so I think: six years earlier, on our way to Bridgeway House, my mother at the wheel and me as navigator, we took a wrong turn and headed east instead of south. When I look back on that fateful moment, I can't help but think of psychoanalyst Carl Jung's assertion that everything that happens to us is a mirror of that which is happening inside us. Perhaps a part of me knew I was already off course, that, as a young woman, mostly unrecovered from my eating disorder and barely able to take care of myself, I could not possibly be for others what I was not for myself.

When I recall the moment I quit my job, and in turn my entire mental health career, I always see myself standing at the kitchen window of my trailer talking to Moira on the phone. It is dusk; the sky is gold and red, and the mares, with foals at their sides, are glowing. Behind me, Jesse, Keithan, and Boomer are asleep in front of the sofa, and my desk is stacked with brightly painted pots, ready to go to my first real art show. A new road is taking shape, and a completely unfamiliar one. Years later, when I am making my living as a potter and a painter, I will recall Mr. Jenkins's comment that nothing a client says is ever lost, that every conversation is a door to the soul. It is the same with roads, I think: all of them, given the chance, lead the way home.

Epilogue

ECLARATIONS OF WAR and their end often come sometime after bombs start and cease to fall. So it is with mental illness, particularly one whose parameters are not clearly in one world or another. In my case, and I suspect in cases both like and unlike mine, there was no single line over which I fell, mad and fractured into illness, or could step artfully back into health. At times I thought I was well when I was not; other times, entertaining what seemed like antiquated demons, I was arguably at my healthiest.

Many years ago, I wrote that illness is a private, fragile thing, and that recovery is a place we come to alone. I no longer believe this. Illness—and here I speak mainly of anorexia—is not private. Whole communities of women and men who have heeded the siren call of starvation do not starve alone. They take with them all of those who love and care and fear for them, parents and friends and spouses and mothers and teachers and counselors, and even bystanders on the street for whom the visuals of anorexia are shocking and disturbing, and suggest a certain truth about our standards of beauty and worth.

Nor is anorexia fragile. Left unchecked, it gathers speed and strength, and as anyone who has suffered from or attempted to treat it knows, is possessed of enormous resolve. Anorexia doesn't give up the fight without a fight.

I write about illness now with twenty-five years' perspective. From this distance, I can see clearly what I could only surmise when I was caught in its grip: that while anorexia is a cruel opponent, it has a noble heart. Its goal is not to destroy us or ruin our families or make us miserable—these are the things we get when we fight any emotional problem or addiction without listening to its message. While the visuals of anorexia are upsetting, and it's tempting to believe that, if we could just fix the eating, we would fix the eater, the visuals are just the road map in, the hieroglyphics, so to speak, of an inarticulate soul. Starvation is what the body wears to match the wardrobe of a thin and ailing mind. Push past this, and you will find a soul in search of repair.

Many years ago, I received a letter from a friend of a friend who was struggling with depression. He wanted to know what had helped me—what, when I looked back on my recovery, did I consider the most important thing I'd learned? I sat down with pen and paper and started writing. By the time I finished and sent the letter, it had been several weeks, and the letter was so long the recipient complained that he hadn't asked for a blow-by-blow account of my recovery, only what I thought was most instrumental to it. It hurt my feelings and embarrassed me at the time, that I had told so much to what turned out to be a disinterested audience. But in trying to get at that "most important" piece of learning, an entire story had emerged.

For anyone recovering from anything, the road in and out is always a story. To think that it is anything less, that the journey is really just a few simple facts around which the dry business of recovery orbits, is not to understand that illness has a beginning, a middle, and if we are lucky, an end.

I went to therapy off and on throughout my twenties, thirties, and forties. As I discovered in my quest to cure and be cured, therapy is part art and part artifice. But there is another part as well: the attempt to synthesize hundreds of therapeutic conversations that included everything from the mysterious fears of childhood to the calorie count of bread crusts, and to find in that mix answers to fundamental questions about existence, demands a belief in alchemy. The impact of therapy as a whole cannot be understood piecemeal; like my sister's demand to know, in an early family session, why some jokes made me laugh while others made me unable to eat, I suspect it is less the particulars of therapy so much as it is the gestalt—the overall mission, the flailing at the gate with many keys—that finally opens the way.

* * *

When I quit my job at the mental health center to pursue an art career, I also quit my fifteen-year, two pack-a-day smoking habit. With the money left to me in my father's will, I made a down payment on a tiny house on ten pasture acres surrounded by Lookout Mountain and Taylor's Ridge. I moved in with my dogs, two of Sally and Ed's horses, and the new vocational director from the mental health center, who would become my husband. I was nervous about all of it. I didn't know anyone personally who had quit a good job to become an artist. My track record with men was spotty at best. I loved cigarettes. Would the dogs adjust to the new place? Could I take care of two horses?

I bought a pottery wheel and set it up in the house. On my pots, I painted detailed black and white images of naked women with large breasts, rounded bellies, prominent nipples, and stylized hands with fingers reaching, grasping, and clasping: depictions of women unapologetically well-nourished and desirous of more. I won a few awards, and I exhibited my pottery, and then my paintings, at art fairs and galleries throughout the US for seventeen years. Today, my paintings are in numerous private, public, and corporate collections, and I continue to paint on commission.

Occasionally, because I am still thin, I am asked what my weight says about my recovery, to which I respond that everyone, eating disordered or not, must make peace with their body in the way that makes the most sense to them. If I were to ask twenty people what I should weigh, I would likely get twenty different answers; a better question, and one that was crucial to my recovery, is *whose dreams, ideals, goals, beliefs, and standards shall I go by, and at what point do I accept authority over my own life?* For the eating disordered, returning our body to a place of physical health and strength must be our priority. Only from there can we truly understand that, at the center of anorexia's noble heart, lies not a number on a scale but an ongoing story—one that is about how we rejoin the world—and in the living years that follow the darkness, pursue a life that is creative, engaged, and deeply felt in our bones.

Acknowledgments

Deepest gratitude goes to Therese Eiben, mentor, editor, and friend, who patiently and lovingly returned me to the essence of my material time and again, and without whom I would not have looked deeply enough or kindly enough.

Sarah McElwain guided me through the first incarnation of this book, gently encouraging me to be "happy to talk."

Sincere thanks goes to the members of my writers group, who read every word of every revision, and who kept the lights on in the hallway: Eleanor Cooper, Linda Voychehovsky, Rachel Schulson, and Jennie Storey. Thank you especially to Suzanne Fisher Staples for believing, and for ushering me into a world of opportunities without my consent.

I am so appreciative of the 2008 CreateHere Literary Arts Grant, which sent me to the Nebraska Summer Writers Conference where I had the opportunity to work on *The Body Tourist* with author and *Los Angeles Times* columnist, Meghan Daum.

Thank you to my friends, who are my family, who have marked every small and large milestone of my adult life with love, encouragement, and great wit: Carol and Frank White, Lawrence and Mada Mathis, George and Theresa Reed, and Martha and Kemmer Anderson. Jack Terpning's friendship was a lifeline all the years of my illness.

And thank you to my family, who are my friends: my sister, poet Julie Shavin Katz, who gave me my first blank book at fourteen and told me to write everything down; and my brother, Mark, for the long walks, the worry, and the invisible flea trick. Thank you also to my father, who was without question a good man. And to Keithan, Jesse, Boomer, Annie, Shark, Bella, and Brie: my dogs, my superheroes.

I am extremely grateful to Cynthia Ceilán and Katherine Boland of Little Feather Books, for believing wholeheartedly in *The Body Tourist* and giving its journey legs.

About the Author

Dana Lise Shavin was born in Atlanta, Georgia, and lives in her father's hometown of Chattanooga, Tennessee. In 1986, she obtained her Master's degree in Clinical Psychology and worked for fifteen years as a therapist, behavior specialist, and psychological examiner. She left the mental health field to pursue a career in art and to focus on her writing. For the past fifteen years, she has made her living as a fine art painter, exhibiting at outdoor art fairs and in galleries throughout the US.

Dana's essays have appeared in *Oxford American* magazine, *The Sun, The Writer, Zone 3, Alaska Quarterly Review, Fourth Genre, Third Coast, Puerto del Sol, Hawaii Pacific Review, Willow Review, Palo Alto Review, Skirt!, Gravy, Chatter,* and numerous alternative health, arts, and entertainment newspapers. She has been a monthly columnist for the *Chattanooga Times Free Press* since 2002, and is the editor of the Chattanooga Jewish Federation newspaper, *The Shofar.* She has been a panelist and workshop presenter at Keystone College's literary conference, *The Gathering,* since 2012, and has spoken and read at venues as diverse as the Unitarian Universalist Church, the Jewish Cultural Center, as part of the University of Women's Speakers Series, the Meacham Writers Workshop, the Hunter Museum of American Art, and at various book clubs, writers groups, and performance venues. She received a MakeWork literary arts grant in 2008. In 2011, Dana returned to her mental health roots and became a certified professional life coach. She specializes in finding balance and fulfillment in life and work, and goal-setting with soul.

Visit Dana Lise Shavin online at www.Danashavin.com, which hosts her blog, *Get My Drift.* You can also find her on Facebook at www.facebook.com/DanaShavinWrites. More information and images of her art can be found at www.Danashavinart.com.

Made in the USA
Charleston, SC
28 August 2015